Feminism in
Eighteenth-Century England

Feminism
in Eighteenth-Century
England

KATHARINE M. ROGERS

UNIVERSITY OF ILLINOIS PRESS

Urbana   Chicago   London

7946890
DLC

11-19-82 JA

ACKNOWLEDGMENTS

Much of the discussion of Defoe in Chapter 2 originally appeared in *Woman in the 18th Century and Other Essays,* ed.
Paul Fritz and Richard Morton (copyright 1976 by A. M. Hakkert
Ltd., distributed by Garland Publishing, Inc.); that of Winchilsea
in Chapter 3, in *Shakespeare's Sisters,* ed. Sandra M. Gilbert and
Susan Gubar (Bloomington: Indiana University Press, 1979); that
of Richardson in Chapter 4, in *Novel* (1976); that of Brooke in
Chapter 4, in *Genre* (1978); that of Inchbald and Smith in Chapter 6, in *Eighteenth-Century Studies* (1977).

LIBRARY OF CONGRESS CATALOGING IN PUBLICATION DATA

Rogers, Katharine M.
    Feminism in eighteenth-century England.

    Includes bibliographical references and index.
    1. Feminism—England—History—18th century.
I. Title.
HQ1599.E5R63   305.4'2'0942   81-16236
ISBN 0-252-00900-2   AACR2

To "the much loved husband of a happy wife"

CONTENTS

༄✿❈ INTRODUCTION ❈✿༄

A significant new interest in woman's nature and position, caused in part by a radical change in attitudes toward marriage, appears in eighteenth-century literature. As Lawrence Stone has demonstrated, the nuclear family as we understand it developed at the end of the seventeenth century.[1] Marriage, which was once considered an alliance between kinship groups pairing people on the basis of birth and wealth without any pretence of consulting their personal preferences, came to be regarded as an intimate lifelong companionship, entered into by men and women seeking partners who would make them happy. According to this new way of thinking, a woman should have a voice in choosing "the man who would control her life," and he should consider and value her as his dearest friend. Moreover, she should be given a good education, to qualify her to be a companion to her husband. However, wives were to remain subordinate companions, and the persisting patriarchal institutions gained emotional force when women were supposed to be bound to their husbands by love more than law.

Besides improving the actual situation of women, the change in attitude must have stimulated feminist thinking by increasing their self-confidence and their expectations, their belief that their minds were comparable to men's and their hopes for happiness and fulfillment. Their improved position made women freer to express their wishes and more aware of the inequities that persisted. This new consciousness brought about by their change in status, together with an enormous improvement in their education, enabled women to articulate their perceptions and claims in unprecedented numbers. For the first time in England, a great many women were expressing themselves privately in letters and diaries, publicly in novels, tracts, and educational works.

Concurrently, late seventeenth-century rationalism undermined some of the conventions restricting women by subjecting them to the test of reason. John Locke, attacking the standard argument that a king rules his country by divine authority as a father rules his family, showed that neither patriarchy had a rational foundation. Seeing reason as the highest value, the rationalists challenged the assumption that women should aim for a distinctively feminine, nonrational ideal. Far from encouraging women to cultivate silliness and helplessness as sweetly feminine, rationalism exposed such qualities as weaknesses unworthy of an adult human being. It also helped people see through the sentimental falsifications which, as affection became more prevalent in the family, tended to obscure exploitation and oppression under the guise of "love."

Several women responded to this spirit of rationalist questioning by applying reason to traditional concepts of woman's nature and role. Mary Astell fiercely argued that woman has equal capacity with man and was not created to serve him (*A Serious Proposal to the Ladies*, 1694), and Lady Mary Chudleigh actually urged women to shun the "wretched state" of marriage and value themselves by despising men ("To the Ladies," 1703).[2] Similar feminist protests appear sporadically through the century, such as *Woman Not Inferior to Man: or, A short and modest Vindication of the natural Right of the Fair-Sex to a Perfect Equality of Power, Dignity, and Esteem, with the Men* (1739) by "Sophia," who contended that women would be entirely capable of holding public office if men did not unjustly deprive them of education.[3]

We do not find another group of feminists, however, until the 1790s, when again reason was being applied to demolish traditional institutions and prejudices. Mary Wollstonecraft's *Vindication of the Rights of Woman* (1792) gained wider attention than earlier feminist works because it was produced and supported by the radical enthusiasm of the French Revolutionary era. When the rights of men were being widely proclaimed, it did not seem so extravagant to extend those rights to women. Ironically, the very movement that gave Wollstonecraft's work prominence was in a few years to discredit it, as the conservative reaction produced by war with France caused a general repudiation of radical thought and thinkers. Widely admired during her lifetime, Wollstonecraft shortly after her death was vilified by her enemies and her work ignored by her friends. Her reputation was so bad by the nineteenth century that several leading feminists repudiated her.[4]

Typically, however, eighteenth-century women were neither so bold nor so systematic in their approach to women's rights as Astell, Chudleigh, "Sophia," and Wollstonecraft. They preferred to base their claims on feeling rather than rational challenge. This approach was better attuned to the growing sentimentalism of the eighteenth century, which, associated with the increase of affection in the family, glorified tender and delicate feelings. It is true that many male authors had no difficulty in combining sentimentality with oppression of women, as they gushed over female self-immolation; with the striking exception of Samuel Richardson, male defenders of women are to be found among the rationalists. But most women made use of the new respect for feelings to articulate the emotions and sanction the values that were important to them as women.

Their new articulate confidence did not, of course, make these women feminists in the contemporary sense; in fact, many of them would have rejected the title. Their feminism tended to be sporadic, ambivalent, or indirectly expressed. Nevertheless, it kept manifesting itself. Hannah More, who vigorously supported the patriarchal status quo, suddenly turned aside from an analysis of women's intellectual limitations to point out that one really could not assess the natural capacities of minds "stinted and cramped" by conventional ladies' education, any more than one could assess the natural walking capacity of Chinese women with bound feet.[5] Jane Barker made her heroine Galesia dismiss learning as useless in women, but before this established her as a convincing intellectual who delights in an independent life of study. Lady Mary Wortley Montagu perversely argued that Turkish women were free, in order to bring into question the remarkable liberty that English women were supposed to enjoy: in fact, she implies, they were not much better off than their Oriental counterparts. Women novelists constantly created situations that criticized society's attitude toward and treatment of women. Charlotte Lennox's intelligent Arabella flies to the world of romance for the importance and excitement denied women in real life. Elizabeth Inchbald shows that her impulsive, self-willed Miss Milner is morally superior to an insipid model of feminine propriety. Charlotte Smith's Celestina has to fend off two suitors who cannot believe that a woman might not be delighted with any proposal of marriage. Fanny Burney's Juliet is victimized by a society that first deprives her of any training to help herself and then constantly takes advantage of her helplessness.

I have found some evidence of feminist feeling in practically all the innumerable women writers of the period, even the most timid and conventional. (Of course writing is necessarily a form of self-assertion, and a woman who looks at the world for herself cannot see it exactly as a man does.) Surely feminism need not be limited to single-minded, systematic campaigning for women's rights, but should include particular sensitivity to their needs, awareness of their problems, and concern for their situation. These early writers helped their contemporaries to formulate their own wishes and needs, and laid the groundwork for the feminist awareness we take for granted today.

NOTES

1. Lawrence Stone, *The Family, Sex and Marriage In England 1500-1800* (New York: Harper and Row, 1977).
2. Quoted *ibid.*, p. 341. Hilda Smith discusses them and other seventeenth-century feminists influenced by rationalism in *Reason's Disciples: Seventeenth-Century English Feminists* (Urbana: University of Illinois Press, 1982).
3. "Sophia," *Woman Not Inferior to Man* (London: John Hawkins, 1740), pp. 27-28. "A Gentleman" answered this with *Man Superior to Woman* (1739), which Sophia refuted with

Woman's Superior Excellence over Man (1740).
4. Ralph M. Wardle, *Mary Wollstonecraft: A Critical Biography* (Lawrence: University of Kansas, 1951), pp. 309, 316-17, 320-22, 339-40. Even Wollstonecraft's friend Hays omitted her from her five-volume *Female Biography* in 1803.
5. Hannah More, *Strictures on the Modern System of Female Education* (New York: Garland, 1974), II, 28.

[1]

THE SITUATION OF WOMEN IN EIGHTEENTH-CENTURY ENGLAND

Despite some improvement in attitudes toward the family, eighteenth-century Englishwomen lived in a traditional patriarchal society, male-centered and male-dominated. It is true that many women acquired education, confident articulateness, and satisfying lives; and that many men genuinely respected women as well as treating them considerately in personal relationships. Nevertheless, all the social institutions supported the interpretation of woman's role voiced by Richard Steele: "All she has to do in this World, is contained within the Duties of a Daughter, a Sister, a Wife, and a Mother." For women are "no other than an additional Part of the Species," and to realize this is "for their own Happiness and Comfort, as well as that of those for whom they were born."[1]

Marriage was more or less forced on women, as their only way to a recognized position in society. Several dreamed of conventual institutions, but such were not available in Protestant England. Lady Mary Wortley Montagu contrasted men, who have "so many roads ... to meet good Fortune, they can no way fail of it but by not deserving it," with her own sex, who have but the one road of marriage, "and that surrounded by precipices, and perhaps, after all, better miss'd than found."[2] For marriage ranged from mild subjection to virtual slavery. Legally, man and wife were considered one person—in effect, of course, the man. This meant that a wife could not sue or make a contract or,

7

more important, control any of the family property: anything she had, inherited, or earned could be spent or wasted as her husband chose.

Montagu, living separately from her husband on an income he allotted her, felt she had to ask his consent in disposing of a two-hundred-pound legacy she had received and could only hope he would permit her to give her jewels to their daughter.[3] If a wife and husband worked together in a family business, it was considered his: he was the entrepreneur and she his (unpaid) employee. Therefore the profits were his, and she was cheating him if she took money from the till to buy something for their children.[4]

A husband controlled his wife's children, her residence, and her way of life. Even after his death, his widow had no rights over their children unless he had made her the guardian. A woman's only escape from an intolerable marriage was a separation, provided her husband could be persuaded to give her enough money to live on. Edward Wortley Montagu did this for his wife, but apparently on condition that she stay away from England, which meant never seeing her beloved daughter and grandchildren. Only if a husband beat his wife so as to endanger her life or denied her necessities could he be forced to allow her a maintenance. If she did not have these excuses, or if she had run away with a man, her husband could legally fetch her back by force and lock her up to prevent her from running again. Theophilus Cibber preferred to hold his wife, the eminent singer and tragic actress Susannah Maria Arne, through financial coercion. Susannah, who had been pressured by her father to marry Theophilus, put up with his flagrant adulteries, appropriation of her entire salary, and sale of her person to William Sloper. But when Sloper and Susannah fell in love and tried to get Theophilus to agree to a legal separation, which would release her from his power, he sued Sloper for alienating his wife's affections. If it had not been for Sloper's distinguished family and Susannah's powerful friends, Theophilus could have forced the two apart by financial pressure, by taking all Sloper's fortune in damage suits and relying on the scandal to keep Susannah from making her living on the stage.[5]

Separation discredited a woman, regardless of the circumstances. Though she acknowledged that Lord Fitzwilliam was peevish and provoking, Mary Delany condemned his wife for leaving him, on the grounds that she brought disgrace to her children: "who will venture on the daughter, when the mother has proved such a wife?"[6] Divorce with the right to remarry, obtainable only by act of Parliament and in effect granted only to husbands who proved their wives had committed adultery, brought social ostracism to women, though no stigma attached to adulterous males. Lady Diana Bolingbroke left her husband for chronic drunkenness, and subsequently fell in love with Topham Beauclerk and bore his child. Bolingbroke divorced her, and she married Beauclerk.[7] The virtuous Samuel Johnson continued to cherish Topham Beauclerk as a friend, but he flatly condemned Lady Diana as a whore. When William Yonge, a notoriously odious and unfaithful man formally separated from his wife, discovered her in adultery, he divorced her and retained all her fortune except a meager annuity. Questioned on the justice of this settlement, the Speaker of the House of Commons declared that, because adultery was punished by death in Old Testament times, "she had forfeited all by Law," and therefore "the taking away half her Fortune was not sufficient Satisfaction for her Husband's Sufferings."[8]

Chastity, narrowly defined, was the all-important factor in determining how a woman was valued, by others and by herself as well. It was equated with virtue or honor in women; and, once lost, it was assumed to be irrecoverable. Johnson, whose attitude toward women was in general benign and rather enlightened, declared that no ill usage could justify a wife's unfaithfulness and that this crime was so pernicious that its perpetrator "should not have any possibility of being restored to good character after losing it."[9] So vital was chastity that a woman must constantly preoccupy herself with preserving its very appearance—avoiding any company, any reading, any actions that could arouse suspicions of her sexual purity in the narrowest mind. A wife must deny herself "even the most innocent liberties" if they happen to arouse jealousy in her husband.[10]

On the other hand, she was expected to graciously overlook adultery in her husband or, if she reacted at all, to examine herself to see how she might have failed to please him. When Lord

Abergavenny turned his wife out of her house after fourteen years of marriage and set the nursery maid at the head of the table, Johnson commented, "I doubt not but it was the Lady's Fault; Women often give great Offence by their Spirit of Non Compliance."[11]

Here we see how the sexual double standard extended from chastity to other virtues as well. It was always the wife's obligation to maintain harmony in the marriage, through whatever degree of sweetness, compliance, and self-sacrifice might be necessary. In a letter to his dearly loved twelve-year-old daughter (*The Lady's New Year's Gift*, 1688), George Savile, Marquis of Halifax, explained in detail how she should accommodate herself to the faults she is *likely* to meet in her husband—namely, adultery, drunkenness, bad temper, avarice, and stupidity. Throughout, he assumed that any type of resistance or retaliation would be as immoral as it was useless.

This attitude persisted throughout the century, reappearing in such works as Bishop William Fleetwood's *The Relative Duties of Parents and Children, Husbands and Wives, Masters and Servants* (1716) and Jane West's *Letters to a Young Lady* (1806).[12] The Church preached that a wife owed her husband obedience to every order that was not actually unlawful (more liberal authorities excepted also those that were patently imprudent); moreover, she was obligated to obey cheerfully. She must never show anger to her husband; if she tried to exert influence, it must be through cajolery or tears. Of course there was also a sound practical reason for a wife to make her marriage a success through sweet compliance. Since her husband was legally entitled to severely restrict her activities, friendships, spending power, and children, it was in her interest to prevent him from wanting to wield his power.

This subjection could have been tolerable in a marriage based on compatibility, mutual love, and respect. Unfortunately, such marriages were not often the norm, although the situation did improve during the eighteenth century. While Halifax assumed that he should choose his daughter's husband with no regard to her preferences and little to the man's character, eighteenth-century parents, particularly among the gentry and middle class, were expected to match their children only with those they could love. But it was still assumed that guardians were better judges on this point than the young women themselves, as we see from the Tatler's account of how he arranged "the disposal of my [twenty-three-year-old] sister Jenny for life." He "told her, that if she kept her honour, and behaved herself in such a manner as became the Bickerstaffs, I would get her an agreeable man for her husband." And in fact he carefully selected a man who would make her happy and give her the necessary judicious guidance (of which, as a female wit, she had particular need).[13] Less conscientious guardians made matches on the basis of birth and wealth and did not scruple to exert emotional and financial pressure to enforce their wishes.

Even when a young woman was theoretically left free, modesty restricted her choice by forcing her into a passive role: she could do no more than respond to a man who indicated interest in her. A mere positive preference on her part was taken as evidence of "somwhat too warm desires."[14] This sinister imputation so frightened women that they hesitated to admit that they loved; Mary Pierrepont insisted to her fiancé, Edward Wortley Montagu: "I rather chuse to use the word Freindship than Love because in the general Sense that word is spoke, it signifies a Passion rather founded on Fancy than Reason."[15] Dr. John Gregory neatly rationalized this denial of freedom in *A Father's Legacy to His Daughters* (1774): since "Nature has not given you that unlimited range in your choice which we enjoy, she has wisely and benevolently assigned to you a greater flexibility of taste on this subject."[16] Thus a woman should find no difficulty in becoming attached to a man who shows interest in her.

Women who married contrary to their parents' wishes were apt to find themselves without portion or inheritance and with reputations damaged by such evidence of uncontrolled passion and willfulness. James Boswell believed that a young woman who married without consulting her parents "ought to suffer," because if such a marriage succeeds, "It gives encouragement to girls of impressionable hearts and light heads to forget the weakness of their sex, to scorn the sage maxims of prudence, and to disturb the settled order of Society." When his wife's sister made a second marriage which he considered low, Boswell forbade his wife to see her, though he did relent when she was dying of tuberculosis.[17]

Theoretically, women did have the right to refuse a marriage; but in practice this was often not so. Mary Pierrepont's father broke off negotiations with Edward Wortley Montagu because he refused to settle his whole estate upon the eldest son of the forthcoming marriage. The father then arranged a marriage with a man Mary knew it would be "impossible to Love." When she protested, he threatened to cut off her support; her other relatives "were sorry I would ruin my selfe, but if I was so unreasonable they could not blame my F[ather] whatever he inflicted on me." They assured her that love was unnecessary: "if I liv'd well with him, that was all that was requir'd of me, and . . . very few women [were] in love with their Husbands and yet a manny happy." Though she was an unusually strong-minded young woman, her father bullied her into a half-acquiescence and then proceeded as if she had freely consented to the match. She recognized that she could not continue resisting if she remained in his house and finally eloped with Montagu. Her father was persuaded to forgive her, but never did hand over the portion to be expected for a woman of her family.[18]

Mary Granville, with less spirit and no lover to rescue her, did not escape. She was a gifted, charming girl of seventeen, whose uncle, Lord Lansdowne, wanted to use her to cement a political alliance. The proposed husband, Alexander Pendarves, was a drunken, surly squire of nearly sixty, and he revolted her. But her uncle, as head of the family, reproached her for objecting to Pendarves "only" because she found him unattractive, and he threatened to cut off her income and her parents' as well. The arguments he used show how the overemphasis on chastity and the enforced economic dependence of women were used to break down their resistance. By telling her she would be "despicable" if she could refuse a man of such "vast merit . . . because he was not young and handsome," he implied that she was being lustful as well as selfish. By urging her to do her duty by getting herself "settled in the world, and ease my friends of an expense and care," he exploited the fact that women had to depend on others for support because they were generally deprived of property of their own." So Mary Granville married Pendarves and spent seven increasingly miserable years with him. Long after his death, when she was forty-three years old, she fell in love with Patrick Delany; but she did not feel free to marry him without the consent of her mother and brother. They were reluctant, because Delany lacked wealth and aristocratic descent, but were finally persuaded to acquiesce.[19]

Montagu and Delany were both aristocrats, but years later the middle-class Fanny Burney found herself in a similar situation, resulting from the financial pressure on women to marry. At the age of twenty-three she narrowly escaped being pushed into marriage by relatives who honestly believed themselves to be acting in her interest. She had happened to meet a Mr. Barlow, who seemed to her dull and faintly ridiculous, and was totally surprised when he sent her a letter of proposal. Though she had no intention of accepting him, she felt she must consult her father, who would not let her write a refusal without further consideration. Barlow called on her and continued to press his proposal; like Jane Austen's Mr. Collins, he persisted in thinking that she was just affecting maidenly skittishness. Meanwhile her grandmother, aunts, eldest sister, and revered friend Samuel Crisp urged her to accept Barlow, pointing out that a portionless young woman like herself had better seize this opportunity for future support, since she was not likely to have another suitor. They thought she was very perverse to refuse a man who had nothing wrong with his character or circumstances. Fanny grew increasingly desperate, hoping that her adored father would not add his voice to the chorus, for she knew she could never resist him. She was pathetically grateful when he abstained from interfering and assured her she might always live with him.[20] When Fanny did fall in love, at forty, with the beautifully compatible Alexandre d'Arblay, her father opposed the match because he was a Roman Catholic émigré without financial resources in England; finally she managed to extract a cold consent (without which she undoubtedly would not have married), but he refused to attend the wedding.

These strangely distorted values influenced everyone's conception of marriage. The elaborate contracts negotiated before an upper-class marriage dealt exclusively with such matters as how large a portion the bride's family was to hand over, what allowance was to be settled on her during the marriage, and what maintenance assured to her in case of separation or widowhood. Women were ashamed to admit that physical attraction affected their preference; equality of birth and wealth were generally accepted as essential. No one criticized Hester Salusbury for marrying a man she hardly knew to please her mother. But when, after Henry Thrale's death, she married Gabriel Piozzi simply because she loved him, her friends and daughters repudiated her. Piozzi was an Italian Catholic musician without wealth, but he was an amiable and respectable man. The outrageous public reaction was evidently provoked by the sight of a woman, a forty-three-year-old intellectual woman, making a marriage which had to be the result of love alone. As Burney saw it, "Children, Religion, Situation, Country & Character—besides the Diminution of Fortune by a certain loss of 800£ a Year were too much to sacrifice to any One Man."[21]

Fortunately, institutions often work out more humanely in practice than theory would suggest. Marriages did occasionally cross class lines with success. Thrale tells how a laboring man's widow with eight children, sent by charity to her former home in the country, married the local squire; and Richardson said that his *Pamela* was founded closely on fact.[22] Though the law gave husbands almost unlimited power, public opinion usually restrained them from flagrantly abusing their wives or denying them money to spend in proportion to the fortune they had brought into the marriage.[23] In the upper class, marriage settlements assured a wife £400 or £500 a year spending money (called pin money) while her husband lived, and a jointure if he died. And courts became increasingly ready to intervene to enforce such provisions (for those who could afford a lawsuit).

More important, eighteenth-century institutions often, somehow, produced good marriages showing mutual help and mutual concessions. Daniel Defoe's moral handbooks are full of incidental pictures of true union in marriage. In *The Family Instructor* (1715), he describes a husband asking his wife why she is in tears, because "there is no affliction can befall thee, but either I must have an equal share in it, or be wanting in affection to thee, which I never was yet, or want a concern for my own happiness; seeing, ever since we have been one by consent . . . I have but one interest, one wish, and one desire with you; and this not by duty only, but by inclination."[24]

The real-life sentimental romance of Richard and Elizabeth Griffith shows how mutually rewarding a traditional marriage could be, as well as how "the rigors of feminine morality were relaxed in actual life." (Elizabeth and Richard generated delicate, tender feelings for each other during years of courtship and marriage, and expressed them in innumerable letters, so interesting to the public that they went through several editions when published under the assumed names of Henry and Frances [1757-70].) Their published letters tell how Henry met Frances in 1746 and was strongly attracted to her, but did not consider proposing marriage because they were both poor. For five years they corresponded secretly three times a week, discussing everything from Henry's hypersensitive cat to Cicero's essays. Henry enlarged Frances's mental horizons, which had been limited by poor education and a narrow social circle; and they argued amicably over feminist issues.

Not armed with the icily impregnable chastity of the heroines of novels, even her own, Frances fell in love with Henry long before it was clear that they would marry. When finally he attempted to seduce her, she was hurt, indignant, and firm in her refusal; but she forgave him because she loved him. She was more seriously angry when he showed her letters to another person, but she later admitted, "I would rather my letters should be read by the whole county, than not be punctually answered by you." Finally she pressed him to make his intentions clear, and he did propose, though when he married her two years later, he insisted on keeping it secret; she, on her side, took care to have the Countess of Orrery witness the ceremony. Henry did not publicly acknowledge the marriage until he made a will two years later, where he declared that, although he would have preferred money, birth, *and* sense in a wife, he realized the third was most important and married accordingly. Moreover, he found he "had so engaged her affections, that no other man could make her happy; and so dallied with her character, that only myself could repair it," so that moral principles "concurred, to what my love and reason had before approved."[25]

The perfect congeniality which originally brought Henry and Frances together kept their love warm through long years of married life. They continued to delight in each other's company and to exchange voluminous letters when Henry was away on business; he made "it a rule to give" her his "observations upon every book" he read. It was not an equal relationship. Frances told Henry, "I am always sincerely pleased, when any little error or weakness of mine gives my ever dear preceptor an opportunity of setting his little pupil right." Nevertheless, Henry thought a wife might exert power as long as she observed decorum: "The Husband should hold the long Reins in his Hand, and *seem* to drive; it looks manly, and saves Appearances; but the Wife should always *underhand* be allowed to take the *leading Rein*."[26] Clearly, the Griffiths had a good marriage in the modern sense, with tenderness and attraction, as well as intellectual companionship, maintained over seventeen years.

In letters to Samuel Richardson, Hester Mulso (Chapone) showed that oppressive law could be reconciled with humane practice if people did not push their authority to the limit. While she would not "suppose a child at liberty to dispose of herself in marriage, without the consent of her parents," she hopes that parents of a daughter over eighteen would not "refuse their consent to a child who, by her wisdom, prudence, discretion, justifies unexceptionably her passion for a particular object." In the same way, although a husband is entitled to his wife's "absolute obedience," an authority that God and custom gave him because man is, in general, naturally superior to woman, nevertheless a generous husband will surely not insist on exerting his authority in any matter where his wife is far more interested than he. Moreover, it is "highly conducive, and, to delicate minds, absolutely necessary to conjugal happiness, that the husband have such an opinion of his wife's understanding, principles, and integrity of heart, as would induce him to exalt her to the rank of his *first* and *dearest friend*"—and friendship is inconsistent with inequality and subjection. Since "Love must always necessarily inspire a constant desire of pleasing and obliging," both husband and wife will "testify their mutual preference of each other's happiness to their own, in the smallest as well as the greatest occurrences of life." For her part, "I would not marry a man, upon whose generosity I could not absolutely depend."[27] Thus Chapone evades the consequences of her traditional principles by assuming that a generous man—and a sensible woman would marry no other—would not think of exerting the control to which he was legally entitled.

It was fortunate that marriages often did work out, for women who were not married, or whose husbands failed to support them, found living difficult. In the first place, they did not get their share of the inheritances that were so important among the upper classes. Normally, the family estate went to the eldest son, on the theory that, as head of the family, he should be as powerful and independent as possible; his sisters' shares were seen as drains on his property. James Boswell entailed the family estate so that his daughters could not inherit it even after his sons, and complacently reflected: "it was a comfort to me to think the estate was now secured to *the sons of Auchinleck.*" His daughters were to be provided for "by frugality"; that is, by savings extracted from the family income.[28] Johnson thought it was ludicrous for a man to will his estate to his three sisters in preference to a remote male heir, for "An ancient estate should always go to males. It is mighty foolish to let a stranger have it because he marries your daughter."[29]

Ladies were prevented from supporting themselves by their lack of access to professional training and by the stigma attached to women who worked for money.[30] A surprising number of careers were considered indelicate; Johnson thought portrait-painting improper because "Publick practice of any art . . . and staring in men's faces, is very indelicate in a female."[31] Earning money at anything made women uncomfortable; Burney felt degraded even at receiving her salary from the Queen.[32] Her case poignantly illustrates the limited options available to women, since, when it appeared that she would not marry, she was considered fortunate to be offered an appointment as Second

Keeper of the Robes to Queen Charlotte. Burney was a highly intelligent woman who had proved herself a successful novelist, yet her family and friends expected her to welcome a career of empty ceremony and devastating boredom. Even more ludicrous was the proposal that the unconventional scholar Elizabeth Carter, translator of Epictetus, accept a position looking after the children of the Princess of Wales. As her best friend begged her to accept this post, she mentioned that Carter was qualified to become a professional tutor at Oxford—but of course that suggestion could be made only in jest.[33]

When Richard Brinsley Sheridan married the spectacularly successful singer Elizabeth Linley, he refused to let her sing for pay, even though they had no money (a decision Johnson considered very manly).[34] A more egregious case was Mary Darby Robinson's father, who wasted most of the family property in a bubble scheme despite his wife's attempts to dissuade him, left his family for a mistress, and stopped sending them money. He was indignant to discover on his return that his wife had set up a little school, considering "his name disgraced, his conjugal reputation tarnished." He forced her to close the school, but continued to live with his mistress, rarely visiting or sending money to his family. When Mary resolved to go on the stage, her father's "stern and invincible sense of honour" was outraged. So Mary married Thomas Robinson, whom she did not love and who turned out to be worthless. Ultimately she did become a very successful actress, and, although Robinson's dissipations consumed most of her earnings, she was exhilarated that she could now support herself honorably—"the consciousness of independence is the only true felicity in this world of humiliations." But her family did not agree: her father and brother could never bear to see her perform, and the sight gave her mother "painful regret."[35]

Unmarried women were more free to conduct girls' schools and thus take advantage of the increasing wealth of the middle class and interest in female education. Both the More sisters and the Lee sisters established schools so profitable that they could retire in middle age with very comfortable incomes. But they needed luck as well as ability, for a school could not succeed without patronage; the Mores were helped by the ducal family of the Beauforts, as well as a wealthy local clergyman. And hired teachers made no fortunes, whether they worked in schools or in private families as governesses. Maria Edgeworth pointed out the discrepancy between the compensation given the tutor of the boys in an aristocratic family and that given the governess of the girls, who did equally important work and came as close to practicing a liberal profession as a woman could. While the governess received a salary insufficient to enable her to retire with dignity, the tutor would be rewarded with a profitable appointment in the Church.[36]

Middle- and lower-class women were better able to look after themselves than ladies, but they too labored under serious disadvantages. The active participation of wives in their husbands' businesses, encouraged by writers such as Defoe, became less common as tradesmen aimed at gentility and furnished their daughters only with useless fashionable accomplishments.[37]

It is true that some women continued to carry on business: a few made fortunes in quack medicine, and many were active in the book trade as printers, booksellers, and keepers of stationers' shops. At first, they predominated in trades catering to women, such as dressmaking and millinery; but later men moved in and, assumed to be better because of their sex, made more money. In the same way, male obstetricians were supplanting midwives for deliveries in the upper-class. They stigmatized the midwives as dirty and ignorant, though actually the women, who were less apt to be carrying lethal pathogens or to misuse forceps, did less damage than male doctors.[38]

Women servants were routinely paid less than men. A fashionable footman, "whose most laborious task is to wait at table, gains, including clothes, vails, and other perquisites, at least £50 per annum, whilst a cook-maid, who is mistress of her profession, does not obtain £20, though her office is laborious, unwholesome, and requires a much greater degree of skill."[39] Finally, working women such as servants and shop assistants were treated as legitimate prey by licentious gentlemen. Both Pepys's and Boswell's diaries show that upper-class men felt privileged to fondle intimately, if not to possess, maids in their own houses and in inns. Once women lost their reputation, they had often no recourse but prostitution—the one field which offered women unlimited opportunities.

In 1739 an anonymous lady addressed these problems in "A New Method for Making Women as Useful and as Capable of Maintaining Themselves as the Men are, and Consequently Preventing Their Becoming Old Maids or Taking Ill Courses," published in *The Gentleman's Magazine*. She deplored the tendency of middle-class men to send their daughters to fashionable boarding schools instead of apprenticing them to shopkeepers in "genteel and easy trades," such as drapers or confectioners. Such businesses are "as creditable . . . for the Daughters of Gentlemen as for their Sons," and women so qualified would "not be forced to a disagreeable match, or even to marry at all."[40]

Several similar proposals, stimulated by the radical social criticism of the end of the century, show that women's economic plight remained unchanged. The best thought out of these is Priscilla Wakefield's *Reflections on the Present Condition of the Female Sex* (1798). After pointing out that women did not get a fair chance even in traditionally feminine occupations such as hairdressing and teaching, she exhorted upper-class women to make a point of patronizing female artisans and shopkeepers, to pay them equitably, and to engage female instructors for their children.[41] She developed a plan for teachers' colleges where women could become genuinely qualified to teach girls and which ultimately would be run entirely by women.

Secondly, Wakefield would expand opportunities for women by letting them into less conventional businesses. She saw no reason why they could not serve in apothecaries' shops, make toys, run inns, or farm. She tells how the two daughters of a gentleman, left with practically nothing and unwilling to marry yokels or live off their relatives, took a farm and for many years ran it with credit and advantage, despite the opposition of the neighboring farmers.[42]

Mary Ann Radcliffe, married to an ineffectual husband, knew at first hand the difficulty of obtaining gainful employment. In *The Female Advocate: Or, an Attempt to Recover the Rights of Women from Male Usurpation* (1799), she argued that a gentlewoman often had literally no way to support herself except prostitution. She proved this by quoting a letter from a former prostitute: "I was reduced . . . to the manifest danger of starving. I would have attempted the most laborious work, but no one would try me, although I offered my labour at half price. . . . I must, they said, be very bad to be reduced to that, and they supposed, I intended to steal the other part of my wages."[43]

Despite this increasing recognition that women had to have better opportunities for supporting themselves, the only profession that actually developed for them was writing. In the 1670s Aphra Behn, the first professional woman author in England, successfully competed with male playwrights. She was followed by Susannah Centlivre, another comic playwright, and Mary de la Rivière Manley and Eliza Haywood, writers of salacious romances and scandal chronicles. They all made an independent living by their writing, but unfortunately contemporaries were less impressed by their professionalism than by the immodesty of their works and the unchastity of their lives. Behn and Centlivre had lovers, Haywood was separated from her husband, and Manley, after being betrayed into a fraudulent marriage, lived as a kept mistress.

These lapses were magnified by prejudice against women who aggressively competed with men, so that Behn was represented as coupling with half the town and Haywood's presumably legitimate offspring were assumed to be babes of love.[44] The women were attacked as if they supported themselves by prostitution (which would have been an easier way than writing). Thus it became customary to associate unchastity with professional competition with men, and these writers did not set a useful precedent for women who had a reputation to lose.

In strong contrast, there is the overidealization of Katherine Philips, "the matchless Orinda," who led a sexually blameless life but also produced only innocuous verses not intended for profit or, she claimed, publication. Even the more assertive Mary Wortley Montagu either circulated her works in manuscript or published them anonymously; she left the manuscript of her major work, the *Turkish Letters*, with a man whom she expected would publish it after her death.[45]

Gradually, however, respectable ladies did begin to write for money, though often anonymously and apologetically. They were accepted and encouraged by prominent people such as Johnson and the Bluestocking hostesses. They published translations from the Greek, history, and criticism, as well as imaginative literature, although some people still believed that such things required a degree of learning beyond woman's grasp.[46] Anna Barbauld brought out a series of editions, including a fifty-volume series of British novels, with professionally competent critical prefaces. Catharine Macaulay, the radical historian, was prominent and widely respected, regarded with better than tolerance even by the conservative Johnson.

However, the overwhelming majority of women wrote novels—partly because this nontraditional form was less intimidating, partly because since Richardson it had specialized in women's experiences and fantasies, partly because it drew on the imagination and sensibility credited to women more than the learning and judgment they were supposed to lack. By the later eighteenth century, there were actually more female than male novelists; Tobias Smollett sourly acknowledged their success in *Humphry Clinker*.[47] A few women attained very gratifying fame and fortune from writing novels. Burney won the attention of the most distinguished society of her day with *Evelina* (1778) and made two thousand pounds from *Camilla* (1796), published by subscription among her influential friends. Without resorting to subscriptions, Ann Radcliffe made five hundred pounds from *The Mysteries of Udolpho* (1794) and six hundred from *The Italian* (1797).

Of course, most novelists, including writers as good as Charlotte Smith, received no such rewards.[48] Smith turned out an average of four volumes per year, but constantly worried about money and was not able to give her nine children a proper start in life. Always struggling to meet deadlines, she had to complete her novels while the first parts were already in print, with obvious damage to their structure. Of course male writers suffered from financial pressure as well, but they did not have to deal with the maternal and household worries that haunted Smith. Besides, they often had other resources, such as legal or clerical income, government positions or sinecures—none of which were available to women.

Although outright hostility to women as authors became less acceptable,[49] it was replaced by a patronizing double standard which was equally damaging. Even Hannah More, who usually erred by minimizing the problems of women, conceded that one aspiring to literary fame would "have to encounter the mortifying circumstance of having her sex always taken into account; . . . her highest exertions will probably be received with the qualified approbation, *that it is really extraordinary for a woman*" and disparaged as "the spontaneous productions of a fruitful but shallow soil."[50] The widespread assumption that novels required less high literary ability than verse, criticism, or scholarship can be explained only by the association of novels with women.

The critics, predominantly male, were all too tolerant of women's novels, because they saw them as necessarily minor productions by unprofessional writers. If the novelist maintained a high moral tone, dealt with the proper feminine material of sentimental romance, and presented her work with due modesty, they praised her. But these conditions implied that she respect convention and disclaim ambition. She might write to support her family, to instruct the young, or to amuse herself—but never to gratify her ego or create a masterpiece.

This combination of indulgence and disparagement led to indiscriminate under- or overvaluing; criticism of women's work shows little evidence of the usual esthetic standards. One would never know from contemporary criticism that Elizabeth Inchbald's *A Simple Story* (1791) was an unusually good novel or that Elizabeth Carter's poems did not equal those of Anne Finch, Countess of Winchilsea, the outstanding woman poet of the century. In John Duncombe's *Feminiad* (1754), a fulsome eulogy of literary women, Winchilsea is buried among a heap of untalented and even forgotten poets. Other women received indiscriminate adulation that blinded them to their talents and limitations: thus Burney was deflected from vivid, colloquial reportage of manners to trite moralizing in pompous style; and More, whose shrewd insight and command of practical detail gave life to her homely stories in the *Cheap Repository Tracts* (1795-98), was led to believe that such works degraded her genius.

In fact, it is these alone that retain interest. Hannah More, a woman of good education and high intelligence but no creative ability, was hailed as a genius for fugitive verse, a priggish tragedy, and what must surely be the most tedious novel in the English language. She was overestimated partly because of her personal charm and influential friends, but mostly because of her irreproachable decorum, high moral tone, and extreme conventionality: she was conservative in politics and rigidly pious, and she vigorously opposed feminism, insisting that the narrow traditional role of women was divinely ordained, socially necessary, and happily suited to their nature. Unexceptionable morality overshadowed literary quality in a woman author, especially since she was not expected to meet the same standards as a man.[51]

This special standard for women's work condoned amateurishness by encouraging the belief that good intentions or financial need were more important than achievement. The anonymous author of The Example: or The History of Lucy Cleveland (1778) did not vainly "hope, that it is deserving of the approbation of the judicious," but trusted that "a candid, a liberal, a generous Public will make the necessary allowances, for the first attempt of a young female Adventurer in Letters."[52] Eliza Parsons tried to disarm criticism of her Mysterious Warning (1796) by confessing that talents and inclination had "no share in her feeble attempts to entertain the Public"; she wrote to support her orphaned children.[53] Such admissions, of course, reinforced the complacency of those who placed women's work in a separate, inferior category.

More important, these statements reinforced the women's suspicions, already planted by the culture, that their work was not only trivial but had to be justified. Sarah Fielding wrote in the preface to David Simple (1744), a novel that a man would have presented without apology: "Perhaps the best Excuse that can be made for a Woman's venturing to write at all, is that which really produced this Book; Distress in her Circumstances: which she could not so well remove by any other Means in her Power."[54] She published the book anonymously; one name appeared on the second edition, that of her brother Henry, who supplied a new preface. However kindly meant, this essay reveals his lack of respect for Sarah's work. After devoting several pages to defending himself against charges that had been made against him, he said he had corrected only a few small errors which no gentleman would censure "in the Writings of a young Woman" and praised the book for two virtues it happens to lack, "vast Penetration into human Nature" and a probable, unified plot.[55] In her preface to *A Simple Story*, one of the best novels of the 1790s, Elizabeth Inchbald deplored the cruel necessity that forced her, against her inclination and capacity, to be an author, attributing her success entirely to good fortune.[56]

Even Jane Austen did not wish to be known as an author outside her own family. She published her novels anonymously and wrote them on a tiny desk in the family sitting room, never once objecting to constant interruptions. To insure that no servant or visitor would suspect her occupation, she wrote on small sheets of paper that could easily be slipped out of sight and refused to have a creaking door fixed because its noise warned her when anyone was coming.[57]

Apologetic and furtive about their creative work, women wrote under conditions unthinkable for a male author. Burney had to rewrite *Evelina* in hours taken from sleep, since her days were filled with transcribing her father's now forgotten *General History of Music*. Since Dr. Burney was a perfectionist, he kept his daughters copying and recopying as he thought of small improvements. Fanny's transcription of her own work was made more laborious by the need she felt to disguise her handwriting, so that no printer could trace her novel to the Burney household and thereby possibly disgrace her father. Even after she had established herself as a successful author, she had to "steal" time to write her comedy "The Witlings" and left the style of *Cecilia* (1782) sloppy and verbose because she could not get time to revise it properly.

Burney, who dutifully worshiped her father, never complained; but Laetitia Hawkins, another novelist daughter of a literary father, was more open: "I was, I will not say *educated*, but *broke*, to the drudgery of my father's pursuits. I had no time but what I could *purloin* from my incessant task of copying, or writing from dictation—writing six hours in the day for my father, and reading nearly as long to my mother."[58]

Burney's attitude toward her writing was always ambiguous. She had been warned in adolescence that even keeping a journal was dangerous,[59] and was persuaded to burn her earliest fiction. Even after *Evelina* had proved a tremendous success, she was embarrassed and annoyed to be recognized as its author and agreed with her revered friend Crisp "that it would be the best policy, but for pecuniary advantages, for me to write no more." Always, she put modesty, delicacy, and conventional morality ahead of such literary values as truth to life. She assured her "Daddy" Crisp: "I would a thousand times rather forfeit my character as a writer, than risk ridicule or censure as a female." This accounts for many of the weaknesses of her novels, as well as the suppression of her best sustained imaginative work, her comedy "The Witlings." Her elders, notably her father and Crisp, convinced her that its satire was improperly cutting for a young lady. So she buried a work of high intrinsic merit that, destined for almost certain success on the stage, would have made it unnecessary for her to accept slavery at Court for financial security.[60]

Practically all the women writers show perpetual anxiety to remain above suspicion. Their heroines never have a libidinous or self-assertive thought; a sexual lapse in a female leads to lingering, remorseful death. Literary convention exerted almost as strong an influence as moral. As authorities on the heart, women were expected to focus on love, although delicacy precluded their dealing with it realistically. A male reviewer actually reproached Anna Laetitia Aikin (Barbauld) because her poems dealt with imagination, knowledge, and benevolence rather than love, "That pleasing passion, by which the ladies rule the world, & which they are thought so perfectly to understand." Of course he would have been horrified if she had actually "breathed . . . her desires given from nature," as he advised.[61]

The economic pressures on some women writers and the psychological inhibitions on all of them certainly limited their achievement. Nevertheless, they succeeded in establishing authorship as a profession by which women could adequately support themselves. They demonstrated that women could write in all genres, as professionally and as profitably as men. And, equally important if professional authorship was to be available to respectable women, they proved by example that publishing one's work could be consistent with the utmost virtue and femininity.

An important reason for the increasing number and competence of women writers was improved education, a development constantly commented on. Johnson spoke of "the amazing progress made of late years in literature by the women," as "he well remembered when a woman who could spell a common letter was regarded as all accomplished; but now they vie with the men in everything."[62] Thomas Gisborne declared that modern education did not merely provide girls with skills such as grammar and spelling, but called "forth the reasoning powers" and enriched "the mind with useful and interesting knowledge suitable to their sex."[63]

A comparison of spelling, punctuation, and sentence and paragraph organization in Dorothy Osborne's letters and Celia Fiennes's journal with the writing in the Bluestockings' letters and Burney's diary, substantiates these claims. Moreover, the Bluestockings' letters are filled with evidence of their enthusiasm for literature, such as Carter's and Montagu's amicable arguments over the characters in Tacitus's history.[64] The bookseller James Lackington testified in 1791: "there are some thousands of women, who frequent my shop, that know as well what books to choose, and are as well acquainted with works of taste and genius, as any gentleman in the kingdom, notwithstanding they sneer against novel readers."[65]

However, one cannot take all the claims at face value. For one thing, Gisborne's "suitable to their sex" indicates that certain knowledge was considered unsuitable—including much of natural history and often mathematics and Latin as well. Hannah More persuaded her father to teach her Latin, but he insisted on terminating her instruction in mathematics when she showed an "unfeminine" aptitude for the subject. When Johnson offered to teach Burney Latin, she was torn between gratification at the great man's interest and apprehension lest she be envied. The project ended when her father forbade her to learn.[66] The objection to the classical languages must have been based on their central importance in higher education, which gave them disproportionate significance in discriminating between the truly and the superficially educated. Many girls struggled to teach themselves Latin to establish their mental equality with men, while men became absurdly uncomfortable about women's learning it.[66]

Moreover, a double standard evidently prevailed in education as it did in writing. Eliza Haywood cheerfully argued that a woman could acquire a competent knowledge of natural philosophy, and aspire to make discoveries worthy to be recorded in the *Transactions of the Royal Society,* "without the least trouble or study." All she needed to do was spend a summer reading a few easy books and go for walks.[67] Burney's Eugenia Tyrold (in *Camilla*) is supposed to be an accomplished classical scholar— at the age of fifteen. Barbauld, a well-educated woman herself and a noted teacher, saw no point in higher education for women, sure that a girl who had not adequately developed her mind by fourteen or fifteen would never do so. Moreover, the competitive atmosphere of a classroom was unsuitable for girls, who could perfectly well "acquire knowledge . . . from conversation with a father, a brother or friend, in the way of family intercourse and easy conversation, and by such a course of reading as they may recommend."[68] Even the radical reformer Mary Hays maintained that "every branch of knowledge" may "be cultivated in a considerable degree, in the . . . domestic scenes of life."[69]

It was probably true that girls could learn more at home than at such schools as were available to them. Higher education was of course closed to women, and the fashionable boarding schools emphasized drawing and music, penmanship, French, and, above all, dancing and deportment. Yet, after years of effort, the girls painted and played less well than the poorest professionals and were unable to converse fluently in French.[70] The improvement in a wife's status from housekeeper to companion might lead merely to replacing useful domestic skills with useless "accomplishments."

A girl could get a good education at home, if she was so

fortunate as to have a learned father, brother, or friend who took an interest in teaching her. The clergyman Arthur Collier taught Latin to Hester Salusbury and Sarah Fielding, as well as to his two daughters. (He told Hester Salusbury Thrale later that Henry Fielding, who encouraged his sister when she read and wrote in English, became jealous when she was able to read Virgil.)[71] Elizabeth Elstob, an early and distinguished Anglo-Saxon scholar, was educated by her brother, and Elizabeth Carter by her father. Elizabeth Montagu's father encouraged her and her sister to vie with their brothers in wit and argument, and Conyers Middleton, her step-grandfather, examined her on the learned conversations she overheard in his company.[72]

Of course these women could not have profited from their opportunities without extraordinary ability and perseverance, since they were given neither the discipline nor the rewards of boys. And always there was the nagging suspicion that cultivating their minds was selfish and unfeminine; the resultant conflict was perhaps responsible for the chronic headaches of More and Carter. Learning for women had always to be justified—no, it did not make them vain or insubordinate or neglectful of their household duties. The young Burney's intellectual activity was rationed as a luxury: since she devoted her mornings to needlework, "my reading and writing in the afternoon is a pleasure I cannot be blamed for by my [step] mother, as it does not take up the time I ought to spend otherwise."[73]

Certainly more women were becoming better educated, but the clearest evidence of progress is the wider recognition that the education of women is important to society. For some time individuals had argued for better education for women—Bathsua Makin in 1673, Mary Astell in 1694, Daniel Defoe in 1698, Richard Steele in 1710, Jonathan Swift in 1726. But by the end of the century, most literary women, as well as many men, seriously considered the subject. Writers from radical Mary Wollstonecraft to ultra-conservative Hannah More recognized that education for girls had to be improved, that superficial accomplishments did not fit them for life or make proper use of their God-given capacities, that they must learn to read solid books, develop intellectual interests, and think for themselves.

The most practical way toward this goal was private reading, and women became an increasingly important element in
the reading public. As more lower-class women became literate
and more upper-class ones interested in reading, more books and
periodicals were directed to them, often with a specific aim of
education. At the end of the seventeenth century, John Dunton's
Athenian Mercury vouched for women's mental equality and
devoted the first Tuesday of every month to answering questions
from and about women, some flippant but others serious and
thoughtful.[74]

By far the most influential works for women were the essays
of Joseph Addison and Richard Steele, one of whose specified
aims was to educate "the fair." As Barbauld testified at the end
of the century: "From the papers of Addison we imbibed our
first relish for wit; from his criticisms we formed our first standard of taste; and from his delineations we drew our first ideas
of manners."[75] Steele and, especially, Addison are patronizing as
they instruct women and conventional as they define what is
feminine and assume women were put on earth to serve men.
Nevertheless, they significantly helped women by devoting so
much attention to their concerns and by constantly exhorting
them to behave according to their nature as rational beings; they
insisted that women had minds that should be developed, and
they gracefully imparted a great deal of cultural information.
Addison rightly claimed that *The Spectator* (1711-12) would help
to raise women's minds above amusements such as "the right ad-
justing of their Hair," which "seem contrived for them rather as
they are Women, than as they are reasonable Creatures; and are
more adapted to the Sex than to the Species."[76]

The Spectator inspired many magazines designed for women,
such as Eliza Haywood's *Female Spectator* (1744-46), Charlotte
Lennox's *Lady's Museum* (1760-61), and *The Lady's Magazine*,
which appeared in 1770 and ran for seventy-seven years. Generally these had some educational element. It is more significant
that *The Gentleman's Magazine* (1731-1914), the most successful
general periodical of the century, regularly carried articles on
women, which were often feminist in discussing women's lack
of educational and economic opportunities, the inequities of marriage, and the equality of the sexes.

An equally important educative force for women was their broadening social life. In the early eighteenth century, men sought domestic comfort or gallantry with women, but turned to their own sex for friendship and intellectual conversation. There was no organized way for a woman to meet others, women or men, who shared her intellectual interests: coffee houses and taverns were closed to her, and mixed social parties were usually assemblies devoted to cards or dancing, with conversation impossible. Visits were a formal obligation more than an opportunity for congenial intellectual discourse. Restricted to the conversation of their own sex, most of whom were poorly educated, women could not expand their minds through social intercourse. A person like Mary Wortley Montagu had no place to mingle with her peers.

To some extent, this pattern persisted through the century, as coffee houses and clubs remained closed to women, and ladies were expected to retire after dinner and leave the gentlemen to converse over their wine. (French observers were shocked by this custom, and feminists like Hays protested against it.[77]) Nevertheless, by mid-century women regularly participated in dinner parties and assemblies where they conversed with men on an equal basis. The *Life of Johnson* (1791) records innumerable such instances, such as Johnson's debate with the Quaker Mary Knowles about sexual distinctions in morality and the nature of friendship. A young woman could reasonably expect that "liberal and enlightened" men would be "not only ready . . . but eager" to share their wider knowledge and experience with "intelligent unassuming females."[78]

Older, more distinguished women associated with men as intellectual equals at the Bluestocking parties. On one occasion, "Mrs. Montagu, Mrs. Thrale, and Lord Mulgrave talked all the talk, and talked it so well, no one else had a wish beyond hearing them."[79] The Literary Club, the most distinguished group of men in England, stopped at Elizabeth Vesey's every other week after dining at the Turk's Head Tavern.[80] The Bluestocking parties created an atmosphere in which men could appreciate women's society in a nonsexual way and demonstrated that women could sustain the interest of intelligent men without the aid of cards or dancing. Though the Bluestockings did not publish much themselves, they helped professional women writers through direct patronage and by introducing them into society.

Bluestocking social life fostered observations like Johnson's on Elizabeth Montagu: "That lady exerts more *mind* in conversation than any person I ever met with. . . . She displays such powers of ratiocination, such radiations of intellectual eminence, as are amazing."[81] While of course the ability to appreciate a woman's mind was not unprecedented,[82] it became far more general as women became more prominent on the intellectual scene. And, in an age when women's success still depended largely upon the good will of men, it was crucially important that many influential men should respect women's intellect and encourage them to achieve. Richardson, a novelist of international reputation, enjoyed talking with intelligent women and urged them to publish their work. He seriously discussed his own work with women, as well as theirs.[83]

Johnson, more influential because his social circle was more distinguished, constantly helped women writers with advice and dedications and gracefully recognized their achievements, as when he organized a party for Lennox on the publication of her *Harriot Stuart* (1750) or greeted More by reciting one of her poems from memory. Flatly opposing the still prevalent view that education imperiled a woman's virtue, he maintained that a woman needed intelligence to be an attractive female or a good wife: "a man of sense and education should meet a suitable companion in a wife. It was a miserable thing when the conversation could only be such as, whether the mutton should be boiled or roasted, and probably a dispute about that."[84] He charged that John Milton's view of women as "subordinate and inferior beings" (so absurdly inconsistent with his championship of liberty for men) showed "something like a Turkish contempt of females."[85] Nekayah in Johnson's *Rasselas* (1759), less bound by her sexual role than any other heroine of eighteenth-century fiction, is actively searching for knowledge and experience precisely as her brother is.[86] Her lady-in-waiting is sent into a harem to demonstrate that even an Arab bandit will find an intelligent woman more interesting than a docile, empty-headed slave.

George Ballard formally celebrated the intellectual achievements of women in his *Memoirs of Several Ladies of Great Britain, Who Have Been Celebrated for Their Writings or Skill in
the Learned Languages Arts and Sciences* (1752). Unmarred by
patronage, it is a well-researched biographical dictionary that
aims to remove "that vulgar prejudice of the supposed incapacity
of the female sex." Ballard discussed sixty-three women, including Astell and Winchilsea; none were living, all were respectable, and none wrote for money. Generally he let the facts speak
for themselves, but on several occasions he explicitly defended
women's authorship of certain works as evidence that they were
capable of understanding Hebrew or developing a tight logical
argument.[87] Later in the century, women began to appear in
general biographical dictionaries, such as the *Catalogue of 500
Celebrated Authors of Great Britain, Now Living* (1788).[88]

The general improvement in attitude is well brought out by
the reception of Carter's translation of Epictetus (1758). A translation from the Greek of a difficult philosopher was far from traditional feminine territory, and it was unblushingly published
for money. Yet it was received with universal acclaim, and the
Monthly Review explicitly drew the conclusion that it would "be
no small mortification to the vanity of those men, who presume that the fair sex are unequal to the laborious pursuit of
philosophic speculation. Those assumers have been ready to
acknowledge the ladies' preeminence with respect to light and
ornamental talents; but, the more solid and noble faculties, they
have reserved as their own prerogative. . . . If women had the
benefit of liberal instructions, if they were inured to study, and
accustomed to learned conversation . . . if they had the same
opportunity of improvement as the men, there can be no doubt
but that they would be equally capable of reaching any intellectual attainment."[89]

Given the opportunity to use their minds and genuinely respected by influential men, some women were able to fulfill
themselves very satisfactorily. Hannah More is a striking example. She traveled freely among the most desirable company, and
her numerous works invariably brought high praise and large

profits. In later life, she did tireless and effective social work, campaigning against the Slave Trade, editing and distributing the enormously successful *Cheap Repository Tracts*, organizing and carefully supervising schools in the toughest districts of rural England. Some of this work took her far from the traditional lady's sphere, as when she and her sister talked to swearing, half-naked men in the "little hell" of a glass factory. But, although her effectiveness was recognized, it was never considered unfeminine. More was able to enjoy the utmost self-fulfillment and public acclaim without ceasing to be a model of feminine modesty and propriety.

She could manage this because she was exceptionally fortunate. Treated from childhood as "the genius" of her family, she was well educated by her father. In adult life four sisters gave her the support that men normally get from wives: namely, admiration and relief from trivial cares. Since she never married, she did not have to concern herself with pleasing a husband or looking after children; yet she was comfortably supported by an annuity from a friend, the profits of the school she ran with her sisters, and the proceeds of her works. With intellect, charm, good connections, and an engaging readiness to admire the right people, she easily won her way into the socially and culturally elite Bluestocking circle. These people helped her directly—her friend David Garrick shepherded her uninspired tragedy *Percy* (1777) to triumphant success—and endowed her unexceptionable conduct with such authority that she was asked by the royal family for advice on educating the princesses. Her exalted social and moral credentials must account for the success of *Coelebs in Search of a Wife* (1808), which despite stupefying dullness went into eleven editions in nine months.

Fortunate as she was, More had no reason to question the status quo. By affirming traditional morality in her life and works, she fulfilled what her society conceived to be woman's particular mission. Her contemporaries were suspicious of exceptional women and reluctant to have their assumptions challenged, but were genuinely pleased to recognize female achievement; hence they welcomed her as a splendid example of intellectual English womanhood. By constantly asserting that women should take no part in politics, More masked the radical implications of educating the poor or attacking the profitable Slave Trade. By seeing that she had no domestic obligations to meet, she could lead an independent and public existence while insisting that woman's proper place was at home looking after her family.[90]

Hannah More was, however, an exception. Few women enjoyed her opportunities, her position of public veneration, her independence of most restrictions and fortunate adaptability to those which remained. More typical was Catherine Talbot, who had nothing to do but be a lady. She delighted in "true . . . friendly . . . improving, or even diverting conversation" and did not object to being called away from intellectual pursuits to talk with a student from her spinning school or to advise a servant; but she felt she was wasting her life in formal chat which "a puppet or a parrot might perform . . . quite as well." Her essential problem, she came to recognize, was enforced idleness: "Because I have little to do, I do nothing with spirit. If Dr. Franklin would come over, and order me to clean the house with my own hands, I should be as happy as he made the Paris ladies by such sort of prescriptions. Or if I was obliged to spend a week in mere reading and meditation . . . Or, if his Majesty would make me a Secretary of State. In short any thing . . . that would take from me the appearance, without the reality, of being quite at my own liberty to do just what I please."[91]

As she saw, freedom for most women could only be apparent. Even in a benign, cultured home like her own, women were loaded with meaningless social obligations and inhibited from committing themselves to serious work. And always, a woman's comfort, fulfillment, and self-respect depended on the good will of the men around her. She could be educated if her father or brother was an educated man who took an interest in her mind; her wishes and judgment could influence her manner of living if her husband permitted them to; she could marry a congenial man if one came into her social circle and her parents approved him; she could have money to spend or give to others if her father or husband had it and would share it with her. Elizabeth Montagu could not have distinguished herself as a hostess, a

philanthropist, and a literary patron if her husband had not indulged her. Without recognizing the appalling consequences of
what she said, Hester Thrale explained why the words *wisely*
and *judiciously* "naturally belong to men," as *discreetly* and
prudently do to women: women "have seldom occasion to act
WISELY and JUDICIOUSLY—adverbs which imply a choice of profession or situation—seldom in *their* power; active principles of
industry, art, or strength—with which they have seldom aught to
do; although by managing PRUDENTLY and DISCREETLY those districts which fall particularly under female inspection, they may
doubtless take much of the burden from their companion's
shoulders."[92]

If a single woman was lucky, she would be supported graciously by her father or brother, and she might be helped by
annuities or legacies from wealthy friends. Sarah Fielding was
supported partly by her brothers, partly by annuities from Ralph
Allen and Elizabeth Montagu, and partly by the modest earnings of her books. Those women who made great profits from
their writing usually published by subscription, a method that
depended on influential connections. Carter made a thousand
pounds from her translation of Epictetus because all her friends,
including the "Queen of the Bluestockings" Elizabeth Montagu
and two bishops, exerted themselves to obtain subscribers.

However personally fortunate she might be, a woman was
under more pressure than a man to conform to conventional
ideas of propriety. Since reputation consists of what is said about
one rather than what one is, since it was so important to women
and so irretrievable once lost, women were terribly dependent
on public opinion. They had to avoid being talked about, however innocent they might be and however irresponsible the
talkers. Mary Wortley Montagu worried about some slanders
that a man might print against her because, "I am too well acquainted with the world ... not to know that the most ground-
less Accusation is allways of ill Consequence to a Woman."[93]
A writer in the *Monthly Review* stated as a matter of course
that women "are far more dependent upon the opinion of others
than men either are, or ought to be."[94]

Since every woman's fate depended on others, every woman
was liable to oppression. Wollstonecraft recognized this when

she made independence her primary claim in the *Vindication of the Rights of Woman*.[95] But most people refused to see the dangers and intrinsic humiliations of dependency. Rather, they rationalized that it was good for woman because suited to her nature. Woman was supposed to be happy in her freedom from the cares and temptations of the outside world and providentially equipped to adapt herself to other people: "Providence, designing from the beginning, that the manner of life to be adopted by women should in many respects ultimately depend, not so much on their own deliberate choice, as on the determination, or at least on the interest and convenience of the parent, of the husband, or of some other near connection; has implanted in them a remarkable tendency to conform to the wishes and example of those for whom they feel a warmth of regard, and even of all those with whom they are in familiar habits of intercourse."[96]

This assumption that woman was created for others, with the assumptions about woman's nature that justified it, unfortunately prevailed through the period, influencing the thought even of otherwise feminist writers. It was always there to block woman's claims to equal rights and equal fulfillment. It led to defining the excellence of women in terms of usefulness to men. Women were supposed to be by nature sprightly and witty to amuse men, refined and tasteful to polish their manners, sweet and compliant to soothe their tempers, pure and self-controlled to elevate their morals. Above all women had to be chaste, in order to sustain the honor and security of their male relatives. A man particularly values chastity, said Addison, because it gives him "a Property in the Person he loves, and consequently endears her to him in all things."[97]

Chastity and all the other qualities were differently interpreted according to the assumed differing needs of women and men. Women were expected to show altruism that no one would have presumed to demand from men. After all, domestic love was considered delightfully easy for a woman, who "has little else to do but (what she is accomplished by the mere gifts of nature) to appear lovely and agreeable to her husband, tender to her children, and affable to her servants."[98] Since her role is so easy and so protected, she can be expected to meet more perfectly the moderate standard required of her. In fiction we see the effects of this assumption in the Booth marriage in Henry Fielding's *Amelia* (1751), where a good wife is totally altruistic, while a good husband is merely affectionate and well intentioned. In life we see it in the general expectation that Thrale, widowed free of her loveless marriage at the age of forty-three, would devote the rest of her life to arranging aristocratic marriages for her daughters and nursing the seventy-year-old Johnson, who had become chronically ill and insufferably peevish. She was called criminally self-indulgent to seek happiness by marrying the man she loved.

The qualities considered feminine were those appropriate to a subordinate class. Steele casually remarked that modesty is "the chief Ornament" of women, integrity of men.[99] Both are virtues, of course, but the first is self-effacing; the second, self-assertive. Women were credited with wit, but this quality was supposed to predispose them to vanity and in any case was constantly made subordinate to the masculine faculty of judgment. Men argued, in a neat circle, that since men are the lawgivers, God must have qualified them with greater strength and reason than women; being better endowed, they should of course rule.[100]

Some writers explicitly identified amiable feminine qualities with inferiority: Edmund Burke declared that perfection cannot be the cause of beauty because "this quality, where it is highest in the female sex, almost always carries with it an idea of weakness and imperfection. Women are very sensible of this; for which reason, they learn to lisp, to totter in their walk, to counterfeit weakness, and even sickness. In all this, they are guided *by nature*."[101] He was not alone in valuing women for weaknesses, which excited men's "most pleasing virtues, generosity, honour, and compassion"[102]—as well as an even more pleasing glow of superiority. It is true that Swift, Johnson, and many women protested this idea that weakness is attractively feminine; but its influence is evident on practically every eighteenth-century heroine.

Defined in relationship to men, women tended to be seen as a homogeneous group separate from humanity in general.

They were evaluated in terms of their limited role in society, and hence expected to conform to a uniform standard for wife and motherhood, while men were free to manifest excellence in different ways. Satirists would write about humanity as male and then devote separate works (such as Pope's *Moral Essay* II, 1735, and Edward Young's Satires V and VI in *The Love of Fame*, 1727 and 1728) to neatly defining the nature and failings of women. Such an approach fostered glib generalizations like "Most women have no characters at all."[103]

Thus limited, women were relegated to a small "feminine" enclave in a society defined in terms of men. Describing his ideal life in "The Choice" (1700), John Pomfret got by and by to the role of women: he would choose to live near "some obliging, modest fair," but would not visit her too often, "For highest cordials all their virtue lose / By a too frequent and too bold an use."[104] "The Fair Sex . . . have Nothing in them which can deserve entirely to engross the whole Man."[105]

Unfortunately, it was Pomfret, Pope, Steele, and Burke who represented the mainstream of eighteenth-century attitudes toward women. Men who could see women as human beings like themselves were as exceptional as women who attained freedom and fulfillment. Social institutions remained thoroughly oppressive, though for fortunate women they might be mitigated by supportive fathers, fair-minded husbands, and enlightened male friends. The institutions were rationalized by assumptions about woman's nature that defined her as a helpmate to man, inferior and properly self-effacing. These assumptions justified men in exploiting and patronizing women and implanted inhibitions and self-disparagement in women themselves.

It was particularly hard to deal with the inequities of woman's lot because they were obscured by a sentimental haze that glamorized dependency and glossed over the pains of self-sacrifice. Few people would admit that the love that was supposed to prevail in marriage could not cancel the effects of oppression or exploitation, or that women could not be expected to find their fulfillment in serving others. That is why the hardheaded rationalism of the late seventeenth century contributed to liberation of women.

NOTES

1. Richard Steele, *The Spectator*, Everyman edition (London:
   J. M. Dent, 1950), III, 70-71. Margaret, Duchess of Newcastle, was an exceptionally assertive woman for her time,
   writing and publishing voluminously, and unabashedly
   avowing her thirst for fame. Yet when she wrote her autobiography, she defined herself as one man's daughter and
   another man's wife; see Patricia M. Spacks, *The Female
   Imagination* (New York: Knopf, 1975), p. 190.
2. Quoted in Spacks, *Female Imagination*, pp. 295-96.
3. *The Complete Letters of Lady Mary Wortley Montagu*, ed.
   Robert Halsband (Oxford: Clarendon, 1965), III, 100, 119,
   133. Hester Thrale Piozzi was grateful to her husband for
   spending on home improvements the money that she had
   brought into their marriage, because he could occupy their
   house only during her lifetime; see *Thraliana: The Diary
   of Mrs. Hester Lynch Thrale (Later Mrs. Piozzi) 1776-1809*,
   ed. Katharine C. Balderston (Oxford: Clarendon, 1951), pp.
   782-83.
4. Hester Lynch Thrale Piozzi, *British Synonymy; or, An Attempt at Regulating the Choice of Words in Familiar Conversation* (London: G. G. and J. Robinson, 1794), I, 419-20.
   The life of Charlotte Turner Smith shows how helpless
   even an able, hard-working woman was to protect her own
   and her children's money. Though she was a good business-
   woman, she could do nothing but watch while her husband
   dissipated the family fortune on harebrained speculations.
   When she left him, he kept her marriage portion of £3000
   and a £2000 legacy she was to receive. She painfully managed to support the family by turning out volume after
   volume of sentimental fiction, though she was not able to
   give her children a proper start in life. Benjamin Smith
   could have seized even her earnings had he not fortunately
   abandoned the family. There were certain limits to a husband's power over his wife's land, if provided for in settlements before marriage; but these affected only wealthy families and could have little practical effect. A wife's property
   could be protected from her husband if vested in trustees
   for her use. Doing this was more usual in the upper class,
   but one watchful middle-class father, the published John
   Newbery, left half his property to his son in trust for his
   stepdaughter in order to keep it away from her improvident
   husband, Christopher Smart; see Arthur Sherbo, *Christopher*

Smart: Scholar of the University (East Lansing: Michigan State University Press, 1967), p. 243.

5. In the end, Sloper's family intimidated Theophilus Cibber; Handel and other powerful patrons enabled Susannah to return to the stage; and the lovers lived together peacefully for over twenty years—but respectable women would never visit Susannah. The whole story is told in Mary Nash, *The Provoked Wife: The Life and Times of Susannah Cibber* (Boston: Little, Brown, 1977). Upper-class women might be in a slightly better position, if their marriage contract stipulated a separate maintenance for the wife if the couple should separate voluntarily.

6. Mary Granville Penderves Delany, *The Autobiography and Correspondence of Mrs. Delany*, ed. Sarah Chauncey Woolsey (Boston: Roberts Brothers, 1879), I, 91-92. Responding to a letter in the *Review*, Defoe advised Mrs. Miserable against leaving her husband because the resultant financial problems and scandal to her reputation would be even more unpleasant than living with him; see *Defoe's Review* (New York: Columbia University Press, 1938), III, 399-400. Though Mary Wortley Montagu had trouble with her own husband, she was "ever astonished . . . that Women can so far renounce all Decency as to endeavour to expose a Man whose name they bear" (*Letters*, II, 395-96).

7. Randolph Trumbach, *The Rise of the Egalitarian Family: Aristocratic Kinship and Domestic Relations in Eighteenth Century England* (New York: Academic Press, 1978), p. 158.

8. Isobel Grundy, quoting the speaker, in "Ovid and Eighteenth Century Divorce: An Unpublished Poem by Lady Mary Wortley Montagu," *Review of English Studies*, XXIII N.S. (1972), 422-24. (In her poem, Montagu pointed out that wives, unlike servants, can never be free of their bondage, that women have the same passions as men, and that "sublimer Virtu" is expected from the supposedly weaker sex than from Cato. Matthew and Laetitia Pilkington both committed adultery, but only she was reduced to beggary and treated as a prostitute. He remarried and obtained a respectable living in the Church.

9. James Boswell, *Life of Johnson* (London: Oxford University Press, 1960), pp. 394, 536; James Boswell, *The Ominous Years, 1774-76*, ed. Charles Ryskamp and Frederick A. Pottle (New York: McGraw-Hill, 1963), p. 287. Boswell agreed with Johnson; soon after this conversation he went off to refresh himself at a bagnio with a whore (*The Ominous Years*, p. 306).

10. [Richard Allestree], *The Ladies Calling. In Two Parts* (Oxford: The Theater, 1673), II, 29.
11. Thrale, *Thraliana*, pp. 178-79. Cf. Boswell, *Life of Johnson*, p. 394.
12. Jane West, *Letters to a Young Lady* (New York: Garland, 1974), I, 67-70, 77-78, III, 143, 145. Elizabeth Griffith, in *Essays, Addressed to Young Married Women* (1782) and Hester Mulso Chapone, in "A Letter to a New Married Lady" (1775), present similar but less unpleasing versions of the wife's obligation to support the marriage by always working to please her husband.
13. Richard Steele, *The Tatler*, No. 75. Jenny Jessamy, the unusually liberated heroine of Eliza Haywood's *History of Jemmy and Jenny Jessamy* (1753), nevertheless declares: "Our parents have not only an undoubted right to dispose of us [in marriage], but also are much better judges of what will make our happiness than ourselves can pretend to be"; reprinted in *The Novelist's Magazine* (London: Harrison, 1785), XVII, 57.
14. [Allestree], *The Ladies Calling*, II, 20.
15. Montagu, *Letters*, I, 96.
16. John Gregory, *A Father's Legacy to His Daughters* (New York: Garland, 1974), p. 82.
17. James Boswell, *Boswell in Holland, 1763-64*, ed. F. A. Pottle (New York: McGraw-Hill, 1952), p. 327; *The Ominous Years*, p. 178.
18. Montagu, *Letters*, I, 47-48, 133-35, 139-41, 151; Robert Halsband, *The Life of Lady Mary Wortley Montagu* (New York: Oxford University Press, 1960), p. 41.
19. Delany, *Autobiography and Correspondence*, I, 4-37, 64, 246.
20. Frances Burney, *The Early Diary of Frances Burney: 1768-1778*, ed. Annie Raine Ellis (London: George Bell, 1907), II, 52-54, 63-64, 69-70, 246-52, 273, 376; Burney, *Diary and Letters of Madame d'Arblay*, ed. Charlotte Barrett (London: Swan Sonnenschein, 1893), III, 214. Burney, who knew Mrs. Delany in old age, protested Alexander Pope's eulogy of the uncle who had treated her so unkindly.
21. Quoted in Miriam J. Benkovitz, "Some Observations on Woman's Concept of Self in the 18th Century," *Woman in the 18th Century and Other Essays*, ed. Paul Fritz and Richard Morton (Toronto: Samuel Stevens, Hakkert and Co., 1976), p. 47. No one found anything to criticize when, some years later, Thrale's daughter married an admiral seventeen years older than she. Elizabeth Robinson was happy to

accept Edward Montagu, an estimable wealthy man twenty-nine years older than she, because he would support her in the style she desired. Shortly after her own love match, Lady Mary Wortley Montagu advised a friend to carefully weigh her parents' choice against her own, and financial advantage against personal preference (*Letters*, I, 177-79).

22. *Thraliana*, p. 115; T. C. Duncan Eaves and Ben D. Kimpel, *Samuel Richardson: A Biography* (Oxford: Clarendon, 1971), p. 88.

23. See, e.g., Eliza Haywood, *The History of Miss Betsy Thoughtless* (London: T. Gardner, 1751), IV, 240, 244; George Farquhar, *The Beaux' Stratagem*, II, i. However, appalling things could happen in isolated areas. According to Maria Edgeworth, Lady Cathcart, in rural Ireland, "was locked up in her own house" for twenty years, "during which period her husband was visited by the neighbouring gentry, and it was his regular custom at dinner to send his compliments to Lady Cathcart." She was not released until her husband's death. See Edgeworth, *Castle Rackrent* (1800; New York: W. W. Norton, 1965), p. 18n.

24. Daniel Defoe, *The Family Instructor, in Five Parts* (Bungay: Brightly and Childs, 1816), p. 51. This is particularly significant because Defoe was not describing an ideal couple; the dialogue reflects what he assumed was the normal attitude of a husband.

25. Richard and Elizabeth Griffith, *A Series of Genuine Letters between Henry and Frances* (London: W. Johnston, 1767-72), I, 57-58, 136, II, 217-18. The letters were probably polished for publication, but are accepted as essentially what they purport to be, genuine.

26. *Ibid.*, II, 63, 115; V, 244. Cf. the driving of the happily mated Crofts in Jane Austen's *Persuasion* (New York: W. W. Norton, 1958), p. 92. On the Griffiths, see J. M. S. Tompkins, *The Polite Marriage* (Cambridge: Cambridge University Press, 1938). Mutual concessions were expected even in less idyllic marriages. The generally submissive Margaret Boswell insisted on seeing James's journal and, having read of his constant infidelities, indignantly refused to cohabit with him any more. Boswell accepted his wife's resentment, was genuinely contrite, and promised to reform, though of course his resolution did not last long; see *Boswell in Extremes 1776-78*, ed. Charles Weis and F. A. Pottle (New York: McGraw-Hill, 1970), pp. 64-65. And on one occasion Johnson urged Boswell to yield to his wife's entreaties to forgo one of his jaunts to London, on the grounds that he "ought

to study the happiness of her who studies [his] with so much diligence" (*Life of Johnson*, p. 560).

27. Hester Mulso Chapone, *The Works* (Boston: Wells and Wait, 1809), II, 47, 82, 118-23. Such a man is Maria Edgeworth's sensible, virtuous Mr. Bolingbroke in "The Modern Griselda," who is made very uncomfortable by his wife's professions of the absolute submission that the handbooks recommended. (These declarations happen to be false, but he would not want them even if genuine.) His ideal is to "live like reasonable creatures," as friends and equals: "I do not desire that my will should govern: where our inclinations differ, let reason decide between us; or where it is a matter not worth reasoning about, let us alternately yield to one another."

28. Boswell, *Boswell in Extremes*, p. 20. Cf. *Life of Johnson*, pp. 666-67.

29. Boswell, *Life of Johnson*, p. 548. Such sentiments make one understand why Samuel Richardson's women characters resent giving up their names on marriage; Boswell's arrangement provides a basis for the attitude of Clarissa Harlowe's odious brother, who resents his sisters as drains on his estate.

30. "Custom . . . allows not the daughters of people of fashion to leave their father's family to seek their own subsistence, and there is no way for them to gain a creditable livelihood" (Chapone, *Works*, II, 94).

31. Boswell, *Life of Johnson*, p. 625.

32. Burney, *Diary and Letters*, ed. Barrett, II, 265-66.

33. *A Series of Letters between Mrs. Elizabeth Carter and Miss Catherine Talbot . . . 1741 to 1770*, ed. Montagu Pennington (London: F. C. and J. Rivington, 1819), II, 63. Fortunately, Carter realized that she was not made for the etiquette and small talk of a Court, and her father (unlike Burney's) did not press her to accept; see Montagu Pennington, *Memoirs of the Life of Mrs. Elizabeth Carter* (London: F. C. and J. Rivington, 1808), I, 182-83.

34. Boswell, *Life of Johnson*, p. 630. She hoped the initial failure of *The Rivals* would make it financially necessary for her to sing publicly again (Oscar Sherwin, *Uncorking Old Sherry: The Life and Times of Richard Brinsley Sheridan* [New York: Twayne, 1960], p. 116), but Richard preferred perpetual financial anxiety to allowing his wife to earn money independently.

35. Mary Darby Robinson, *Memoirs of Mrs. Robinson, "Perdita,"* ed. by her daughter (London: Gibbings and Co., 1895), pp. 28-29, 31-32, 36, 42, 141-43, 151-52.

36. Maria and Richard Edgeworth, *Practical Education* (New York: Garland, 1974), pp. 548-49.
37. Daniel Defoe, *The Complete English Tradesman* (1725), in *The Novels and Miscellaneous Works*, ed. Sir Walter Scott (Oxford: D. A. Talboys, 1841), *passim*; "A New Method for Making Women as Useful and as Capable of Maintaining Themselves as the Men Are," quoted in Robert Palfrey Utter and Gwendolyn Bridges Needham, *Pamela's Daughters* (New York: Macmillan, 1937), pp. 229-30; Mary Ann Radcliffe, *The Female Advocate* (New York: Garland, 1974), p. 431.
38. Women such as Jane Sharp (1671), Elizabeth Cellier (1687), and Elizabeth Nihell (1760) vigorously argued the superior competence of midwives in normal deliveries.
39. Priscilla Wakefield, *Reflections on the Present Condition Of the Female Sex; With Suggestions for Its Improvement* (New York: Garland, 1974), pp. 150-53. Cf. Boswell, *Life of Johnson*, pp. 512-13.
40. Quoted in Utter and Needham, *Pamela's Daughters*, pp. 229-30.
41. Wakefield, *Reflections*, pp. 150-54. Carter also deplored this situation; see *Letters from Mrs. Elizabeth Carter to Mrs. Montagu*, ed. Montagu Pennington (London: F. C. and J. Rivington, 1817), II, 58-59.
42. Wakefield, *Reflections*, pp. 171-75.
43. Radcliffe, *Female Advocate*, p. 458. Johnson's *Rambler* No. 12 describes the humiliations and ultimate frustration of a poor gentleman's daughter seeking employment as a lady's maid; she is gratuitously insulted as dishonest and unchaste.
44. Alexander Pope, *The Dunciad*, II, lines 157-58. Direct hostility to women as authors is reflected in Behn's and Centlivre's charges that men sneered at women's plays and tried to make them fail. See Behn, preface to *The Dutch Lover*; Centlivre, Dedication to *The Platonick Lady*; and introduction to *The Works of the Celebrated Mrs. Centlivre* (London: John Pearson, 1872, apparently a reprint of the 1761 ed.), I, viii.
45. Anne Finch, Countess of Winchilsea, similarly left her collected poems in manuscript, hoping they would be published. Montagu at least was influenced by her ideas of propriety for an aristocrat as well as for a woman.
46. See, e.g., Elizabeth Inchbald's diffidence about the perfectly competent prefaces she supplied for *The British Theatre* and her biographer's disapproval of the enterprise, in *Memoirs of Mrs. Inchbald*, ed. James Boaden (London: Richard Bentley, 1833), II, 84.

47. Tobias Smollett, *The Expedition of Humphry Clinker*, ed. Angus Ross (Baltimore: Penguin Books, 1967), p. 160. It was said that male authors sometimes posed as women to get better sales.

48. Successful playwrights got more money for less labor, but it was very difficult for a woman without contacts to get a play produced. Inchbald, a professional actress, had to persist for a long time before being accepted as an author. Hannah More made £750 from *Percy*, but its production was lovingly supervised by her friend David Garrick.

49. It had by no means disappeared, as we see from Elizabeth Hamilton's statement, "The women fear and hate, the men ridicule and dislike" female writers, in her *Translation of the Letters of a Hindoo Rajah* (London: G. G. and J. Robinson, 1796), II, 285.

50. Hannah More, *Strictures on the Modern System of Female Education* (New York: Garland, 1974), II, 12-13.

51. The same phenomenon occurred earlier in the century with Elizabeth Rowe, whose insipid romances enjoyed high praise and lasting popularity because her demeanor was so modest and her morality so edifying. For an analysis of her appeal, see John J. Richetti, *Popular Fiction before Richardson* (Oxford: Clarendon, 1969).

52. Quoted in J. M. S. Tompkins, *The Popular Novel in England, 1770-1800* (Lincoln: University of Nebraska, 1961), p. 117.

53. Quoted in Philippe Séjourné, *Aspects Généraux du Roman Féminin en Angleterre de 1740 à 1800* (Aix-en-Provence: Publications des Annales de la Faculté des Lettres, 1966), p. 89.

54. Quoted in Irvin Ehrenpreis and Robert Halsband, *The Lady of Letters in the Eighteenth Century* (Los Angeles: University of California, 1969), p. 34. This was the preface to the first edition, replaced in the second, "corrected" edition by Henry Fielding's preface.

55. Sarah Fielding, *The Adventures of David Simple . . . in the Search for a True Friend* (London: A. Millar, 1754), I, vii-ix.

56. A reviewer singled out this absurdly self-disparaging preface for special praise, in the *Monthly Review* of April 1791; quoted in William McKee, *Elizabeth Inchbald, Novelist* (Washington: Catholic University of America, 1935), p. 25. Elizabeth Griffith's novels have lasted better than anything by her husband, but their voluminous correspondence discusses his work far more than hers, and she made a point of insisting that she wrote strictly from necessity (*Genuine*

Letters, IV, 30). Charlotte Smith, too, repeatedly insisted that she wrote novels only from financial need.

57. R. W. Chapman, *Jane Austen: Facts and Problems* (Oxford: Clarendon, 1948), pp. 130, 132-33. Male critics often commend Austen for working under these trying conditions. Maria Edgeworth also wrote in the family sitting room.

58. Quoted in Burney, *Early Diary*, I, lxviii.

59. *Ibid.*, I, 19-20.

60. Burney, *Diary and Letters*, ed. Barrett, I, 102, 170. Much as Burney deserves sympathy for the sacrifice of her work on "The Witlings," she was surely perverse to choose intellectual women for the object of her satire. She did not even want to be recognized as an intellectual, and tells of a time when, after picking up a translation of Cicero while alone in a library, she put it away instantly when someone came in, "because I dreaded being thought studious and affected" (*ibid.*, I, 22). Cf. Johnson's remark that he never saw her reading (*ibid.*, I, 82).

61. William Woodfall in *The Monthly Review*, 1773; quoted in Betsy Rodgers, *Georgian Chronicle: Mrs. Barbauld and Her Family* (London: Methuen, 1958), pp. 58-59.

62. Burney, *Diary and Letters*, ed. Barrett, I, 160. Cf. Boswell, *Life of Johnson*, p. 979. Hester Thrale said her own good education was exceptional, for in her youth, "Education was a Word . . . unknown, as applied to Females"; quoted in James L. Clifford, *Hester Lynch Piozzi (Mrs. Thrale)* (Oxford: Clarendon, 1952), p. 9.

63. Thomas Gisborne, *An Enquiry into the Duties of the Female Sex* (1797), (New York: Garland, 1974), pp. 58-59.

64. *Letters from Carter to Montagu*, I, 261-64.

65. Quoted in Séjourné, *Roman Féminin*, p. 50.

66. Thrale, *Thraliana*, p. 502. Burney delicately satirized the disproportionate emphasis placed on Latin by ascribing it to the dunce Sir Hugh Tyrold in *Camilla*. Cf. Edgeworth: she did not, "though a woman, set too high or too low a value upon the learned languages," in "The Good Aunt," *Moral Tales for Young People* (New York: Garland, 1974), II, 3.

67. Eliza Haywood, *The Female Spectator*, 1744-46 (Glasgow: Chapman and Duncan, 1775), III, 134.

68. Anna Laetitia Barbauld, *The Works*, ed. Lucy Aikin (London: Longman, 1825), I, xviii-xxi. Note how she echoes misogynistic St. Paul.

69. Mary Hays, *An Appeal to the Men of Great Britain in Behalf of Women* (New York: Garland, 1974), p. 250.

70. Hamilton, *Translation of the Letters of a Hindoo Rajah*, I, 132-34.
71. Thrale, *Thraliana*, pp. 78-79.
72. *Elizabeth Montagu, Queen of the Blue-Stockings: Her Correspondence from 1720 to 1761*, ed. Emily Climenson (London: John Murray, 1906), I, 6-7. Lady Mary Pierrepont (Wortley Montagu), provided by her father with instruction in needlework and carving, read voraciously in his library and taught herself Latin; ultimately she was helped by Bishop Gilbert Burnet, a friend of the family.
73. Burney, *Early Diary*, I, 15. Elizabeth Carter offered the most engaging refutation of the argument that learning interferes with housewifery, in telling how she learned to bake. After a disaster fifteen years before, "The children all set up their little throats against Greek and Latin ... So to stop their clamour, I happily applied myself to the forming a special good sweet cake, with such success, that the former mishap was forgot, and I was employed to make every christening cake that happened in the family ever after and ... several grave notable gentlewomen of unquestionable good housewifery have applied to me for the receipt" (*Letters between Carter and Talbot*, I, 181-82).
74. Florence M. Smith, *Mary Astell* (NY: AMS Press, 1966), pp. 46-47. More unconventional was Beighton's *The Ladies Diary* (1703-26), which challenged women with mathematical puzzles, often involving algebra or geometry. See Myra Reynolds, *The Learned Lady in England* (Boston: Houghton Mifflin, 1920), pp. 327-28.
75. *Selections from the Spectator, Tatler, Guardian, and Freeholder*, ed. Anna Laetitia Barbauld (London: Edward Moxon, 1849), I, vi-vii. She did, however, recognize that Addison's "pleasantries betray a contempt for women" (xv-xvii).
76. *Spectator*, I, 33. Cf. *Spectator* No. 323, on the lady's week, which "shews the Disagreeableness of such Actions as are indifferent in themselves, and blameable only as they proceed from Creatures endow'd with Reason" (III, 6).
77. Séjourné, *Roman Féminin*, pp. 22-24; Mary Hays, *Memoirs of Emma Courtney* (New York: Hugh M. Griffith, 1802), II, 31. A male character in Edgeworth's "Letter from a Gentleman" points out that only men can "converse freely with all classes of people, with men of wit, of science, of learning, with the artist, the mechanic, the labourer. . . . From academies, colleges, public libraries, private associations of literary men, women are excluded, if not by law, at least by custom"; in Maria Edgeworth, *Letters for Literary Ladies*

(New York: Garland, 1974), pp. 6-7. There was a ladies' coffeehouse in Bath (where in general women had more freedom), which Elizabeth Montagu much enjoyed; and in 1765 a group of ladies established Almack's, a mixed club.

78. Maria Edgeworth, *Patronage, in Tales and Novels* (New York: AMS Press, 1967), VIII, 15.

79. Burney, *Diary and Letters*, ed. Barrett, I, 234. Burney vividly describes an assembly at Elizabeth Vesey's, where Sir William Hamilton might be describing Pompeii, Elizabeth Carter and Hannah More discussing some new author, and Edmund Burke reading aloud a pamphlet with incomparable eloquence; in *Memoirs of Dr. Burney* (Philadelphia: Key and Biddle, 1833), p. 192.

80. M. G. Jones, *Hannah More* (Cambridge: Cambridge University Press, 1952), p. 58.

81. Quoted in *Mrs. Montagu, Queen of the Blues: Her Letters and Friendships from 1762 to 1800*, ed. Reginald Blunt (Boston: Houghton Mifflin, 1923), I, 10.

82. John Locke wrote that Lady Damaris Masham "is so well versed in theological and philosophical studies and of such an original mind that you will not find many men to whom she is not superior"; quoted in Smith, *Mary Astell*, p. 110.

83. Sarah Fielding wrote him her appreciation: Miss Collier and I "were at dinner with a hic, haec, hoc man who said, 'Well, I do wonder Mr. Richardson will be troubled with such silly women,' on which we thought to ourselves . . . if Mr. Richardson will bear us and not think us impertinent in pursuing the pleasure of his correspondence, we don't care in how many languages you fancy you despise us"; quoted in Joyce M. Horner, *The English Women Novelists and Their Connection with the Feminist Movement* (Northhampton: Smith College Studies in Modern Languages, XI, 1929-30), p. 34.

84. Boswell, *Life of Johnson*, pp. 445, 719. Cf. pp. 406, 859. For the importance of intelligence to attractiveness, see pp. 845, 1070. Johnson was disgusted with Barbauld for wasting her cultivated intellect in her husband's "infant boarding-school" (pp. 662-63).

85. Samuel Johnson, *Lives of the English Poets* (London: J. M. Dent, 1954), I, 93.

86. Harrison R. Steeves, *Before Jane Austen: The Shaping of the English Novel in the Eighteenth Century* (New York: Holt, Rinehart and Winston, 1965), p. 230. Johnson also displayed sympathy and respect for women in *Rambler* No. 18, where he showed that unhappiness in marriage often re-

sults not from deficiencies in women themselves but from selfishness or poor judgment on the part of the men who chose them for wives; when he advised Boswell to let his daughters learn all they could, for "it is a paltry Trick indeed to deny Women the Cultivation of their mental Powers" (Thrale, *Thraliana*, p. 172); and in the Dictionary, where he quoted from several women to illustrate the use of words.

87. George Ballard, *Memoirs of Several Ladies of Great Britain* (Oxford: W. Jackson, 1752), p. 321. See his articles on Mary Herbert, Countess of Pembroke, and Lady Dorothy Pakington.

88. Women authors are also listed in *Letters Concerning the Present State of England* (1772), *A New Catalogue of Living English Authors* (1799), *Literary Memoirs of Living Authors of Great Britain* (1798), *New Biographical Dictionary* (1796), and Theophilus Cibber's *Lives of the Poets* (1753). Regrettably—and surprisingly, considering his support of female authors—Johnson included not one woman in his *Lives of the English Poets* (1779-81).

89. *Monthly Review*, XVIII, 588, quoted in Séjourné, *Roman Féminin*, p. 29.

90. Even so, some people viciously attacked More for exerting too much influence on religion through her Sunday schools. See Mary Alden Hopkins, *Hannah More and Her Circle* (New York: Longmans, Green, 1947), pp. 192-93.

91. *Letters between Carter and Talbot*, II, 112, 322. Carter accepted formal visiting as a social duty, but recognized its irksomeness: "I have a very laudable affection for *conversation*, but . . . I mortally hate *talking*, and consequently I have no natural talents for a visit" (*Letters from Carter to Montagu*, II, 140).

92. Thrale, *British Synonymy*, II, 367-68. Cf. Boswell, *Life of Johnson*, p. 1089.

93. Montagu, *Letters*, II, 14. She illustrated her statement with the case of Griselda Murray, who resolutely prevented a footman from raping her, but then made the mistake of prosecuting him. The resulting trial attracted so much ribald publicity that she felt she had to leave home, writing to her father: "It cuts me to the soul to see you think I've even had the appearance of doing anything to the dishonour of your family." It is painful to add that Montagu herself exploited the situation in a lubricious "Epistle from Arthur Gray, the Footman, to Mrs. Murray." See Robert Halsband, "Virtue in Danger: The Case of Griselda Murray," *History Today*, 17 (1967), 693-96, 700.

94. *Monthly Review* (November, 1797), quoted in Séjourné, *Roman Féminin*, p. 69.

95. Cf. Thrale's description of the uncomfortable position of Frances Reynolds, who was supported by her brother, Sir Joshua. Thrale marveled at the poor lady's noble resolution "not to keep her Post by Flattery if She cannot keep it by Kindness;—this is a Flight so far beyond my power that I respect her for it, and do love dearly to hear her criticize Sir Joshua's Painting" (*Thraliana*, pp. 79-80).

96. Gisborne, *Enquiry*, p. 116.

97. *Spectator*, I, 306.

98. Steele, *Tatler* No. 175.

99. *Spectator*, I, 21.

100. Gisborne, *Enquiry*, pp. 19-23; George Savile, First Marquess of Halifax, *The Complete Works*, ed. Walter Raleigh (New York: Augustus M. Kelley, 1970), p. 8. Colley Cibber's very popular comedies constantly enforce the idea that a husband must rule his wife because he is wiser; the best example is *The Provoked Husband*.

101. Edmund Burke, *A Philosophical Enquiry into the Origin of Our Ideas of the Sublime and Beautiful* (1757), ed. James T. Boulton (London: Routledge and Kegan Paul, 1958), p. 110. Italics mine.

102. Richard Griffith, in *Genuine Letters between Henry and Frances*, I, 49. Cf. Alexander Pope's "Fine by defect, and delicately weak" ("Of the Characters of Women," line 43)—a line which infuriated both Wollstonecraft and More.

103. Pope, "Of the Characters of Women," line 2. Hays recognized the self-serving nature of such generalizations (*Appeal*, p. 31).

104. John Pomfret, "The Choice," lines 101, 136-37. In the same way, Matthew Green would use women as a remedy for "The Spleen" (1737), when his mind required relaxation by their frivolous gossip (lines 182 ff.).

105. Eustace Budgell, *The Spectator*, IV, 98.

❧ [2] ❧

THE LIBERATING EFFECT
OF RATIONALISM

The political upheavals in seventeenth-century England encouraged a spirit of rationalist questioning that ranged from the fashionable cynicism of Restoration courtiers to the theoretical analyses of John Locke. Even though these thinkers did not aim at achieving social change for women, they laid essential foundations for it by questioning the sacredness of traditional patriarchal institutions and exposing the sentimental falsifications that obscured their oppressive nature.

Locke's attack on the divine right of kings in *Two Treatises on Government* (1689, written about 1679) applied to patriarchy in the home as well as the state, since Locke's opponent, Sir Robert Filmer, had grounded the allegedly divine authority of the king in the state upon that of the father in the home. Locke's rational questioning of authority that had no clear basis in nature and restrictions that had no practical necessity could be used (though it rarely was) to undermine the oppressive hierarchical structure of the family. He did argue that a parent has authority over a child only so long as the child is too immature to judge for himself (or, presumably, herself), and that a married couple need stay together only so long as was necessary to raise their joint children.[1] He also swept aside irrational customary beliefs about sexual distinctions in education. Girls as well as boys should have plenty of fresh air and exercise, since robust health is more desirable than delicate beauty. Latin is not the essential distinction of an educated person; nor need there be any mystique about learning it, for an intelligent mother can easily teach herself enough to ground her son in Latin.[2]

Contemporary dramatists of manners shared Locke's rationalism if not his seriousness. The court wits surrounding Charles II, already disposed to ridicule the morality of female subordination because it was associated with middle-class puritanism, extended to women the right to plain-speaking and pleasure-seeking they claimed for themselves. Thus, without systematic concern for the rights of women, aristocratic literature challenged traditional restrictions upon their freedom and supported women in evading them. Its characters not only violate the conventions unscathed, but explicitly question them. George Etherege's Gatty (*She Would If She Could*, 1668) describes the favored position of men under the sexual double standard as "those privileges which custom has allowed 'em above us."[3] Women's chastity and reputation appear as the useful commodities they in fact were, rather than priceless spiritual values whose loss meant irremediable ruin. Although women recognize that their actions must be controlled by the double standard, their minds are as free as men's—in contrast to those of later eighteenth-century heroines, who accept the double standard as naturally right. This mental liberation is particularly evident in high comedy, where the characters' intellect and emotions are relatively untrammeled by mundane circumstance.

Though women in Restoration comedy generally appear only in courtship situations—that is, in relationship to men—within this sphere they have unlimited scope for capacity and self-will. Not only are they shrewd and enterprising, they are admired for these qualities. Far from modestly suppressing their own wishes and passively awaiting the disposition of senior relatives, they take charge of the most important decision of their lives. They work to get the man they choose, as is usual in romantic comedy; and they show a new articulateness as they protest against arranged marriage and defend their right of choice. Hillaria in Edward Ravenscroft's *The Careless Lovers* (1673) rebuffs her uncle's matchmaking with, "Do you think, Uncle, I ha'nt as much Wit to choose a Husband as you?" Women are no longer the "poor sneaking sheepish Creatures" they were in his young days; "in this Age, we know our own strength, and have wit enough to make use of our Talents. If I meet with a Husband makes my Heart ake, I'le make his Head ake." Hillaria denies that man and wife make one person in marriage, since "in Arithmetick . . . one and one makes two." She rebuts her cousin Jacinta's shocked protest on the grounds that women have "Rational Souls as well as Men" and were passive in former ages only because "Dotage then was counted Wisdom."[4]

After finding the man they want, the women in these works make him eager to marry them, despite his rakishness, through their wit, self-control, and force of character. When Hippolita in William Wycherley's *The Gentleman Dancing Master* (1672) is about to be forced to marry a fool, she does not weep or implore or pray for resignation. Instead, she tells herself, "Courage . . . thou art full fourteen years old, shift for thy self."[5] She contrives to find a more desirable suitor (even though her father keeps her isolated from men), to get the suitor into the house, to charm him into wanting to marry her, to test him to make sure he values her rather than her fortune, and to marry him under the noses of her father and her fiancé.

It is wit, not canine devotion, which holds the interest of a Restoration comic hero. Thus Olivia of Sir Charles Sedley's *The Mulberry Garden* (1668) declares that "The only way to oblige most men" is to tease them "a little now and then . . . it gives 'um an Opinion of our wit; and is consequently a Spur to theirs."[6] These playwrights dramatized courtship as playful opposition, for they recognized that interests occasionally conflict in all relationships. They expected neither the self-forgetfulness imagined by romantic writers nor the unconditional devotion demanded by contemporary moralists. Hence they saw no reason why an injured wife should not retaliate. In Wycherley's *The Country Wife* (1675), a neglectful husband, an abusive husband, and an inconsiderate fiancé are systematically deprived of their women, whose independence in finding satisfaction elsewhere is applauded by author and audience. Both this play and *The Mulberry Garden* emphasize the point that freedom and experience do not threaten woman's virtue; the only chaste woman in *The Country Wife* has always enjoyed "the innocent liberty of the Town."[7]

The concept of mutual rights in marriage becomes explicit in the proviso scenes that dot Restoration comedy. These show women justifiably hesitating before the total commitment that marriage required of them and intelligently trying to retain some autonomy even in a situation where their identity would be legally merged into their husband's. John Dryden's Florimel (*Secret Love*, 1667), reluctantly consenting to marry, stipulates that she and Celadon are to retain "two wills." They agree to love "as long as we can; and confess the truth when we can love no longer," and to abstain from prying into each other's affairs, whether his gambling debts or her male acquaintances.[8]

The classic proviso scene between Millamant and Mirabell in William Congreve's *The Way of the World* (1700) is far more serious, despite its surface flippancy. Dryden's pair are not necessarily laying the foundation of a good marriage, for they are joined by nothing more than immediate sexual attraction, and they define their freedom mainly in sexual terms. Mirabell, on the other hand, is a judicious and responsible man, whose relationship with Millamant has been established before the play opens. They are in love, but they are more concerned about personal privacy (on her side) and healthy childbearing (on his) than gross sexual derelictions. Developing their principles with greater and more realistic detail, Millamant and Mirabell provide a framework for marriage that could apply to actual life— and could almost be said to prefigure the marriage contracts of today.

Millamant's apparently frivolous requirements are a fanciful expression of her real need to retain personal independence in marriage. She wants to keep hearing "the agreeable fatigues of solicitation" because she sees that wives are often taken for granted. She protests against conjugal togetherness, as if husband and wife could not be free to enjoy visits and plays separately; she owns no obligation to consort with uncongenial people because they happen to be his connections; and she wants to do things on whim without being called on for an explanation. She wants the privacy necessary for an independent existence: to visit and correspond as she likes without questions or even "wry faces" from him, and to have a room of her own: "wherever I am, you shall always knock at the door before you come in." She does not want to be overborne by his judgment, even if it may be superior: "I shan't endure to be reprimanded nor instructed: 'tis so dull to act always by advice, and so tedious to be told of one's faults." Though Mirabell is wiser than she, since he enjoys the benefit of more education and experience than were available to women, Congreve lets her express a natural distaste for living with a perpetual mentor. Mirabell accepts her demands as "pretty reasonable," and his own counterprovisos would not limit the freedom of spirit she claims.[9] That Mirabell can accept her provisos without loss of manliness shows that Congreve did not share the usual assumption that men must dominate in marriage.

Through a mask of feminine coquetry and inconsequence, Millamant intelligently seeks to protect her personal identity in a repressive social role. The apparent frivolity of her claims doubtless made them more acceptable to the contemporary audience, but also made it easier to discount them as the whims of a silly coquette. High comedy can be dismissed as an artistic game with no relevance to real issues. Certainly it did not provide workable solutions to actual social problems. Wycherley lets us enjoy the country wife's brief fling with Horner without concerning himself about what will happen when her husband, Pinchwife, gets her back to the country. Restoration high comedy raises possibilities of liberation, but does nothing directly to implement them. In realistic comedy, such as Thomas Shadwell's *Bury Fair* (1689), women were firmly subordinated.

Shadwell liked to condemn comedy of wit in a high moral tone and called its typical leading characters "a Swearing, Drinking, Whoring, Ruffian" and "an impudent ill-bred *tomrig.*"[10] This attitude became more and more prevalent in the eighteenth century, as middle-class moral standards came increasingly to dominate. Assertiveness in women appeared even more offensive than adultery in rakish heroes. Jeremy Collier's *Short View of the Immorality and Profaneness of the English Stage* (1698) includes among its horrible examples John Vanbrugh's Lady

Brute, because she considers accepting a lover to console herself for her beastly husband (*The Provoked Wife*, 1697).[11] As conventional morality (patriarchal of course) was treated with increasing solemnity, women found it harder to justify retaliation and self-assertion even in their own minds.

There may seem little common ground between modish playwrights who jeered at traditional sexual morality and a conscientious clergyman who not only upheld it but despised feminine artifice and represented even licit sexuality as repulsive. Yet Jonathan Swift grew up in the tough-minded atmosphere of the Restoration and shared some of its attitudes. Like the playwrights, he expected women to be as strong and capable as men, to be able to direct their lives and look after themselves. Like them, he derided high-flown conceptions of romantic love and insisted that women were flesh and blood human beings. He hoped a newly married lady did "not still dream of Charms and Raptures, which Marriage ever did, and ever will, put a sudden end to" ("A Letter to a Very Young Lady on Her Marriage").[12]

Swift's ideal for marriage was rational friendship, in which sexual distinctions, as well as sexuality, were ignored as far as possible: "a Wise Man . . . soon grows weary of acting the Lover and treating his Wife like a Mistress, but wants a reasonable Companion, and a true Friend through every Stage of his Life." If the young lady will educate herself by following Swift's reading program and associating with well-informed people, her husband "will have a regard for" her "Judgment and Opinion in matters of the greatest weight"; and they will always "be able to entertain each other" without the help of others.

Swift insisted, rightly, that women could not be reasonable companions unless they were better educated. Despite the scolding tone that predominates, his writings reveal far more respect for women than does the patronizing praise offered by contemporaries like Steele; for he criticized them from the same high standard he applied to men. He was disgusted by the low level then considered good enough for women: "not one Gentleman's daughter in a thousand" can "read or understand her own natural tongue."[13]

He personally devoted much effort to forming the minds and values of young women to meet his high standards. These pupils, from his beloved Esther Johnson ("Stella") through the adventuress Laetitia Pilkington, accepted his often rough criticism because they recognized that it indicated genuine respect for their capacity. Though Pilkington was naturally coquettish, she "would at any time give up any pleasure or gaiety for the more rational entertainment of the Dean's conversation." Once, when she had left his house upset by his bullying, Swift wrote to her: "You must shake off the leavings of your sex. If you cannot keep a secret and take a chiding, you will quickly be out of my sphere. Corrigible people are to be chid; those who are otherwise may be very safe from any lectures of mine."[14]

When he constructed utopian societies in *Gulliver's Travels* (1726), Swift made a point of including organized educational systems for girls (in contrast to contemporary practice, which left them to pick up what they could at home). In Lilliput both girls and boys are educated in boarding schools run by the state. The girls' female attendants, whose only function is to dress them when they are small, are strictly forbidden to tell them "frightful or foolish Stories," so that "the young Ladies ... are as much ashamed of being Cowards and Fools, as the Men; and despise all personal Ornaments beyond Decency and Cleanliness." There is no essential difference in the education of girls and boys, except that the girls' exercises are slightly less robust and their learning slightly less academic, to leave room for lessons in household management. "For, their Maxim is, that ... a Wife should be always a reasonable and agreeable Companion, because she cannot always be young."

Among the more ideal Houyhnhnms, even less difference is made between males and females, who are alike distinguished by reason, friendship, and benevolence. They are all trained to "Strength, Speed, and Hardiness" and compete regularly in games, which are sometimes won by females. Gulliver's Houyhnhnm master "thought it monstrous in us to give the Females a different Kind of Education from the Males, except in some Articles of Domestick Management; whereby ... one Half of our Natives were good for nothing but bringing Children into the World: and to trust the Care of their Children to such use-less Animals, he said was yet a greater Instance of Brutality."[15]

As Swift drew utopian educational systems that developed the same human qualities in girls and boys, he admired these qualities in the two women he loved, Stella and Vanessa. When Stella devotedly nursed him during an illness, he did not praise her for "womanly" softness and self-sacrifice, but for "manly" honor. He did not define honor as military glory, which women could not attain, nor as chastity, to which they were usually limited, but as integrity, which is available to any person of character—just weighing of a moral issue, free of external influence, self-interest, and every unworthy passion: "How shall I act? is not the Case,/ But how would *Brutus* in my Place?" Stella's honor also shows itself in courage, honesty, absolute faithfulness to her word, love of freedom, and indignation against tyrannical rulers. In short, she has "The Fire that forms a manly Soul" as well as a "Fund of Wit and Sense" that most people are surprised to find in a woman ("To Stella, visiting me in my Sickness," 1720). Vanessa is also endowed with "Knowledge, Judgment, Wit . . . Justice, Truth and Fortitude"—qualities that her frivolous society has not the sense to appreciate. Swift concludes there is a need "to reform the Men" so they can value a truly superior woman ("Cadenus and Vanessa," 1713).[16]

In his "Letter to a Very Young Lady," Swift roundly declared that "there is no quality whereby Women endeavour to distinguish themselves from Men, for which they are not just so much the worse."[17] This scorn for "feminine" qualities must be interpreted in terms of the conventional ideal of his time, as expressed for example by Steele: "a right Woman . . . should have gentle Softness, tender Fear, and all those parts of Life, which distinguish her from the other Sex; with some Subordination to it, but such an Inferiority that makes her still more lovely" (*The Spectator*, 1714).[18] If femininity is to be identified with weakness and inferiority, the feminist will demand that women be like men. Accordingly, Swift told the young lady: "I am ignorant of any one quality that is amiable in a Man, which is not equally so in a Woman . . . Nor do I know one vice or folly which is not equally detestable in both," including the female prerogative of cowardice. He even discommended the blind approval that was considered becoming in a wife. Esteem your husband for the good qualities he has, but do not "fancy others in him which he certainly hath not," he wrote. "For although this latter is generally understood to be a mark of Love, yet it is indeed nothing but Affectation or ill Judgment."

Though Swift was contemptuous of all-female society—he "never yet knew a tolerable Woman to be fond of her own Sex" —this shows realistic evaluation rather than misogyny. When women were encouraged by every social force to be weak and frivolous, an intelligent woman would naturally feel out of place among them. Moreover, Swift was not sneering at the company of women, which he greatly enjoyed; and he went on to deplore the custom of isolating the sexes, stating that a well-chosen mixed group could be very agreeable. "As little respect as I have for the generality" of women, he pitied the lady of the house who had to withdraw immediately after dinner "as if it were an established Maxim, that Women are incapable of all Conversation. In a Room where both Sexes meet, if the Men are discoursing upon any general Subject, the Ladies never think it their business to partake in what passes, but in a separate Club entertain each other, with the price and choice of Lace and Silk, and what Dresses they liked or disapproved at the Church or the Play-house."[19] This statement does not express contempt for women, because it is plainly based on an exceptionally high standard of what women should be.

Swift never patronized women, but insisted that they be rational and virtuous just as men should be, which implies of course that they have equal natural capacity. He found their empty-headedness disgusting because he saw no more excuse for failings in women than in men. Extreme delicacy, exaggerated modesty, tearfulness, and cowardice, far from being naturally appropriate to the female sex, were just as contemptible in women as in men, and also undoubtedly the result of affectation, though Swift could not imagine why women should think it attractive to affect fears of nonexistent dangers or harmless animals.

While Swift's exhortations to women to be like men are positive in the sense that he acknowledged no inferiority intrinsic in their sex, they are negative insofar as he condemned everything that is distinctively female. Intelligent women should avoid the society of their sex, and feminine influence is always bad. Beauty should be ignored and romantic love is a "ridiculous Passion which hath no Being but in Play-Books and Romances." So little sanctity has motherhood that "Parents are the last of all others to be trusted with the Education of their own Children."[20] In fact, Swift repudiated female sexuality altogether, most graphically in such poems as "The Lady's Dressing Room" and "Strephon and Chloe." His descriptions of breasts are invariably disgusting, and he was obsessed with the bad smells that flow from the female body.[21] Thus he accepted women as equals, and indeed greatly enjoyed their friendship—but only to the extent that they made themselves like men by divesting themselves of distinctively feminine characteristics.

Daniel Defoe, like Swift, combined Restoration tough-mindedness about women and love with middle-class morality and concern with everyday life. Typical in expressing the new emphasis on love in marriage, which was particularly strong among liberal Dissenters, he was unusually aware of the difficulties in achieving that ideal. He devoted far more attention than did Swift to the practical problems of women, such as living with bad husbands or supporting themselves in a society that denied them training and opportunities. Because his examination of women's situation was so honest, full, and detailed, he was even led to question some of the moral laws which governed them, though by implication rather than direct challenge. Like Swift in believing that women could and should be abler and stronger than they were, Defoe took a more positive attitude: instead of scolding women for their weaknesses, he explicitly laid the blame on a male-dominated society. He was, unlike Swift and the Restoration dramatists, purposefully a feminist.

In his first important book, *An Essay upon Projects* (1697), Defoe proposed academies for girls analogous to the public schools for boys, declaring that women's apparent folly came from poor education rather than from natural inferiority. Women "are only beholden to natural parts for all their knowledge. Their youth is spent to teach them to stitch and sew or make baubles. They are taught to read indeed, and perhaps to write their names or so, and that is the height of a woman's education. And I would but ask any who slight the sex for their understanding, what is a man . . . good for that is taught no more?" He asked why anyone should consider ignorance "a necessary ornament in a woman," reminded men that education would cure the pride and impertinence they reprehend, and suspected they "denied women the advantages of education for fear they should vie with the men."[22]

Defoe agreed with Swift that the chief aim of education for women should be to make them more intelligent companions, that "they may be as profitable in their conversation as they are pleasant." Though he declared he "would deny no sort of learning" to girls "whose genius would lead them to it," he unfortunately did not specify a curriculum. Concentrating rather on the objection that would loom above all others in contemporary minds, possible imperilment of the girls' chastity, he described in great detail the precautions that would be taken to keep men away from the academy. He also made a point of disclaiming any intention of "exalting the female government in the least"; but he went on to question the rationale for masculine government by pointing out that once women were properly educated, they would no longer be weak in judgment.[23]

Defoe's voluminous discussion of marriage—domestic commentary in *The Review* (1704-13) and other newspapers and three manuals on family life, *The Family Instructor* (1715), *Religious Courtship* (1722), and *Conjugal Lewdness* (1727)—shows the same candid recognition of friction between spouses and the same refusal to expect women to give up their rightful claims that we find in Restoration comedy, with a more responsible facing of the real-life issues. Defoe conspicuously avoided references to the wife's duty to submit and obey (even though he fully endorsed the analogous domestic duties of children to parents and servants to masters) and constantly insisted that the responsibilities, duties, and rights of marriage are mutual. Throughout *Conjugal Lewdness* (which despite its title is not primarily concerned with sex) he insisted upon the necessity for mutual respect in marriage, mutual forbearance, and natural compatibility between the partners. He recognized that women risk more than men in marriage, but nowhere suggested that this greater commitment meant that they should be the only ones to yield in order to make their marriages work. Both men and women, he said, should resolve beforehand "to disband all Humours and ill Tempers, and sacrifice every Inclination to their Family Peace, . . . to study each others Humours, and to endeavour so to match their Tempers, that the Marriage may Unite their Souls as well as Bodies."[24]

Indeed, Defoe was "so little a Friend to that which they call Government and Obedience between the Man and his Wife" that he refused even to discuss subordination in marriage. "The great Duty between" man and wife is love, and the only obedience is obligingness on both sides: "Love knows no superior or inferior, no imperious Command on one hand, no reluctant Subjection on the other." Instead of assuming that woman was created to be a helpmate to man, Defoe believed the two should constantly help one another; instead of assuming that womanly love involved submission, he insisted that love could only be genuine and satisfying between equals. Without loving friendship, Defoe maintained, neither virtue, nor fidelity, nor "Conscience of the Conjugal Duty," nor religion, nor submission on the wife's part could create a good marriage.[25]

Just as obligations are mutual in a good marriage, blame usually is in a bad one. When a correspondent to *The Review* asked "for Directions what to do with a bad Wife," Defoe gave him no sympathy whatever. "She is a very bad Wife, that a kind good Husband cannot reclaim . . . there are such Abundance of good Wives call'd bad ones, or made bad ones by bad Husbands," that Defoe is reluctant to believe a woman a bad wife on her husband's word. Possibly the man's complaints of his wife's extravagance proceed from his own stinginess; or perhaps he holds her responsible for the entire expense of the household, while he squanders far greater sums on his private vices or follies.[26] If a man marries before he is ready to support a family, he has no right to blame his wife for the inevitable household expenses. If he conceals his financial situation from her, he cannot blame her for spending beyond their income. However tradesmen may "endeavour to excuse themselves ... by loading their wives with the blame of their miscarriage ... as old father Adam in another case did before them," Defoe is confident that a woman will not reduce her family to poverty if her husband "truly and timely" explains their financial position. Defoe refused to condemn out of hand even the wife who committed the paramount sin of adultery, declaring it was a man's business "to preserve the Affection of his Wife entire." A husband's wickedness does not justify his wife's adultery (as it would have in a comedy by Wycherley), but it does stop "his Mouth very much."[27]

Defoe's awareness of the oppression of women in marriage can be matched only by a woman, the passionate advocate of celibacy, Mary Astell. He went to the length of questioning why a woman would marry at all except to have children: "take a married Life, with all its *Addenda* of Family Cares, the trouble of looking after a Houshold, the hazard of being subject to the Humours and Passions of a churlish Man," or possibly of

> a Tyrant, and a Family-Brute; with still more the apparent hazard of being ruined in Fortune by his Disasters if a Tradesman, by his Immoralities if a Gentleman, and by his Vices if a Rake ... she would be next to Lunatick to marry, to give up her Liberty, take a Man to call Master, and promise when she takes him to *Honour* and *Obey* him. What! give herself away for nothing! Mortgage the Mirth, the Freedom, the Liberty, and all the Pleasures of her Virgin-state, the Honour and Authority of being her own, and at her own dispose ... to be ... a Wife without Children.[28]

Notice that Defoe refrains from sentimentalizing over the joys of loving submission, or the bliss of sexual fulfillment, or the forlorn state of a woman without a man to look after her.

Defoe showed his respect for women in a more positive way through his presentation of the wife's role in *The Complete English Tradesman* (1725). Again like the comic writers, he encouraged women to be independent, although his emphasis is economic rather than sexual. He thought a wife should participate in her husband's trade rather than passively consume his gains and should be prepared to fend for herself in case of widowhood. Women, like everyone else, should do all they can to avoid the role of passive victim. Although some women may be too foolish or proud to concern themselves with trade, the fault more commonly lies with the husband, who may take foolish pride in keeping his wife an idle lady with nothing to do but make visits. Some husbands think the appearance of their wives in their shops would debase their trades by making them seem "less masculine"; and some "unkind . . . and imperious" men fear to make their wives useful lest they "value themselves upon it, and make themselves . . . equal to their husbands."

Defoe ended this section with an inspiring tale of a young woman left by the sudden death of her husband with a flourishing business, five small children, and another on the way. Far from passively desponding, the widow applied "her mind to carry on the trade herself," improved the knowledge she had started to acquire during her husband's lifetime, and capably directed the employees. She built up the business steadily until her son grew up, then shared it equally with him and an apprentice whom she married to her daughter. How much better than if the family had merely divided what the father left, which would barely have kept them alive. Women, Defoe concluded, "when once they . . . think fit to rouse up themselves to their own relief, are not so helpless and shiftless creatures as some would make them appear."[29]

This resourceful heroine has something in common with Moll Flanders (1722) and Roxana (1724), as Defoe's insistence that a wife prepare herself for widowhood presages their preoccupation with comfortable survival in any eventuality. Defoe's novels, like his marriage manuals, stress the problems of marriage (especially the economic problems) and the need and capacity of women to be active and independent in order to cope with the disadvantages society imposed on them.

More significant, in the novels he seemed to feel freer to pursue his feminism beyond the bounds of respectable thought. Assuming the persona of a disreputable woman, he suggested a truly radical criticism of marriage and accepted standards of feminine behavior. From insisting that the obligations of marriage are mutual and equal, he proceeded to look at women just as he looked at men. From sympathetic recognition of women's difficulties in marriage, he proceeded to raise the question of whether they should marry at all or would do better to lead an independent life. This in turn raised the question of whether women could be independent without casting off the moral restrictions placed on their sex.

The plots of *Moll Flanders* and *Roxana*, focusing relentlessly upon economic necessity, demonstrate that women were made helpless by Defoe's society and that it might often be impossible to reconcile proper feminine behavior with survival. When Moll as a child expresses her reasonable desire to make an independent living, she learns that she cannot possibly support herself no matter how industriously she sews or spins.[30] It soon becomes apparent that she will have to depend on a man; if one man leaves her, she must find another.

Yet women cannot rely on men to support them. The respectably married Roxana (wed at fifteen to a fool her father mistakenly chose for her) can only watch while her inept, idle husband lets his business collapse; she is helpless to prevent the financial ruin she plainly sees coming. She cannot even inherit money, since her father will not leave her a legacy that would fall under her husband's control; instead, he leaves it under the care of her brother, who proceeds to lose it by going bankrupt.

Defoe's preoccupation with the economic aspect of marriage is not uplifting, but it was essential to cut through sentimental illusions that perpetuated the victimization of women by concealing their helplessness to earn or control money. Defoe had withering scorn for men who failed to support their families. If society deprives a woman of the opportunity to support herself, then the husband who does not support her is failing a vital responsibility, no matter how affectionate he may be.

When her husband deserts the family, Roxana is left with five small children to support. Their father, his relatives, and society at large leave them on her hands—"let her that brought them into the World, look after them if she will." Yet as a woman she is deprived of any means to do so. If she had one child or two she would have tried to support the family by needlework—provided people had kindly given her some to do—but for "one single Woman not bred to work, and at a Loss where to get Employment, to get the Bread of five Children" is, as she says, impossible. All she can do is sell her possessions one by one and beg from relatives who regard her as a troublesome parasite —forced to these degrading expedients only because she is a woman.

Thus Roxana must get rid of the children if any of them are to survive. It is only after they are gone that the kindly landlord comes forward to help her. As a respectable lady, conventionally brought up, Roxana is naturally horrified at the idea of prostituting herself to him "for Bread." But of course she has no other means of support, and—as her maid Amy says— chastity "is out of the Question when Starving is the Case." Since a woman's only source of support was a man, a woman who was not able to marry had to defy the law of chastity and become someone's mistress. Roxana's claim that she would have been happy if she had kept her chastity "tho' I had perish'd of meer Hunger; for, without question, a Woman ought rather to die, than to prostitute her Virtue and Honour" is surely to be read ironically.[31] It is better to become a nice man's mistress than to starve.

Moll too repeatedly finds herself in a position where she must choose between morality and survival: she can starve as the deserted wife of the linen draper who has squandered her fortune, or she can marry another man bigamously; she can starve as the widow of the ruined banker, or she can take to stealing. As long as they live as respectable women, Moll and Roxana are passive victims.

Casting off chastity not only enables Roxana to survive but increases her comfort and even her self-respect. She finds by experience that "a Wife is treated with Indifference, a Mistress with a strong Passion . . . a Wife must give up all she has; have every Reserve she makes for herself, be thought hard of, and be upbraided with her very *Pin-Money*," whereas the mistress can command her lover's property as well as her own; "the Wife bears a thousand Insults, and is forc'd to sit still and bear it, or part and be undone; a Mistress insulted, helps herself immediately, and takes another." Roxana immediately proceeds to disavow these "wicked Arguments for Whoring," but she cannot refute them. As a mistress, she is free to direct her life as she sees fit, for example to weigh coolly the advantages and disadvantages of marriage to the Dutch merchant who expected to coerce her into marriage by making her pregnant.

When the merchant argues that a woman should not object to giving up her liberty in marriage because in return she gets freedom from worldly cares, the fallacy is apparent because of the vivid picture of Roxana's marriage which has opened the book. When he goes on to argue that "where there was a mutual Love, there cou'd be no Bondage," she effectively exposes his sentimentality: "the Pretence of Affection, takes from a Woman everything that can be call'd *herself*; she is to have no Interest; no Aim; no View; but all in the Interest, Aim and View of the Husband." This conception of love reduces the woman to a "passive Creature," who lives "by Faith (not in God, but) in her Husband." That Defoe agreed with Roxana's arguments is suggested first by the merchant's concession that she "was right in the Main";[32] second, by Defoe's own use of similar arguments when he questioned why a woman would marry if not for children.

As a mistress, moreover, Roxana can enjoy ego gratification from professional success, which would not have been available to a woman in respectable domestic life. She wants public acclaim and wealth, and prostitution happens to be the only field in which she can use her talents to pursue her aims. In the same way, Moll Flanders, driven by necessity to be a thief, soon begins to take pride in her professional skill and success: "I grew the greatest artist of my time." Incongruous as her professional attitude is, it brings out the valid point that only in crime could a woman exercise the skill, resourcefulness, and application which would advance a man in honest trade. As a thief, also, she can make full use of her superior capacities by escaping the respectable woman's dependence on others: "I was seldom in any danger when I was by my self, or if I was, I got out of it with more dexterity than when I was entangled with the dull measures of other people."[33]

Defoe was exceptionally realistic and fair-minded in his recognition that women have the same ego drives which are condoned if not approved in men. He presented women fulfilling their ambition in the only way then open to them, and we wonder whether they are really more vicious than men who fulfill theirs by business deals or political maneuvering. Although Defoe's heroines lack such conventional attributes of femininity as delicacy, emotionality, and self-immolating devotion, they are unequivocally female, as evidenced by their sexual attractiveness and symbolized by Moll's discomfort when she wears men's clothes.[34] Presenting women in the same terms as men, Defoe implied that they were equally capable and equally entitled to self-determination and self-fulfillment.

In striking contrast to the traditional representation of women as being totally absorbed in romantic love, or sexual gratification, or preservation of chastity, Defoe showed sexual motivation as comparatively unimportant in Moll and Roxana, despite their profession. His lack of emphasis on chastity is particularly significant. Where most eighteenth-century writers, even feminists like Samuel Richardson, made a woman's chastity the central concern of her life, Defoe sensibly showed that it is not all that important. He laid relatively little stress on physical fidelity even in his treatises on marriage, and in his novels he repeatedly showed that a woman who lost her chastity was not necessarily ruined, and could in fact prove to be an excellent wife.[35] (I believe that Defoe's development of his plots is more to be trusted than the self-condemnations he put into the mouths of his characters.)

By showing that women's lives need not be determined by their sexual status, Defoe demonstrated his recognition of their full humanity and his wish to free them from sexual as well as economic dependence on men. Moll and Roxana, early divested of their chastity, are free to adapt themselves to situations so as to survive as well as possible, to choose whether or not they will have a man, and to remake their lives after any catastrophe. The significance of their stories increases when we remember how consistently eighteenth-century writers reinforced women's inhibitions by showing sexual desire leading inevitably to seduction, and seduction to ruin. In Defoe's novels, sexual experience frees women from inhibitions and emboldens them to deal more effectively with the world, as it is likely to do in real life; in most literature of the period, it imprisons them ineluctably in guilt and shame.

Obviously, Moll and Roxana were too disreputable to function as role models for eighteenth-century ladies. The price they paid for their freedom was too high. Their mercenary values and callousness are dismaying even to modern readers. Nevertheless, they demonstrate what emancipation is possible to women when the usual moral inhibitions have been removed. By creating realistic fictional situations in which such women could flourish, Defoe opened up possibilities of independence that are exhilarating even today.

Defoe had a more positive attitude toward love than Swift did, for he considered it the "one essential and absolutely necessary Part" of marriage, without which "I think [it is] hardly lawful, I am sure [it] is not rational, and . . . can never be happy."[36] But his position was not so different as the words suggest, since the love he meant was solidly grounded on merit, compatibility, and mutual help, as well as economic sufficiency. He shared Swift's contempt for people who married for romantic attraction alone.[37] Both were well aware of the potential difficulties of marriage, though Defoe dealt with these more from the woman's point of view, Swift from the man's. We find the same devaluation of sex and romance, the same acute awareness of the problems of marriage, in the first systematic feminist in England, Mary Astell.

Astell maintained a strongly conservative position both in religion and politics: "in a State of Ignorance and Pravity such as ours is, there is not any thing that tends more to Confusion than Equality."[38] But this did not inhibit her from radical thinking about the nature of her sex, which produced *A Serious Proposal to the Ladies* (1694), a project for establishing a "monastery" or "religious retirement" for women, and *Some Reflections upon Marriage Occasioned by the Duke and Duchess of Mazarine's Case* (1700), inspired by the Duchess's apologia for eloping from her crazy husband. Both books were popular enough to go through several editions. The *Proposal* attracted considerable attention, much of it respectful, but met the fate Astell feared

for it when she said she would rather "find her Project condemn'd as foolish and impertinent, than . . . find it receiv'd with
some Approbation, and yet no body endeavouring to put it in
practice."[39] The institution she proposed was too much like a
Roman Catholic convent, and for most people, even feminist
sympathizers like Defoe, the dangers of popery far outweighed
the interests of women.

The institution did indeed resemble a liberal and enlightened convent, except that its explicit aim was self-development.
All that would be required of its occupants would be "to be as
Happy as possibly you can, and to make sure of a Felicity that
will fill all the capacities of your Souls!" This would include
emotional fulfillment in the form of virtuous friendship, "a
Blessing, the purchase of which were richly worth all the World
besides! . . . a love that . . . makes no distinction between its
Friend and its self, except that in Temporals it prefers her interest." Astell's emphasis upon friendships among women is
highly significant, since her contemporaries expected women to
focus their affections on men and children and even denied that
they could have strong feelings independent of biological ties.

Within this female community, celibate women could lead
fulfilling lives and girls could be educated until they were ready
for marriage. All would be relieved of pressure to marry, since
they would be provided with a desirable alternative. They would
divide their time among prayer, study, teaching, and good works.
Education would consist of reading substantial works—French
philosophy rather than French romances—and conversing in such
a way as to "enlarge their prospect, rectify their false Ideas, form
. . . adequate conceptions of the End and Dignity of their Natures," and understand their religious principles.

Astell made short work of the usual arguments against
educating women. "A smattering of Learning" might "make
Women vain and assuming"—as, she notes, it does men—but a
solid education will decrease talkativeness by teaching women
to speak only to the purpose. And, since ladies generally have
plenty of leisure time, learning will not draw them away from
their household affairs but from fashionable idleness: "is not the
fitting our selves to do Real Services to our Neighbours, a better

expression of our Civility than the formal performance of a thousand ridiculous Ceremonies, which every one condemns and yet none has the Courage to break through?" Finally, a woman should certainly not be held back by the fear of outshining her husband. If she knows more than he, it is his own fault because of his greater opportunities for improvement, "unless he be a natural *Block-head*, and then such an one will need a wise Woman to govern him."

As aware as Swift of the follies of her sex, Astell was more insistent that these proceeded entirely from poor training. There is no natural reason why women "should be content to be Cyphers in the World, useless at the best, and in a little time a burden and nuisance to all about them"; but as things now stand, they "are from their very Infancy debar'd those Advantages, with the want of which they are afterwards reproached, and nursed up in those Vices which will hereafter be upbraided to them." If a poor young lady is taught "that 'tis Wisdom enough for her to know how to dress her self, that she may become amiable in his eyes, to whom it appertains to be knowing and learned; who can blame her" if all she cares about is outshining others in dress?[40] How can women develop proper values when they are persistently discouraged from learning? While boys are carefully taught and rewarded with fame, authority, and riches, girls who want to learn are frowned upon or laughed at. "If, in spite of all Difficulties, Nature prevails . . . they are stared upon as Monsters, censur'd, envied, and every way discouraged."[41]

Properly educating women would not only free them from vanity and pettiness, but would "render them more agreeable and useful in company" and capable of amusing themselves when alone. They would be better wives, for a husband who can be entertained with his wife's conversation at home "needs not run into Temptations in search of Diversions abroad." They would be better mothers, for bringing up children requires not only tenderness, but a thorough understanding of human nature.[42]

This last is to be acquired from practical experience as well as books. The accepted policy that a young man should gain knowledge of the world, so as to know whom to trust and what to conceal, holds equally for a young woman—more so, even, since reputation is more vital to her.[43] Most contemporary writers, assuming woman's virtue was too fragile to withstand exposure to evil, identified it with innocence—innocence that must be unceasingly protected by others. Astell would have women acquire experience so they could protect themselves.

Finally and most important, no one who is ignorant can be truly religious and moral, for belief must be founded on understanding. Women must not merely "know whats Commanded and what Forbid, without being inform'd of the Reasons why. . . . For we find a Natural Liberty within us which checks at an Injunction that has nothing but Authority to back it."[44] The natural instinct to question arbitrary authority, on which English males prided themselves, was not generally conceded to women. Astell, one of the few people to apply Locke's libertarian teaching to the family, derided this inconsistency in the liberal politicians: "how much soever Arbitrary Power may be dislik'd on a Throne, not *Milton* . . . nor any of the Advocates of Resistance, would cry up Liberty to poor *Female Slaves*, or plead for the Lawfulness of Resisting a private Tyranny." And English women were slaves, "if the being subjected to the *inconstant, uncertain, unknown arbitrary Will* of Men, be the perfect *Condition of Slavery.*"[45]

Astell differed from her male contemporaries in grounding her arguments for educating women more on their own self-development than on their usefulness to others. More explicitly than any writer of her time, she insisted that women should be independent of men. As the coquette values herself too little when she bases her self-esteem on "the pitiful Conquest of some worthless heart," so does the wife whose highest moral aspiration is to obey her husband.[46] Repudiating the accepted doctrine that woman was created to be a helpmate to man, Astell denounced "those who think so Contemptibly of such a considerable part of *God's* Creation, as to suppose that we were made for nothing else but to Admire and do them Service, and to make provision for the low concerns of an Animal Life."[47]

Astell's preference for celibacy, along with her conservative acceptance of established law, accounts for her relative indifference to improving the lot of women in marriage. While she argued passionately that women were not created inferior to men, she agreed that they were subject to their husbands. It follows that a wise woman will remain single. One who does not choose to do so must accept marriage as it is; and since it is intrinsically oppressive, it does not much matter whom she makes her master. Therefore a girl should agree to any convenient match which her family arranges, "Modesty requiring that a woman should not love before Marriage, but only make choice of one whom she can love hereafter; She who has none but innocent affections, being easily able to fix them where Duty requires."[48] Astell sympathized with the woman who, rightly in her opinion, would not sacrifice her independence for the moderate satisfaction that marriage could offer; she did not concern herself with the woman who wanted a richer emotional life, or who was forced to marry by family pressure or economic need.

Accordingly, *Some Reflections Upon Marriage* draws a grim picture of the wife's situation but offers no suggestions for improving it. A man who courts a woman

> wants one to manage his Family, an House-keeper, one whose Interest it will be not to wrong him, and in whom therefore he can put greater Confidence than in any he can hire for Money. One who may breed his Children, taking all the Care and Trouble of their Education, to preserve his Name and Family. One whose Beauty, Wit, or good Humour and agreeable Conversation, will entertain him at Home when he has been contradicted and disappointed Abroad; who will do him that Justice the ill-natur'd World denies him; that is, in any one's Language but his own, sooth his Pride and flatter his Vanity, by [being] always . . . on his Side. . . . Who will . . . make it her Business, her very Ambition to content him. . . . In a word, one whom he can intirely Govern . . . who . . . cannot quit his Service, let him treat her how he will.[49]

Even more clearly than Defoe, Astell realized the consequences of centering a relationship on only one of its parties, of defining one person's virtue in terms of her usefulness to another person.

This is woman's situation in a fortunate marriage, when her husband has good sense and character. But many poor women find themselves "yok'd for Life to a disagreeable Person and imperious Temper, where Ignorance and Folly . . . tyrannizes over Wit and Sense." They are "perpetually contradicted for Contradiction-sake, and bore down by Authority, not by Argument," denied their "most innocent Desires, for no other Reason but the absolute Will and Pleasure of a Lord and Master, whose Follies a Wife, with all her Prudence, cannot hide." Like Defoe and unlike their contemporaries, Astell recognized stupidity as the worst of faults in a husband who was legally master, and she saw that such a man's unreasonableness could not be tactfully managed; it would only be reinforced by unlimited compliance from his wife.

Astell took pleasure in pointing out that such sacrifices, routinely expected of women, would be extolled as peculiar heroism in men: "that Woman must be endow'd with a Wisdom and Goodness much above what we suppose the Sex capable of, I fear much greater than any Man can pretend to, who can so constantly conquer her Passions, and divest herself even of innocent Self-love, as to give up the Cause when she is in the Right, . . . even when she clearly perceives . . . the Imprudence, nay, Folly and Madness of such a Conduct." Since men cannot deprive women of their natural good sense, they had best train it to the stoical virtue necessary to endure a life of total resignation. After all, even "the great and wise *Cato*" committed suicide rather than submit to a triumphant conqueror.

The only course of action Astell can recommend to a wife is stoical resignation; the only consolation, the belief that her sacrifices contribute "to bring Glory to *God*, and Benefit to Mankind." Indeed, she sometimes sounds like the most conservative preacher of wifely submission: "She then who Marries, ought to lay it down for an indisputable Maxim, that her Husband must govern absolutely and intirely, and that she has nothing else to do but to Please and Obey."[50]

While such statements appear to give reassuring support to the status quo, they must of course be interpreted in context. Though Astell would not go so far as to suggest changing the laws of marriage, believing them determined by Church and State, her stark presentation of their oppressiveness functions as a tacit criticism. Her constant implication that women would enjoy more happiness and dignity if they abstained from marriage is a more radical, though still implicit, attack on her society's concept of woman's role. It is possible that her conventionally proper statements were intended to be ironic. Certainly there are times when she allowed her tone to slip into sarcasm, as when she asked how a woman could possibly "forbear to admire the Worth and Excellency of the Superior Sex," who have done "all the great Actions that have been performed in the World": "Have they not founded Empires and over-turned them? . . . Their vast Minds lay Kingdoms waste. . . . All that the wise Man pronounces is an Oracle, and every Word the Witty speaks, a Jest. It is the Woman's Happiness to hear, admire and praise them, especially if a little Ill-nature keeps them at any time from bestowing due Applauses on each other!"[51]

Astell reconciled her feminism with her conservatism by refraining from direct attacks upon the law. (This resolution was easier for her because she herself evaded the pains as well as the joys of marriage by remaining single.) Even in her *Proposal*, she took care not to question the institutions of society. First, the strongly religious orientation of her plan for a community of women accorded with traditional views of woman's role in its stress on devotional reading and good works, although her insistence on understanding rather than passive acceptance is distinctively feminist. Second, while the "monastery" would provide congenial surroundings for study and self-development, there was no thought of practical application or external recognition. Astell explicitly denied any desire to expand women's opportunities for careers and must have assumed that the ladies would be supported by their families, since she made no mention of gainful employment. However, though she declared women had no business in the pulpit, at the bar, or in Parliament, she did not concede that this implied any inferiority, considering the absurdity of men's pursuits: men "may busy their Heads with Affairs of State, and spend their Time and Strength in recommending themselves to an uncertain Master, or a more giddy Multitude, our only endeavour shall be to be absolute Monarchs in our own Bosoms. . . . And whilst they have un-rival'd the Glory of speaking as *many* Languages as *Babel* afforded, we only desire to express our selves Pertinently and Judiciously in *One*."[52]

Thus Astell was able to combine acceptance of the external status quo with radical questioning of the alleged natural superiority on which men based their prerogatives. Not only did she insist on woman's natural equality to man and essential similarity in mind and character, but she did so with blunt aggressiveness, uninhibited by the modesty and tact considered appropriate to her sex. Recognizing that the timid conventionality of women is as destructive as the selfishness of men, she denounced those who smugly acquiesced in their own degradation, who were "wise enough to love their Chains, and to discern how very becomingly they fit." Let such women "enjoy the great Honour and Felicity of their tame, submissive and depending Temper! Let the Men applaud, and let them glory in this wonderful Humility!" Let the women pride themselves on "having the Prudence to avoid that audacious Attempt of soaring beyond their Sphere! Let them Huswife or Play, Dress, and be pretty entertaining Company! Or, which is better, relieve the Poor to ease their own Compassions, read pious Books, say their Prayers, and go to Church, because they have been taught and used to do so." But, she vehemently concludes, "let them not judge of the Sex by their own Scantling: For the great Author of Nature ... never design'd that the Mean and Imperfect, but that the most Compleat and Excellent of His Creatures in every Kind, should be the Standard of the rest."[53] Astell demolishes the superficial goodness on which conventional women pride themselves and acutely recognizes that conforming mediocrity can support self-satisfaction quite as well as unusual superiority. "The Humblest Person that lives has some Self-Esteem, nor is it either Fit or Possible that any should be without it." But let it be grounded on genuine worth.[54]

Women justify their passivity by appealing to tradition: "why shou'd we think so well of our selves as to fancy we can be wiser and better than those who have gone before?" Astell summarily dismissed such appeals (at least in the private sphere) in accordance with the rationalism of her age, testing customs and beliefs by reason as Locke did. We must discard prejudices, she insisted, no matter how many people have maintained them, nor how dear they have been to us. After all, our ancestors were no better than ourselves, equally liable to short-sightedness and self-interest; besides, it is not wise people but the crowd who make custom. Therefore, women should bravely stem the tide, should attempt the glorious though difficult conquest "over foolish and ill-grounded Maxims and sinful Customs."[55]

The Restoration court wits, as well as Swift and Defoe, would have agreed with Astell that opinions must "be cashier'd if they stand not the test of a severe Examination and sound Reason."[56] Such rational examination helped women by exposing the pious conventions that oppressed them and the sentimental fictions that exploited them. It suggested that a marriage should be evaluated like any other social relationship, that an institution that gave every advantage to one party was apt to be oppressive, and that this oppression could not be dispelled merely by the presumed affection between the parties. Since oppression of women was based on ill-defined moral assumptions or alleged natural differences, any clear-headed examination of their situation was potentially liberating.

Only potentially, however, since no one thought of changing society to improve the position of women—of changing the laws which subjugated married women, for example, or enabling women to enter the professions. It was because they thought in terms of private life and personal development that conservatives like Astell and Swift could be feminists even as they supported the established order in Church and State. Astell advocated total mental independence for women but did not suggest extending it into the practical sphere. The heroines of Restoration comedy and of Defoe's novels have a freedom and equality not to be enjoyed by dramatic or fictional heroines for generations to come, but the first were separated from ordinary life by the conventions of high comedy, the second by their outlaw status.

Still, these authors laid the groundwork for women's claims to equal treatment by insisting that there is a single human standard of mind and character. As Restoration cynics derided romantic idealization of women, they freed them to be people rather than angels, recognized in them the same ego as men have, and encouraged them to function independently in the world. As rationalists esteemed Reason the highest faculty of rational creatures, they exhorted women to follow it rather than some specifically "feminine" standard such as delicacy, affection, or "instinctive" rectitude.

Locke acknowledged "no difference of sex ... relating ... to truth, virtue and obedience."[57] Defoe assumed that resourcefulness and self-fulfillment were equally important to men and women, and Swift deplored all efforts of women to differentiate themselves from the general (male) standard of excellence. Astell grounded her argument on the injustice of denying women the opportunity to develop mental qualities they shared with men. Both the Restoration comic playwrights and Defoe recognized that a woman could survive the loss of her reputation, or even her chastity—a very important point considering that the assumed need to preserve these precious things was to inhibit women throughout the eighteenth century.

On the other hand, all these writers presented too one-sided a view of women to provide adequate role models. The Restoration playwrights restricted them to an entirely sexual role, played in artificial situations. Defoe applied himself to practical problems, but in the process largely eliminated romance, as well as tenderness. His fictional heroes, male and female, sacrifice their emotional life to their financial well-being. While his nonfictional handbooks present a more positive picture of marriage, they too overstress economic facts, economic rights, and precautions against being cheated.[58]

Swift and Astell, reacting against the immorality and frivolity of the Restoration, denied women sexual expression. Swift savagely degraded female physicality in his poems, dismissed love as a ridiculous passion, and assumed suitable marriages were to be arranged by the couple's relatives. Astell explicitly stated that a virtuous young woman should be able to prefer the husband her relatives have selected for her. In effect, they grant women human equality at the expense of their womanhood.

It is obvious that general suitability could not be enough to satisfy women in a relationship that was to dominate their lives, and that tenderness and sensibility had to supplement reason in their daily living. With all its negative effects on ideals for women, sentimentalism did improve their position by giving respect to their feelings. Moreover, as long as women's role in society was radically different from men's—most obviously, because their welfare and fulfillment centered on emotional relationships in the home—a masculine standard could not satisfy their needs.

NOTES

1. John Locke, *Two Treatises of Civil Government* (London: J. M. Dent, 1924), pp. 142-43, 148, 155-56. Hester Mulso Chapone quoted this passage to support her argument to Samuel Richardson that there are limits to the obedience a daughter owes her parents. Though Locke spoke only of sons, he surely included daughters, she says: "since the duty of a child is equally imposed on both, and since the natural liberty Mr. Locke speaks of arises from reason, it can never be proved that women have not a right to it, unless it can be proved that they are not capable of knowing the law they are under"; *The Works of Mrs. Chapone* (Boston: W. Wells and T. B. Wait, 1809), II, 39.
2. John Locke, *The Educational Writings*, ed. James L. Axtell (Cambridge, Eng.: Cambridge University Press, 1968), p. 344.
3. George Etherege, *She Would If She Could*, ed. Charlene M. Taylor (Lincoln: University of Nebraska Press, 1971), p. 20.
4. Quoted in Jean Gagen, *The New Woman: Her Emergence in English Drama 1600-1730* (New York: Twayne, 1954), pp. 121-24.
5. William Wycherley, *Complete Plays*, ed. Gerald Weales (Garden City, N.Y.: Doubleday, 1966), p. 155.
6. Sir Charles Sedley, *Poetical and Dramatic Works*, ed. V. de Sola Pinto (London: Constable, 1928), I, 119. Wit was expected in actual women, as well as in the comedies. According to the eighteenth-century journalist Eliza Haywood, King Charles was instantly put off by the lumpish replies of a beautiful woman whom he addressed in the Mall. Despite the deplorable promiscuity of the Restoration, Haywood continued, its requirement of intelligence in both men and women indicated "a certain Delicacy in Amours which cannot be alledged in Favour of the present"; *The Female*

Spectator (Dublin: George and Alexander Ewing, 1747), II, 249-50.

7. Wycherley, *Plays*, p. 274.

8. John Dryden, *Four Comedies*, ed. L. A. Beaurline and Fredson Bowers (Chicago: University of Chicago Press, 1967), pp. 97-98.

9. William Congreve, *Complete Plays*, ed. Alexander Ewald (New York: Hill and Wang, 1956), pp. 320, 344-47. Not all the proviso scenes in Restoration comedy are serious enough to be considered feminist—e.g., those between Monsieur and Flirt in Wycherley's *Gentleman Dancing Master* (which concerns keeping a mistress rather than marriage) and between Isabella and Sir Timorous in Dryden's *Wild Gallant*. Congreve's work as a whole does not demonstrate feminism, though Cynthia in *The Double Dealer* palely shares Millamant's apprehensions about marriage. Angelica in *Love for Love* anticipates Millamant's skillful one-upmanship, but the bracing effect is dissolved in the sentimentality of her final acceptance of Valentine.

10. Thomas Shadwell, Preface to *The Sullen Lovers*, in *The Complete Works*, ed. Montague Summers (London: Benjamin Blom, 1968), I, 11.

11. Jeremy Collier, *Short View . . . of the English Stage*, in *Critical Essays of the Seventeenth Century*, ed. J. E. Spingarn (Oxford: Clarendon, 1909), III, 257.

12. Jonathan Swift, *Satires and Personal Writings*, ed. William A. Eddy (London: Oxford University Press, 1932), p. 66.

13. *Ibid.*, pp. 66, 68.

14. Laetitia Pilkington, *Memoirs*, ed. Iris Barry (New York: Dodd, Mead, 1928), pp. 74-75, 87.

15. Jonathan Swift, *The Writings*, ed. Robert A. Greenberg and William B. Piper (New York: W. W. Norton, 1973), pp. 41-43, 233-35. (The description of Lilliputian education is, of course, in the short utopian passage interpolated in Book I.) Swift's utopian educational systems owe much to Locke.

16. Jonathan Swift, *The Poems*, ed. Harold Williams (Oxford: Clarendon, 1937), II, 693, 700, 713-14, 724-26.

17. Swift, *Satires and Personal Writings*, p. 70.

18. *The Spectator* (London: J. M. Dent, 1950), I, 436.

19. Swift, *Satires and Personal Writings*, pp. 64, 67, 69-71.

20. *Ibid.*, p. 66; Swift, *Gulliver's Travels*, in *The Writings*, p. 41.

21. Besides the poems mentioned in the text, see "A Beautiful Young Nymph Going to Bed," "Cassinus and Peter," Books II and IV of *Gulliver's Travels*.

22. Daniel Defoe, *Earlier Life and the Chief Earlier Works*, ed. Henry Morley (London: George Routledge, 1889), pp. 144-45.
23. Ibid., pp. 148, 152.
24. Daniel Defoe, *Conjugal Lewdness . . . A Treatise Concerning the Use and Abuse of the Marriage Bed* (Gainesville, Fla.: Scholars Facsimiles and Reprints, 1967), pp. 25-27, 32-33; Daniel Defoe, *The Review*, ed. Arthur Secord (New York: Columbia University Press, 1938), V, 34.
25. Defoe, *Conjugal Lewdness*, pp. 26-28.
26. Defoe, *Review*, X, 223-24.
27. Daniel Defoe, *The Complete English Tradesman*, in *The Novels and Miscellaneous Works*, ed. Sir Walter Scott (Oxford: D. A. Talboys, 1841), XVII, 91-94; Defoe, *Conjugal Lewdness*, p. 79; letter to *Applebee's Journal* in William Lee, *Daniel Defoe: His Life, and Recently Discovered Writings* (London: J. C. Hotten, 1869), III, 295.
28. Defoe, *Conjugal Lewdness*, p. 129. For Astell's views on marriage, see pp. 75-76.
29. Defoe, *Complete English Tradesman*, pp. 216, 219-23, 226.
30. Daniel Defoe, *Moll Flanders*, ed. James Sutherland (Boston: Houghton Mifflin, 1959), p. 13.
31. Daniel Defoe, *Roxana: The Fortunate Mistress*, ed. Jane Jack (London: Oxford University Press, 1969), pp. 15, 20, 28, 29.
32. Ibid., pp. 132, 149, 153.
33. Defoe, *Moll Flanders*, pp. 186, 191-92.
34. Ibid., p. 186.
35. Besides Moll and Roxana, there are the two good wives of Colonel Jack.
36. Defoe, *Conjugal Lewdness*, p. 28.
37. E.g., Defoe, *Review*, II, 347.
38. Mary Astell, *Moderation Truly Stated* (London: Richard Wilkin, 1704), p. 59.
39. Mary Astell, *A Serious Proposal to the Ladies For the Advancement of Their True and Greatest Interest* (London: R. Wilkin, 1694), p. 51.
40. Ibid., pp. 6, 11-12, 15-16, 20, 32-33, 37-38, 58, 131.
41. Mary Astell, *Some Reflections upon Marriage* (London: William Parker, 1730), p. 172.
42. Astell, *Proposal*, pp. 19, 38, 128. The laborious task of raising children devolves on women not because of natural law, but because fathers are usually not sufficiently interested, and besides, "Precepts contradicted by Examples seldom prove effectual."
43. Astell, *Reflections*, pp. 87-88.

44. Astell, *Proposal*, p. 128.
45. Astell, *Reflections*, pp. 44-45, 150. The Whig Shadwell made his heroine Gertrude say, "I ... have ever held non-resistance a doctrine fit for all wives, though for nobody else" (*Bury Fair*, 1689).
46. Astell, *Proposal*, p. 4; *Reflections*, pp. 90-91.
47. Astell, *Proposal*, p. 158.
48. *Ibid.*, p. 35. She added a long Appendix to *Reflections upon Marriage* to prove from the Bible that God did not create woman inferior to man.
49. Astell, *Reflections*, pp. 54-55.
50. *Ibid.*, pp. 4-5, 52-53, 82, 86, 123.
51. *Ibid.*, pp. 81-82.
52. Astell, *Proposal*, p. 159.
53. Astell, *Reflections*, pp. 175-77.
54. Astell, *Proposal*, p. 158.
55. *Ibid.*, pp. 66, 73. Astell's contemporary, Lady Mary Chudleigh, who was also conservative in politics and ardently religious, advanced similar views. In *The Female Preacher* (1699?) and *The Ladies' Defence* (1701) she defended women against the misogynistic preacher John Sprint, asking why wives alone should be expected to practice passive obedience and maintaining that women had a right, even an obligation, to be educated. In the preface and first essay of her *Essays upon Several Subjects* (1710), she exhorted women to cultivate their minds.
56. Astell, *Proposal*, p. 71.
57. Locke, *Educational Writings*, p. 344.
58. E.g., in *Religious Courtship* Defoe advises a woman considering marriage: "You must have his Estate appear, your Part be settled, and the Land bound to you ... you will have it under Hand and Seal, so that he shall not be able to go back" (London: E. Matthews, 1722, p. 198).

DIVERSE EXPRESSIONS OF FEMINISM
IN EARLY WOMEN WRITERS

Two of Mary Astell's contemporaries shared her indignation at conventional disparagement of women, though neither was a systematic feminist. They both wrote in personal, private genres obviously suited to women—lyrics and letters—and, like Astell, they did not write for money. Their primary motive was to express their ideas and feelings.

Anne Finch, Countess of Winchilsea, was in many ways a typical Augustan poet, writing in the traditional genres and consistently upholding reason. Yet, because she was a woman, her poems are subtly different from those of her male contemporaries. She obviously could not fit into the tradition, derived from the Roman erotic poets, in which Augustan love poetry presented love for a woman as a superficial feeling based on desire. Women appeared in this poetry only as more or less unworthy love objects, existing for the amusement of men and never individualized as human beings. For a woman, on the other hand, love was not a trivial pastime, but her major source of fulfillment; her husband, the only man a reputable woman could write to, was too important to her not to be individualized. Therefore, Winchilsea's poems express deeper feeling and give a far more vivid sense of a mutual relationship than do most men's poems to women.

For example, one poem opens, with passionate simplicity, "This to the Crown, and blessing of my life,/ The much lov'd husband, of a happy wife." She loves him, and he has made her happy. Their love is of paramount importance, and it gives, as love should, perfect happiness. She goes on to express her appreciation for the "constant passion" with which he conquered her initial resistance (perhaps she had resented the generally exploitative and superior attitude of contemporary men in love) and with which he now flouts fashionable convention by combining the status of a husband with the attentiveness of a lover. For his sake, she will even undertake "What I in women censure"—evidently, conforming to conventionally feminine frivolity and fashionable accomplishments. What emerges here is a real relationship, based on deep love, involving mutual concessions (his efforts to win her "stubborn, and ungratefull heart," her yielding to convention to please him), and irradiating both their lives equally.[1]

In "To Mr. F. Now Earl of W." she cleverly makes use of the conventions to express her own deeper feelings. Her husband is away and has asked her to greet him on his return with a poem. In typical Augustan manner, she appeals to the Muses, who are ready to assist until they discover, to their amazement and shock, what she is asking them to do—to help her express love for her husband! No, they cannot lend their aid to such an outlandish enterprise. They all send excuses, but Urania, the muse of heavenly love, tells the poet in confidence that heartfelt love can be expressed without the Muses' inspiration. So Winchilsea relies on her own feelings, realizing that to express tenderness for one you truly love requires no aid of Muse or convention. Always preserving Augustan form and Augustan restraint in these poems to her husband, Winchilsea achieved an unusually personal, genuine tone simply by looking at their actual relationship directly. Her expression of uncomplicated wholehearted pleasure in the company of a loved spouse, free of pretentiousness in feeling or diction, is unique in her period. Since it was impossible for a woman to be comfortable in the contemporary conventions of love poetry, she could not follow them without question as the men did. Since the men's poems were seldom sincerely felt and rarely achieved more than technical cleverness, her inability to follow their conventions was beneficial, in a sense forcing her to be original. Winchilsea could look directly at her feelings and describe them sincerely, thereby producing poems which were not only distinctively natural but refreshingly free of the superficiality and cynicism that tainted most love poetry in her time.[2]

"Ardelia's Answer to Ephelia" (c. 1690), one of Winchilsea's few satiric poems, is her personal adaptation of a popular Restoration form, in which the poet meets a fool who aims at being socially pleasing and who takes possession of him or her for a long tedious time. But, unlike the typical Restoration satirist, Ardelia (the poet) sees herself not as a perfect mistress of society's standards of wit and breeding, but as an outsider: she prides herself upon being outside of a society whose rules she considers immoral and irrational. Almeria, the butt of her satire, is a fool not because she cannot achieve true fashion, but because she fits perfectly the pattern of a sophisticated Restoration lady.

Almeria has a talent for seeing faults—"she discerns all failings, but her own"—but is effusively complimentary to one's face: she embraces Ardelia, protests she has pined hourly for her company, and insists she come to dine, though in fact she considers her an old-fashioned prude. After dinner they ramble about in Almeria's coach to see the fashionable sights—or, actually, "any thing, that might the time bestow." Ardelia stops to enter a church, while Almeria "Flys round the Coach" in order to display herself to the best advantage to any passing beau.

Almeria lists Ardelia's many faults to one of these fops—and thereby exposes herself, since she represents contemporary fashion in contrast to Ardelia's Right Reason. She has no interest in Almeria's most absorbing concern—those trifles on which most women built their egos, as indeed convention encouraged them to. Almeria prides herself on judgment shown in such things as placing "a patch, in some peculiar way,/ That may an unmark'd smile, to sight betray,/ And the vast genius of the Sex, display." She is mortified that Ardelia drank tea without a single "complement upon the cup," even though Almeria had braved a storm at sea in order to get her first choice of the china on an incoming ship. Instead of gratefully attending when Almeria advised her about clothing shops, Ardelia cut her off with "I deal with one that does all these provide,/ Having of other cares, enough beside."

Winchilsea was equally contemptuous of the housewifely occupations that frittered away women's lives. In her "Petition for an Absolute Retreat" she made a point of specifying that her table was not only to be simply provided (as was usual in such poems), but "spread without my Care." Unlike male authors, women had to supervise their own housekeeping. Even more ridiculous were the foolish pseudo-arts to which women were expected to devote themselves: to

> . . . in fading Silks compose
> Faintly, th'inimitable *Rose*,
> Fill up, an ill-drawn *Bird*, or paint on Glass
> The *Sov'reign's* blurr'd and undistinguish'd Face,
> The threatning *Angel*, and the speaking *Ass*. ("The Spleen")

Her withering view of the traditional feminine occupations was exceptionally uncompromising; for even the feminist Richardson and the intellectual Lady Mary Wortley Montagu carefully insisted that every woman must know how to use a needle.

Almeria rushes Ardelia from the church to Hyde Park, lest they should "loose e're night, an hour of finding fault." There Almeria sneers at a lovely girl because she is unsophisticated and a gifted writer because he does not compliment the ladies and her "best of friends" because she is rumored to be disgracefully in love. Finally Almeria sees the most ridiculous creature of all—a woman poet ("They say she writes, and 'tis a common jest"). Ardelia asks whether the poet is conceited or spiteful. Otherwise, what is wrong with a woman's writing? At length Ardelia manages to escape, to return to the country the next day.

Like any Augustan poet, Winchilsea satirized deviations from reason. But her enforced detachment from the fashionable world—attributable mostly to her sex—sharpened her ability to see where accepted social norms diverged from reason. As an outsider, she was better qualified to evaluate the ideals of the dominant group. Though she could satirize women very sharply, her satire is always modified by coming from a right-minded woman rather than a male censor of the sex. Thus she avoided patronizing generalizations and expected women to meet a universal human standard rather than a specifically "feminine" one.

She showed herself, as Ardelia in the "Answer" or the speaker in "On Myselfe," as one with sufficient rational morality to despise the frivolity charged to women, to value what is truly important and, if necessary, to live on her own resources. Moreover, she pointed out that society pressed women to be foolish: women are "Education's, more then Nature's fools" ("The Introduction"). Small-minded Almeria conforms to conventional standards; it is Ardelia who is the social misfit. Winchilsea's male contemporaries constantly twitted women for idle visiting; by specifying that no idle visitors were to invade her "Absolute Retreat," she indicated that formal visits were a tiresome burden imposed by society's view of ladylike behavior. Finally, Winchilsea saw follies primarily as a waste of women's time and resources, rather than as an annoyance to men. Ardelia scorns shopping not because it is expensive or takes her away from home and family, but because she is more interested in intellectual pursuits.

Winchilsea's feminism became explicit when she considered the plight of the female poet. Arguing women's right to express themselves rather than their right to compete with men in the marketplace, she was particularly concerned with inward factors—domestic pressures and inhibitions. More emphatically than any other eighteenth-century writer, she protested against the petty details that distracted the female author and the widespread assumption that it was presumptuous for a woman to write poetry. She was unusually outspoken in maintaining that a creative woman has a right to express herself because it is wrong to force anyone to bury a talent. Far from apologizing for taking time to fulfill herself by writing, she roundly declared that the approved feminine occupations were unworthy of an intelligent person.

Her "Introduction," written for a manuscript collection of her poems, not published by her but wistfully left for publication, argues her right to be a poet. Starting with the common Augustan attack on carping critics, she soon closes in on the charge all critics will find: her verses are "by a Woman writt." For most people believe that "a woman that attempts the pen" is "an intruder on the rights of men," since women should devote their minds to "Good breeding, fassion, dancing, dressing, play."

> To write, or read, or think, or to enquire
> Wou'd cloud our beauty, and exaust our time,
> And interrupt the Conquests of our prime;
> While the dull mannage, of a servile house
> Is held by some, our outmost art, and use.

In other words, men do not want women wasting time and energy on anything that does not contribute to their usefulness to men, whether as sexual objects or household managers; nor do they want them to rise above trivia, lest they develop ideas of their own. But Winchilsea's confidence falters when she considers the present state of women, and she comes to a depressing conclusion. Debarred from education, instead expected and actually trained to be dull, few women can rise above the mass. And if one is pressed by "warmer fancy, and ambition" to try, she cannot help wavering: "So strong, th' opposing faction still appears,/ The hopes to thrive, can ne're outweigh the fears." She concludes that she had best keep her muse's wing "contracted," keep her verses to herself and a few friends, not aspire to laurel groves but remain in her absolute retreat.

Such expressions of discouragement, and even more her occasional self-disparagement, when she calls her vocation a feminine foible or says her works would not merit publication regardless of her sex, show that Winchilsea was not completely easy in her unconventional role.[3] But most of the time she insisted not only that she was a serious poet, but that poetry was the most important thing in her life. When she suffered her periodic bouts with depression—to which her ambivalence as a woman poet may have contributed—her most painful fear was that her poetry was degenerating, and even that those who decried her writing as "An useless Folly, or presumptuous Fault" might be right ("The Spleen").

Defending a woman against the unthinking sneers of Almeria, who follows fashion by viewing a female poet as a ridiculous object, Winchilsea asked: "Why shou'd we from that pleasing art be ty'd,/ Or like State Pris'ners, Pen and Ink deny'd?"[4] Thus she made a bold equation between the legal restrictions on a prisoner (either deserved or imposed in flagrant violation of traditional English liberty) and the customary restrictions on a woman, imposed simply because of her sex. Winchilsea was particularly concerned with liberty—not the public liberty so constantly cited in British literature, freedom from autocracy and oppressive laws; but rather the domestic liberty that was harder to establish, especially for a woman, freedom from the petty restrictions of convention and trivial obligations. In the "Absolute Retreat," she petitioned that "the World may ne'er invade . . . My unshaken Liberty."[5]

Considering Winchilsea's emphasis on liberty, it is tempting to read her tale "The Bird and the Arras" as an allegory. A bird is caught in a room and mistakes the pictured scene on a tapestry for a real one, but, trying to alight on a tree, only beats herself against the flat surface. She rises to the pictured sky, seeing the pictured birds apparently flying there and glorying in her ability to rise above them. But then she strikes the ceiling and plummets to the ground. She flutters around "in endlesse cercles of dismay" until a kind person directs her out of the window "to ample space the only Heav'n of Birds." The bird imprisoned in a man-made room suggests a woman imprisoned in man-made conventions; the bird that makes doomed efforts to rise through the ceiling, the poet who "wou'd soar above the rest" of her sex, only to be "dispis'd, aiming to be admir'd."[6]

At the end of her "Nocturnal Reverie," description of the animals' activity at night leads her to delicate sympathy with their "shortliv'd Jubilee, . . . Which but endures, whilst Tyrant *Man* do's sleep." She is not deprecating obvious cruelty (as Pope did in "Windsor Forest"), nor even any specific oppression, but just the restrictions imposed on domestic and wild animals by man's dominion. The poet, too, enjoys an unaccustomed liberty in this peaceful solitary scene. In the subdued moonlight, she feels free from the distractions of day and able to respond to the spiritual influences that speak to her true nature; her "free Soul" can feel at home even "in th'inferiour World." The soul's affinity and longing for Heaven is of course a traditional religious idea, but one thinks also of the imprisoned bird finally escaping into "ample space."

Winchilsea's resentment of the restrictions on women's intellectual life, expressed indirectly in her claims for liberty, found its most direct statement in her wistful vision of the easy comradeship of men exchanging witty conversation and knowledgeable criticism at a London tavern:

> Happy you three! happy the Race of Men!
> Born to inform or to correct the Pen
> To proffitts pleasures freedom and command
> Whilst we beside you but as Cyphers stand
> T'increase your Numbers and to swell th'account
> Of your delights which from our charms amount.

Her regrets for what she is missing lead her to open protest against the assumption that women are a mere peripheral part of the human race; it is little consolation to be men's occasional love objects, if that is all they can be.[7]

But it is unlikely that such restrictions significantly cramped Winchilsea's creative development. The forms she found congenial could be adapted to fit her distinctive talent and point of view. She could write love poems in which woman is not an object to be idealized or fantasized about, but a human subject expressing her own feelings. She could write poems on friendship in which women, seen outside of sexual relationships, give ardent affection or wise guidance to one another.[8] She could write satire on women in which the satirist is not a censor scolding or instructing an inferior class, but a right-minded person criticizing fellow human beings for degrading themselves below the standards that all should meet. Winchilsea's experiences as a woman heightened her sensitivity to many things less evident to male contemporaries, especially the social restrictions upon human liberty. It is possible that she gained as much as she lost by her isolation from the masculine tradition, that this isolation, freeing her from conventional thought and feeling, helped her to develop her unique poetic voice.

Winchilsea's younger contemporary Lady Mary Wortley Montagu shows the effects of greater involvement in fashionable society and its expectations, sharpened perhaps by the caution advisable in a woman living separated from her husband. For, despite brilliant insights and indirect protests, Montagu never so emancipated herself from society's standards of propriety for women, even though she was a personal friend of Mary Astell. She wrote primarily for herself and her friends, but even so her feminism is typically veiled in apology or flippancy.

Montagu experienced the oppression of women in her society, for she had to educate herself, was bullied by a father who wanted her to marry a man she could not love, and was exiled from country and family when she could no longer live with the man she did marry. But she seems to have accepted this situation as inevitable and therefore to be endured without protest by a woman of breeding: "tis allwais the Fate of Women to obey."[9] She constantly professed that it was a wife's duty to obey her husband and conceal his faults from public view, and she was punctilious about complying with Edward Wortley Montagu's wishes after their separation. However radical her ideas might be—she once said the authority of parents and husbands "is built on grosse impositions upon Mankind"—she insisted that women maintain outward decorum. She even approved Lord Halifax's advice to his daughter "that a Husband's Kindness is to be kindly receiv'd by a Wife even when he is drunk, and thô it is wrapp'd up in never so much impertinence."[10]

Montagu prided herself on being a properly conducted aristocrat and a tough-minded rationalist, and she ruthlessly suppressed feminist feelings that seemed to conflict with these ideals.[11] She was deeply moved by Richardson's Clarissa, but called herself "an old Fool" to weep over Clarissa's fate and attributed her emotion merely to her own experience of almost being forced into a distasteful marriage. She found Richardson's more overtly feminist characters, Anna Howe and Charlotte Grandison, pert and odious. She derided the delicacy of his heroines, whose mental distress pushes them into picturesque madness; for "Madness is as much a corporal Distemper as the Gout or Asthma, never occasion'd by affliction, or to be cur'd by the Enjoyment of their extravagant wishes."[12]

When Montagu did protest against the situation of women

in "the paradise of wives," she adopted a mask of "feminine" perversity. In the letters written when she accompanied her husband on his embassy to Constantinople, she constantly remarked on the liberty of Turkish women, evidenced chiefly by their freedom to carry on adulterous affairs while going about concealed under veils. Of course she must have realized that this was a frivolous proof of liberty and that Turkish women were even more restricted and less valued than English ones. But this was how she made the point that English women were only supposed to be free. In fact, she had written to Wortley before their marriage, wealthy young women in England "are sold like slaves, and I cannot tell you what price my Master [her father, then engaged in prenuptial financial arrangements] will put on me." Resisting the request to take off her clothes in a ladies' bath, Montagu showed the ladies her stays, the long corset worn by Englishwomen. At last the Turks thought they understood, as they concluded the stays were a sort of chastity belt that only her husband could unlock. This apparently ingenuous anecdote, which Montagu recounts with relish, points to the actual restrictions upon eighteenth-century Englishwomen, aptly symbolized by the rigidity of their dress. In the same vein, she tells the story of a Spanish lady who, captured and raped by a Turkish admiral, chose to remain as his beloved wife rather than returning to Spain, where sympathizing relatives would have shut her up in a convent for life as the only means to cancel her disgrace.[13]

Typical of her class and period, Montagu accepted as proper, or at least inevitable, the institutional restrictions on women. At the same time, she saw through the automatic pieties and sentimental illusions that supported them. Accordingly she did protest directly against contempt for women. In her periodical *The Nonsense of Common Sense* (1737-38), she attacked with equal vigor the husband who expects blind obedience from his wife, thinking "he lessens the Opinion of his own Understanding, if he . . . condescends to consult" hers, and the indulgent man who says "that Women's Weakness must be complied with, and it is a vain troublesome Attempt to make them hear Reason." By lowering women's self-respect, by encouraging them to accept themselves as foolish, such men render their wives "useless

Members of the Common-wealth, and only burdensome to their own Families."

Montagu attributes this widespread denigration of women either to the ignorance of writers who have never known well-bred women or the self-interest of those who consider only what will sell. And unfortunately they calculate correctly, for in "the Coffee-houses . . . there is hardly one Man in ten but fancies he hath some Reason or other to curse some of the Sex": either he has to support a sister or mother, or he is tired of his wife, or the woman he courts does not want him, or he needs justification for preferring the society of his hounds to that of his wife. She concluded with Astell's point that women in fact require more greatness of mind than men because their trials are more severe. They must be strong without external encouragement: "some Women have suffered a Life of Hardships with as much Philosophy as *Cato* traversed the Desarts of *Africa,* and without that Support the View of Glory offered him"; for a sensible woman knows "that Mankind is too much prejudiced against her Sex, to give her any Degree of that Fame which is so sharp a Spur to their greatest Actions."[14]

A brilliant intellectual who loved learning—she found "every branch" of knowledge "entertaining"—Montagu early concluded that women had a right to solid education. Thanking Bishop Gilbert Burnet for encouraging her study of Latin, she complained that "My Sex is usually forbid studys of this Nature, and Folly reckon'd so much our proper Sphere, we are sooner pardon'd any excesses of that, than the least pretentions to reading or good Sense. . . . our Natural Deffects are every way indulg'd, and tis look'd upon as in a degree Criminal to improve our Reason, or fancy we have any." This attitude is so entrenched that a woman is forced to find excuses for learning, "as if it were a thing altogether criminal not to play the fool in Consort with other Women of Quality, whose Birth and Leisure only serve to render them the most uselesse and most worthlesse part of the creation." (However, she hastens to add that she is not arguing for sexual equality: "any Woman who suffers her Vanity and Folly to deny" that she owes men obedience "Rebells against the Law of the Creator and indisputable Order of Nature.")[15]

Years later, after her intelligence had attracted numerous misogynistic attacks, Montagu's attitude toward learning for women became more cautious and negative. Although she strongly recommended that her daughter encourage an intellectual granddaughter to read, she presented education as a palliative for the inevitable miseries of woman's lot. Though it "is as necessary for the Amusement of Women as the Reputation of Men," girls must not "expect or desire any Applause from it. Let their Brothers shine, and let them content themselves with makeing their Lives easier by it, which I experimentally know is more effectually done by Study than any other way."[16] She does not suggest that their education might be useful to society, even in forming better wives or mothers.

After tracing the intelligence hereditary on both sides of the family—mentioning only men—Montagu recommends that her granddaughter learn the classical languages and read much poetry (for the oddly frivolous reason that she can then recognize whether a suitor is sending her plagiarized verses). But she must be sure "to conceal whatever Learning she attains, with as much solicitude as she would hide crookedness or lameness. The parade of it can only serve to draw on her the envy, and consequently the most inveterate Hatred, of all the he and she Fools, who will certainly be at least three parts in four of all her Acquaintance."[17] Notice the hostility to the majority which accompanies this counsel of submission.

Montagu's next letter opens apologetically, lest her daughter, or more likely her son-in-law, share the general belief that a learned education for daughters is "as great a prophanation as the Clergy would" consider exercise of the functions of the priesthood by the laity. But gradually she works herself into a truly radical position. First she compares the education of a lady to that of a prince (as Wollstonecraft was to compare the education of women and soldiers), for neither gets a substantial education, and both are given praise for insignificant achievements. This leads her to speculate that sexual superiority comes from education more than nature: "The same characters are form'd by the same Lessons, which inclines me to think (if I dare say it) that Nature has not plac'd us in an inferior Rank to Men, no more than the Females of other Animals, where we see no distinction of capacity, thô I am persuaded if there was a Common-wealth of rational Horses [like Swift's Houyhnhnms] . . . it would be an establish'd maxim amongst them that a mare could not be taught to pace." While in this revelatory mood, she even confesses that her "true vocation was a monastery." Had she been mistress of an independent fortune at fifteen, she would have established a monastery (like the one Astell projected) "and elected my selfe Lady Abbess."[18]

Anger repeatedly breaks the surface of Montagu's decorous acceptance of the status quo. Telling how an Italian Cardinal could not believe she had published nothing, she commented: "the character of a learned Woman is far from being ridiculous in [Italy], the greatest Familys being proud of having produce'd female Writers." "To say Truth," she pursued, "there is no part of the World where our Sex is treated with so much contempt as in England." This time she protested that women's "knowledge must rest conceal'd and be as useless to the World as Gold in the Mine." She went on to praise the critic Longinus for choosing his two examples of sublime writing "from a Jew . . . and a Woman."[19]

Winchilsea and Montagu were the best women literary artists of their time, partly because they did not have to rely on public approval. Some of their contemporaries demonstrated that women could successfully compete in the marketplace, but, as this entailed using forms developed by men, they had either to ignore their feminine perceptions and write as men or to weaken the masculine forms by trying to adapt them to their own vision.

Aphra Behn, considered the first professional woman writer in England, not only demonstrated that she could write plays as well as a man, but vigorously asserted her right to be valued equally. She boldly claimed that she wrote for fame as well as for economic necessity, and she quickly moved from defending her position to attacking those who sneered at female writers. In the "Epistle to the Reader" prefacing *The Dutch Lover* (1677), she establishes that comedy can be written without the formal education denied to women and yet is at least as valuable as the learned works only men can write: "I have heard the most of that which bears the name of Learning, and which has abused such quantities of Ink and Paper, and continually employs so many ignorant, unhappy souls for ten, twelve, twenty years in the University (who yet poor wretches think they are doing something all the while) . . . are much more absolutely nothing than the errantest Play that e'er was writ." She proceeds to lampoon "a sorry Animal" that announced at the play's first performance that it would certainly be woeful, "for it was a woman's."[20]

In the Preface to *The Lucky Chance* (1687), she defended herself against charges of obscenity on the grounds that they were made only because she was a woman. What really offends her critics, she claims, is her success. Her specific defense of a titillating scene is disingenuous, but it is certainly true that her works are no bawdier than those of male contemporaries like Dryden and Shadwell. "All I ask," she concludes, "is the Priviledge for my Masculine Part the Poet in me, (if any such you will allow me) to tread in those successful Paths my Predecessors have so long thriv'd in."[21]

"The poet in Behn" was indeed masculine: her consciousness of herself as a woman appears almost entirely in these explicit defenses of the woman author, which are in no way integrated into her creative works. These show values and perceptions hardly distinguishable from those of the male writers with whom she competed.

Indeed, Behn's most famous play, *The Rover* (1677), reveals a more masculine set of values than do the works of Etherege or Wycherley. Willmore, the Rover, presented as the most attractive male in the play, is a bully, a drunkard, and an unabashed exploiter of women. But Behn suggests no criticism of his behavior, and rewards him with Hellena, the most desirable of the women, who brings him a fortune of 300,000 crowns. Willmore echoes Wycherley when he asks, "what the Devil should I do with a virtuous Woman?—a sort of ill-natur'd Creatures, that take a Pride to torment a Lover," or finds "Kindness," by which he means availability, "is better Sauce to Woman than Beauty!" But Wycherley put such words into the mouth of a contemptible fop, Sparkish, not the hero.[22] Behn's lively youths twice threaten to rape the virtuous Florinda, desisting only because they learn that she is their friend's fiancée; in other words, his property.

Even though Hellena has sprightliness and wit, she is far from Willmore's equal. She teases him only very mildly, and not to establish any rights—only to attract and catch him. He thinks of her seriously only after he learns she can bring him a fortune. Unlike Etherege's Harriet (*The Man of Mode*, 1676), who holds her own with the masterful Dorimant, makes him look foolish, and finally makes terms with him, Hellena never scores points in her wit combats and is only too happy to present Willmore with herself and her fortune. In Part II, when Hellena has died, Willmore does not even bother to affect sorrow.

Though Behn does assert the right of women, as well as men, to win the people they love, she seems to accept men's emotional domination as natural and proper. She makes Willmore declaim against mercenary calculation in affairs of love, but fails to note that he is more coldly exploitative than any woman in the two plays. Thus, paradoxically, the major plays of the major female playwright of the Restoration afford a striking example of the callous attitudes which later sentimentalists rightly rejected as antifeminist. Willmore is the embodiment of the rake who uses women without the slightest consideration for their rights and feelings, who sees nothing in a woman but her body and makes every effort to enjoy it without offering her any return. Behn seems to accept without criticism this callous world in which the strong dominate the weak and her own sex is consequently victimized.[23]

The only evidence of feminism within Behn's plays is her relatively sympathetic presentation of intelligent older women, such as Lady Knowell in *Sir Patient Fancy* (1678). Lady Knowell contrasts strikingly with learned ladies in men's plays, such as Shadwell's Lady Fantast in *Bury Fair* (1689)—totally negative characters, who are ignorant and conceited, neglect their domestic obligations, and maliciously obstruct the legitimate love interests of the attractive young people. Such plays made it clear that learning was out of woman's reach, and to attempt it made her odious and unnatural.

Lady Knowell, on the other hand, was not put in the play to

demonstrate that learning is beyond women; for she is affected but not ignorant. Only the sour Puritan Sir Patient Fancy seriously objects to her reading. Lady Knowell is, throughout, on the side of the young people, opposing the conventionally restrictive views of Sir Patient, who does not care about love, for "Pious Wedlock is my Business." It is not the female intellectual who is humiliated at the end of the play, but her antifeminist adversary. Comic though she is, Lady Knowell is infinitely more human than the learned ladies of Molière and his imitators; and she is ridiculed for foibles such as conceit, not for the mere fact of having intellectual interests. Among the few middle-aged females in Restoration drama, she stands out as a mature intelligent woman drawn by another mature intelligent woman.[24]

Susannah Centlivre, like Behn, succeeded in the theater by writing like a man. Her plays, full of ingenious intrigue and comic bustle, are competent rather than brilliant and show no evidence of a distinctive personal view, feminine or otherwise. For example, she accepts without criticism the conventional assumption that English wives enjoyed perfect liberty and she frequently contrasts their happy state with that of women in Spain and Portugal.[25] It may be significant that her plays are notably unsentimental for her period, the early 1700s, and carry on such Restoration comic features as spirited heroines who successfully pursue what they want and a relatively relaxed attitude toward sexual misbehavior. And perhaps there is a hint of feminism in Centlivre's version of the learned lady, the enthusiastic young scientist Valeria in *The Basset-Table* (1706). Though comic, the "little She Philosopher"[26] remains charming; and her folly is balanced not against virtuous domesticity, but against the far more dangerous folly of gambling, in the conventional Lady Reveller.

Neither Behn nor Centlivre, however, nor the other successful women dramatists of the century, wrote plays distinguishable from men's. They might protest vigorously against sexual discrimination in their prefaces, but they followed literary forms that provided no scope for feminine perceptions or feminine experience.

Mary de la Rivière Manley and Eliza Haywood were equally

successful writers. Manley's *Atalantis* (her scandal chronicle *Secret Memoirs and Manners of Several Persons of Quality, of Both Sexes; From the New Atalantis,* 1709-10) became a household word, and Haywood's *Love in Excess* (1719) enjoyed a popularity comparable to that of *Gulliver's Travels* and *Robinson Crusoe*.[27] Like Behn and Centlivre, they wrote to support rather than to express themselves, and their works do not show any particular feminine insight. It is true that they prided themselves upon writing as women. But what this actually meant was that their fictions consist of an endless series of love intrigues, developed with much explicit detail. It does seem plausible that women would have particular skill in describing love, which was so much more central in their lives than in men's. But no such skill appears in Manley and Haywood, who used not personal experience, but stereotypes available to anyone. Haywood gave herself away in her dedication to *The Fatal Secret* (1724): "But as I am a Woman, and consequently depriv'd of those Advantages of Education which the other Sex enjoy, I cannot so far flatter my Desires, as to imagine it in my Power to soar to any Subject higher than that which Nature is not negligent to teach us. Love is a Topick which I believe few are ignorant of . . . a shady Grove and purling Stream are all Things that's necessary to give us an Idea of the tender Passion."[28]

Moreover, by presenting romantic love as an irresistible force, Manley and Haywood reduced its subjects to mere sexual puppets. And by emphasizing its greater importance to women, they tended to reduce women especially to helpless victims. Typically, Manley shows an innocent young woman enslaved by love to a man of greater experience and higher social position, who by virtue of these circumstances controls the situation. In *The New Atalantis* a Duke falls in love with his young ward, Charlot, who has been brought up totally innocent. He rapes her, thus initiating her sexually while preserving her innocence, but triggering her desires so that she falls blindly in love with him and loses all thoughts of her own self-interest. By and by the Duke grows tired of her, marries a less passionate woman, and leaves Charlot to pine away. Manley exalts absolute devotion such as Charlot's as the ultimate virtue, contrasting it with the ambition and self-interest of men; but clearly such exaltation does not help women. It merely gives a strongly sexual tinge to the self-immolating devotion which has traditionally been expected of them. Repeatedly, Manley depicts female innocence victimized by male power and egotism;[29] but her glorification of the sacrifice and her depersonalization of the victims prevent her portrayals from becoming feminist protests. Indeed, her procession of unindividualized female victims, whose experience is described in such luscious detail, is designed to appeal more to masculine than feminine fantasy. They are closer to the depersonalized victims in Gothic novels like Matthew Lewis's *The Monk* (1796) than to the sensitive heroines of women novelists later in the century. Passion is not a liberating force in Manley's women, but only makes them helpless slaves of the men they love. The self-controlled women of later fiction, aware of the real consequences of yielding to lovers without marriage, are both more realistic and more creditable to their sex than Manley's creatures of passion.

Eliza Haywood's *Love in Excess* likewise shows how romance centering on love for women need have no connection with feminism. Its amiable hero is overpowered by love at first sight of his ward Melliora; that is to say, he must have her, regardless of his obligations to a wife who loves him or Melliora's feelings for him. She is so impressed by his physical and emotional force—he practically rapes her on three occasions—that she soon responds to his passion.

Though the romances of Manley and Haywood show a more masculine than feminine point of view, Manley at least was vividly aware of the oppression of women and protested against it not only in prefaces but in passages inserted in her works, though never incorporated in the central fantasy. She had personally experienced oppression, for, robbed of fortune and reputation by a sham marriage at the age of fifteen, she had to subsist as a kept mistress and a hack writer and was constantly abused for the enforced looseness of her life and works. Nevertheless, like a Defoe heroine, she managed to survive quite comfortably; and unlike them, she boldly justified her conduct. In her fictionalized autobiography, *The Adventures of Rivella*

(1714), she took just credit for wit, courage, and generosity, which, she argued, amply compensated for her lack of the traditional feminine virtues of beauty and chastity.

Manley constantly defended women's right to be authors and to discuss politics, but her most original contribution to feminist thought was an acute analysis of the degradation intrinsic in economic dependence. She described a fictitious Sarmatia, where wives must implore their husbands whenever they need money, "for the Women never keep the Purse, and are forced to content themselves to have all Things provided to their Hand; the Men are the sole Managers, so that the Ladies have nothing to do but *Dress, Divert, Eat, Drink,* and make *Visits,* which last are always perform'd with splendid Ostentation.... The Women seldom cross the Way without a Coach, six Horses, and a numerous Train of Servants; yet have they no Money, but upon every Occasion are forc'd to kneel and implore their Husbands, who take a Pleasure in being importun'd."[30] No contemporary saw so clearly that economic dependence is oppressive even if the subject class is financially comfortable, and therefore that giving economic control to one party in a relationship is necessarily unjust.[31]

Writing under relentless financial pressure, these playwrights and romance-writers naturally turned to the conventional forms that would be profitable. Their need sharpened their resentment of the prejudices that impaired women's chances of making a living, but it precluded the free experimentation that would have encouraged them to modify the male-created forms to express new feminine insights.

Jane Barker and Mary Davys, however, gave a distinctive turn to the romantic tale, perhaps because they were not pressed to write for bread. Jane Barker, who lived on a small pension, created an original situation in the frustrated relationship of a self-doubting intellectual, Galesia, with her cousin Bosvil. In *Love Intrigues; or, The History of the Amours of Bosvil and Galesia* (1713) Galesia (representing Barker herself) tells how she fell in love with Bosvil but never brought him to propose marriage—partly because of his sadistic tendency to lead on and then disappoint her, partly because of her own pride, as well as the reserve enjoined on all women. Although Barker did not develop these motives clearly, she made an effort to discard sexual stereotypes and honestly observe a female character.

Galesia comes to life when Bosvil's marriage to another woman drives her to seek consolation in reading, which she finds amply compensates for loss of his company. She can almost bless false Bosvil, "Whose Crimes conduc'd to this my Happiness./ Had he bee true, I'd lived in *sottish Ease*,/ Ne'er study'd aught, but how to *love* and *please*." However, she characteristically keeps questioning her intellectual vocation, being unable to free herself from the traditional view that learning is unsuitable for women. She is really happy studying medicine under her brother's guidance, as she reads Harvey on the circulation of the blood, learns to write professional prescriptions, and heals the sick (though not, of course, for payment or fame). But when her brother dies, she contrasts the death of this useful professional man with her own survival—"useless to the World; useless to my Friends, and a Burden to myself."[32]

Galesia is delighted to find a closet in the attic, a room of her own, where she can converse with her old friends the medical authors and write poetry. But it all ends on the day a ruined young woman enters from the roof and Galesia's mother prohibits her "Garret-Closet ... lest I should encounter more Adventures." Instead of openly resenting this senseless deprivation of her only real fulfillment, Galesia moralizes "how useless, or rather pernicious, Books and Learning are to our Sex. ... for by their Means we relish not the Diversions or Imbellishments of our Sex and Station, which render us agreeable to the World, and the World to us."[33]

Her mother follows up this prohibition by persuading Galesia to submit entirely to convention and marry, to employ her "Parts in being an obedient Wife, a discreet Governess of your Children and Servants; a friendly Assistant to your Neighbours, Friends, and Acquaintance: This being the Business for which you came into the World."[34] So Galesia listens to two suitors. But it turns out that both are grotesquely unfitted to become heads of households, and both die in time to release her from marriage. The first man commits a robbery as an idle prank and gets hanged for it, while the second, unable to extricate himself from a leechlike mistress, shoots himself. Noting that something seems to happen to everyone who might marry her, Galesia reflects that she is not destined for happiness. But actually it looks more as if happiness for Galesia is the single life. She has created a satisfying life for herself with her intellect and has no need for a husband. No man is shown, from the unreliable Bosvil to the childish later suitors, who could serve as the responsible director that an eighteenth-century husband was supposed to be. If men are in fact incapable of filling this role, the whole rationale for woman's subordination in marriage is destroyed.

But Barker was no more ready than Galesia to draw these implications. She created a partially liberated heroine with a genuine mental life, who loved learning but was half ashamed of her love, who questioned propriety but doubted her right to question it. She raised possibilities for a different kind of life from that described by Galesia's conventional mother. But her ambivalence spoiled the construction of her story: motives remain undeveloped and conflicts unresolved, and the plot tails off without any conclusion.[35]

Mary Davys, a widow who supported herself by keeping a coffee house at Cambridge, also raised the possibility that a woman might do better not to marry, in her *Familiar Letters betwixt a Gentleman and a Lady* (1725). Her Berina wants to keep Artander as her friend and is surprised and annoyed by his proposal of marriage. Davys left the situation open, letting her readers decide whether Berina would "dwindle into a wife" or remain independent, presumably because she recognized the restrictions imposed by marriage but was not prepared to declare that women were better off single.

Davys's *The Accomplished Rake, or the Modern Fine Gentleman* (1727) is more artistically satisfying than *Familiar Letters* because it is unclouded by such ambiguity. The feminist message of this novelette is not at odds with convention, since the eighteenth-century reformation of manners had discredited the rake as glorified in *The Rover*. Sir John Galliard is much like

Willmore—witty and sexually attractive, self-indulgent and callous to the welfare of others, especially women. But, far from triumphing, he is sternly evaluated and ultimately humiliated. He consorts constantly with women of the town, but instead of falling helplessly in love with him, they make him drunk and cheat him. When virtuous Belinda is too sophisticated to succumb to his flattery, he plots to rape her. Her sensible and eloquent arguments leave him unmoved, but he is frustrated by her maid's resourcefulness. Galliard is thoroughly discomfited—equally ashamed of himself for attempting Belinda's honor and chagrined at his failure, torn between his attraction to her and his unthinking aversion to marriage. She lets him know that, in any case, he could not be assured of her consent.

Ultimately, after adulterous affairs have led him to accident and disease, he has to propose to a girl whom he has raped, even though he had previously decided it would be too much of a sacrifice to "marry the girl to redeem her honor while I entail a slavery upon myself for life."[36] She accepts him, but not with gratitude; she makes it clear that she wants only to give her beloved child a father. Galliard is driven to reform by defeat in all his other affairs, and he is not rewarded for it.

Although The Accomplished Rake does not question fundamental assumptions about women, it is distinctively feminist in its icy contempt for the rake, who is reduced to ridiculous defeat by all the women he attempts to prey on. It is significant that the women defend themselves: Belinda is no helpless victim who must be protected by some man, but as spirited and self-assured as a Restoration comic heroine. She is saved from Galliard by her maid, and in turn shrewdly brings justice to a servant maid who has been deceived by his friend. Davys's original presentation of her theme is matched by her fresh realistic technique, including plausible motivation, sensible morality, and crisp natural English instead of the faded heroic diction of the conventional romance writers. Avoiding the artistic clichés of her genre, she likewise avoided stereotyped attitudes toward men, women, and love.[37]

Successful as far as it goes, The Accomplished Rake is of course limited. Women soon turned to the full-scale novel, with its greater scope for character development. At the end of her career, Eliza Haywood tried the new form, which stimulated her to original vision, as well as to improved technique.[38] Her *History of Miss Betsy Thoughtless* (1751) has the makings of an interesting study in woman's desire for liberation and difficulties in achieving it. The heroine, an attractive orphaned heiress of fourteen, sees that she can have more fun as a courted virgin and her own mistress than as a wife, subject to the direction of her husband. But she is forced to choose between marrying immediately or losing Trueworth, the man who would be right for her. Angry at her coquettish temporizing, he marries a more decorous girl.

By this time, the family decides indiscreet Betsy had better be settled and presses her into marrying Munden, who proves to be oppressive and stingy. The marriage fails for financial rather than sexual or sentimental reasons, as Munden meddles with Betsy's spending of her pin money, which should be her private affair. Finally she leaves him, taking with her all property that was hers before marriage—a step which Haywood presents as justified since it would be "mean" to let her husband deprive her of what is due her by the marriage contract.[39] By this time Betsy is purged of her vanity and thoughtlessness, Munden and Mrs. Trueworth obligingly die, and the reformed Betsy is married to the right man, who of his own volition settles eight hundred pounds a year on her in case of death or separation.

Haywood's sympathy for her strong-willed heroine is innovatively feminist. She shows Betsy's vanity and thoughtlessness balanced by her essential virtue and goodness of heart, just as they would be in a man. She balances Betsy's exploitative attitude toward the opposite sex by her generous friendship for her own. She endows Betsy with a natural desire to keep her independence and a resentment of encroachments by her marriage partner which conventional writers would allow only to men. Unfortunately, however, Haywood fails to engage the reader's sympathy for Betsy. She never convinces us that Betsy is, apart from a little vanity, "the most deserving of her sex."[40] Betsy's clinging to independence appears less a rational program for preserving individuality than a selfish adolescent's craving to enjoy unlimited parties and play off one man against another. She appears a mere selfish minx, whose troubles with an overbearing husband are just what she deserves.

To develop her theme successfully, Haywood required more substantial characterization (so Betsy's merit and Munden's odiousness would be convincing) and new values in sexual relationships. The position of women would be improved not with a female version of the Restoration rake's callous freedom, but with tenderness and consideration on the part of both sexes. These necessary feelings were to be developed by later generations of women novelists. Elizabeth Inchbald's Miss Milner, in *A Simple Story*, is a deeply touching version of the character for which Betsy is a crude sketch.

Charlotte Lennox's *The Female Quixote* (1752) is another interesting study of woman's needs which fails to fulfill its potential for lack of adequate form. The heroine, Arabella, sees life in terms of the romances of Madeleine de Scudéry, in which people devote their lives to exquisitely refined love affairs, and peerless virgins are courted for years by humbly devoted suitors, whom they reward with marriage after innumerable exploits and distressing adventures. Arabella is indignant that her father has chosen Glanville as a husband for her, even though he is suitable in every way; and even more so when Glanville proceeds directly to court her to be his wife, instead of proving himself worthy by years of noble deeds. "What Lady in Romance ever married the Man that was chose for her? In those Cases the Remonstrances of a Parent are called Persecutions; obstinate Resistance, Constancy and Courage; and an Aptitude to dislike the Person proposed to them, a noble Freedom of Mind." She would like to discourse for hours about beauty and love, but as Glanville says, "all that can be said" of either "may be comprised in a very few Words."[41]

Thrown into ordinary eighteenth-century society by the death of her father, Arabella misjudges everything and gives Glanville endless trouble because she expects him to behave like a hero of romance. Finally a kind and sophisticated Countess begins to open her eyes to real life, and a wise clergyman convinces her that the romances are not only false but morally pernicious for encouraging unreasonable expectations and socially irresponsible behavior.

Arabella learns that she is not to have the exciting adventures of a romance heroine, for, as the Countess tells her, "The Word Adventures... can hardly with Propriety be apply'd to those few and natural Incidents which compose the History of a Woman of Honour, and when I tell you... that I was born and christn'd, had a useful and proper Education, receiv'd the Addresses of my Lord ——— through the Recommendations of my Parents, and marry'd him with their Consents and my own Inclination, and that since we have liv'd in great Harmony together, I have told you all the material Passages of my Life."[42] This restrictive outline, accurate in rendering the limited scope of an eighteenth-century lady, reflects also the limitations of life itself; Arabella is conceited as well as unrealistic when she expects the world to offer her endless excitement and attention.

Yet Lennox does not present her with unqualified derision, for the romances, however inappropriate to actual life, answered a real psychological need of women. Arabella's affectionate father regards marriage as a necessary business to be dispatched and, as a matter of course, has selected a husband for her; not wishing to coerce her, he tells Glanville, "Gain her Heart as soon as you can, and when you bring me her Consent your Marriage shall be solemnized immediately."[43] It does not occur to him that she might not consent, or that he should investigate her feelings about the most important decision of her life. In the romance world, on the other hand, men had to win women's consent, and personal feelings took priority over patriarchal law and custom; a woman was a precious individual rather than a necessary social unit. A more realistic version of these values was to be seriously asserted in the sentimental novels of the later eighteenth century.

Because Arabella's fantasies respond to a legitimate psychological need, and a need characteristic of idealistic women, she is never ridiculed like Molière's *Précieuses ridicules* (1659) or Steele's Biddy Tipkin in *The Tender Husband* (1705). When she is contrasted with conventional women, it is not so often to

expose her aberrations as to show her superiority. Her unconventional values free her from the pettiness, spite, and mental
insipidity of the typical fashionable young lady, Miss Glanville.
When Mr. Glanville and Arabella discuss Grecian history for
two hours, Miss Glanville can only hum and tinkle the harpsichord. One day Miss Glanville, "having spent four long Hours
in dressing herself" in hopes of eclipsing Arabella, is "extremely
mortified" to find her looking lovely despite "the Haste and
Negligence she made her Woman use in this important Employment." When Arabella ingenuously praises her appearance, Miss
Glanville looks in the mirror to see whether something is
wrong.[44]

It is significant that Arabella is not humiliated out of her
errors, but reasoned. She puts up intelligent arguments to the
clergyman who reforms her, though his prove to be the stronger.
In the end she marries Glanville, and Miss Glanville marries a
deceitful rake; the latter couple are "married in the common
Acceptation of the Word; i.e., they were privileged to join Fortunes, Equipages, Titles, and Expence; while Mr. *Glanville* and
Arabella were united, as well in these, as in every Virtue and
laudable Affection of the Mind."[45]

Arabella's conspicuous superiority suggests that she is not
merely an addict of silly fiction, but a woman of intellect capable of rising above conventional limitations, whether frivolous
or humdrum. She rightly prefers reading to dressing and formal
visits, she takes an interest in subjects larger than petty sexual
rivalry, she likes to listen to discussion of ideas and can interest
an intelligent man with her own conversation. Still, the only
books we know she reads are foolish romances. Her intellectual
achievement is undercut by her romantic delusions, just as
Galesia's was by her constant self-deprecation. Barker and Lennox admired intellect in women, but were not prepared to ap-
prove it unequivocally.

Sarah Fielding, herself a scholar who translated Xenophon,
wholeheartedly advocated learning for women. Cynthia, the
leading woman and most intelligent character in her *David
Simple* (1744), illustrates the frustrations of the intellectual
woman as well as the misery of economic dependence. For

David Simple expresses not women's wish-fulfilling fantasies, but their unhappy consciousness of enforced passivity and dependence. (Fielding herself, who never married, depended for support on her brothers and patrons.) David, the pure-minded, considerate hero, is constitutionally incapable of aggression; and he is surrounded by women, who were socially inhibited from action.

Without meaning harm, Cynthia's parents constantly thwarted her curiosity ("such Things were not proper for Girls of my Age to know") and deprived her of any but the most inane reading ("poring on Books, would never get me a Husband"). Thus she wasted her childhood in acquiring trivial accomplishments, "without being indulged in any one thing I liked." Her brother had to "be cajoled or whipp'd into Learning, while it was denied me, who had the utmost Eagerness for it." And her envious sisters sneered that a witty woman must be a libertine, or at least deficient in judgment, common sense, and fulfillment of her domestic obligations.[46]

Cynthia's father orders her to marry a clod who likes her person, has heard she has had a sober education, and wants an heir; he expects her to look after his household and comply with his humor, in return for which he will be kind to her and see that she and her children are financially comfortable. She answers that she has "no kind of Ambition to be his *upper Servant*," and would take no more pleasure in fine clothes purchased to gratify her husband's vanity than his horse does in gaudy trappings. Furious, Cynthia's father throws her out; and she has to become a lady's companion—or, to put it more bluntly, a toadeater.[47]

Cynthia is balanced by Camilla, a more conventional woman (who will marry David, as Cynthia will marry Camilla's brother, Valentine). Camilla has been victimized by a harsh stepmother, who finally persuaded her father to throw her out of his house. She laments that "there is no Situation so deplorable . . . as that of a Gentlewoman in real Poverty," but there is a real question whether Camilla has suffered more from her sudden violent afflictions, or Cynthia from the perpetual smaller frustrations of her whole life. Cynthia wishes "she had gone thro' all the Miseries Poverty could have brought upon her, rather than have endured half what she had done for living in Plenty at another's Expence."[48]

The two couples form a happy community of unworldly people, delighting in intelligent conversation, in which Cynthia usually takes the lead; for Sarah Fielding explicitly opposed the contemporary view that a woman, however intelligent, must be passive and self-deprecating. Cynthia "always employed her Thoughts in what manner she could best amuse her Company," and "every Person of this Party delighted in hearing her talk." Though she is not conceited, "*Cynthia* did not put on a silly Affectation of not knowing the Strength of her own Understanding."[49] Recognizing the unreality of this idyll, in the second part of *David Simple* (1752), Fielding showed her pleasant social group destroyed, as conventionally worldly people cannot leave it alone.

Fielding's *History of the Countess of Dellwyn* (1759) presents an even more explicit analysis of the degradation produced by women's economic dependence. Although the Countess's father "seldom absolutely refused her any thing tolerably reasonable," he granted her requests with such ill-humor that she hated to ask. "It is a common Practice of Persons, who are endowed with the Power of either bestowing or withholding Benefits, to make all Complaints of them apparently without a Cause, by declaring they have never refused any thing they were asked"; but they ignore "the Heart-aches that are endured before the Request . . . and the Pain that is given by a Compliance, which they make more afflicting to a gentle Mind than a mild Refusal."[50] While embittering every grant he makes his daughter, the father makes no effort to teach her prudence in restricting her expenses. Thus encouraged to develop a taste for dissipation and luxury, she has to marry for money an old nobleman, whom she does not love. She is destroyed not by innate feminine worldliness, but by values corrupted by a father who preferred docility to virtue.

All these intelligent, articulate authors asserted woman's mental capacity and protested, directly or indirectly, against her situation in society. But their expressions of feminist awareness tend to be obscured or undercut both by their personal self-doubt and by their lack of a suitable form. Those who wrote for profit, especially, could not adequately express their feelings as women because they used forms shaped by men's values and experience. Behn and Manley wrote essentially like men, relegating their feminist protests to prefaces or isolated passages. The better novelists did express more of their individual perceptions, but were hampered by trying to fit their material into the picaresque form developed by Defoe and Henry Fielding. Instead of focusing on Cynthia, the intellectual woman whom she could have understood from the inside, Sarah Fielding focused on a man, who comes across as flat and unrealistic and whose experience is thin. Instead of developing Arabella's feelings so as to make her illusions plausible, Lennox contrived a long series of silly mistakes, which become increasingly tedious and far-fetched. Only when Samuel Richardson had given romance a solid realistic underpinning did women have a form which they could use with confidence because it was suited to expressing what they had to say.

NOTES

1. All Winchilsea's poems are quoted from *The Poems of Anne Countess of Winchilsea,* ed. Myra Reynolds (Chicago: University of Chicago Press, 1903).

2. Even when Winchilsea was writing on more modish themes, she introduced a refreshing feminine point of view. Considering men's constant complaints that marriage is a ball and chain, oppressive to the natural freedom of the male, it is nice to see a woman making exactly the same claim in "The Unequal Fetters." Aphra Behn had made the same point in a song in *The Emperor of the Moon;* see "A Curse upon that faithless Maid," *The Works,* ed. Montague Summers (London: Heinemann, 1915), III, 396. Despite the vast social and moral distance between them, Winchilsea made a point of commending Behn, though admitting that she wrote "a little too loosly" ("The Circuit of Apollo").

3. In the "Preface" that follows her "Introduction," Winchilsea declared that she could not help writing and showing her works to friends, thus implying that a poet's talent could

not (and should not) be suppressed. But she went on to suggest that her poems represented lapses from rational conduct and that she withheld them from publication not only to avoid abuse as a woman author, but because they were not worthy of publication.

4. Winchilsea, *Poems*, p. 45.

5. Declining an invitation to London, she suggests that the country be "Our place of meeting, love, and liberty" (*Poems*, p. 39). She and her friend cannot express their thoughts and affection amid the fashionable conventions operating in London.

6. "The Introduction." For Winchilsea, limitation seems to have had a special meaning, expressed in poems such as "The Nightingale": it was not the Augustans' decorous acceptance of human limits, but the Romantics' painful awareness of the discrepancy between human beings' aspirations and achievement. Perhaps her sex made Winchilsea particularly aware of the restrictions upon human beings.

7. "A Poem, Occasion'd by the Sight of the 4th Epistle Lib. Epist: 1 of Horace."

8. E.g., "The Losse," a lament for a woman friend who has died; "Friendship Between Ephelia and Ardelia," which sets the highest possible standard for friendship between women; "Some Reflections. In a Dialogue Between Teresa and Ardelia," Teresa's wise correction of Ardelia for a lapse in faith; the section of "The Petition for an Absolute Retreat" in which she tells how Arminda's love has helped her. She frequently compared the love between herself and a woman friend to that of David and Jonathan, there being no Biblical or literary precedents for friendship between women. The generally conventional poems of Molly Leapor, strongly imitative of Pope, nevertheless include a strong defense of woman's capacity for friendship, "Essay on Friendship."

9. *The Complete Letters of Lady Mary Wortley Montagu*, ed. Robert Halsband (Oxford: Clarendon, 1965), I, 12.

10. *Ibid.*, II, 40; III, 96.

11. It is true that she abandoned both standards when she fell violently in love with Count Francesco Algarotti, but this passion was out of character for her and soon terminated.

2. Montagu, *Letters*, III, 8-9, 95-96. Henry Fielding was also too sentimental for Montagu, who condemned *Tom Jones* and *Amelia* for placing "a merit in extravagant passions" (III, 66). Richardson condemned Montagu's hard-headed contempt "for the generality of the fair Sex" (II, 33-34) by

attributing it to his unpleasantly mannish Miss Barnevelt in *Sir Charles Grandison*.

13. Montagu, *Letters*, I, 64, 314, 328, 407-8.
14. Lady Mary Wortley Montagu, *The Nonsense of Common Sense*, ed. Robert Halsband (Evanston: Northwestern University Press, 1947), pp. 25-28. Despite this acute feminist defense, she sprinkled conventional denigrating references to women through other papers in this series. Though most of the works Montagu published in her lifetime could just as well have been written by a man, she did anonymously publish a poem attacking Swift's "Lady's Dressing-Room" and another sympathizing with a divorced wife and protesting the double standard. See Robert Halsband, " 'The Lady's Dressing Room' Explicated by a Contemporary," in *The Augustan Milieu* (Oxford: Clarendon, 1970), and Isobel Grundy, "Ovid and Eighteenth Century Divorce: An Unpublished Poem by Lady Mary Wortley Montagu," *Review of English Studies*, XXIII N.S. (1972), 424-25.
15. Montagu, *Letters*, I, 44-45; III, 25.
16. *Ibid.*, II, 449-50.
17. *Ibid.*, II, 22-23.
18. *Ibid.*, III, 25, 27, 97.
19. *Ibid.*, III, 38-40. She refers to Longinus's treatise "On the Sublime," which quotes from Sappho and the author of Genesis.
20. Behn, *Works*, I, 221, 223-24; III, 187.
21. *Ibid.*, I, 187. She similarly defended herself against the charge of bawdiness in the epistle "To the Reader" attached to *Sir Patient Fancy* (1678), which also has a belligerent feminist epilogue.
22. *Ibid.*, I, 70, 127. Cf. William Wycherley, *The Country Wife*, in *Complete Plays*, ed. Gerald Weales (Garden City, N.Y.: Doubleday, 1966), pp. 301, 335.
23. Despite its aggressively feminist preface, *The Dutch Lover* presents a totally unenlightened view of sexual relations: there is no criticism of the appalling way in which the male characters treat women as property and threaten to execute them for violating the family honor, while the men practice sexual freedom themselves. The most dramatic indication of Behn's male-oriented outlook is her poem "The Disappointment," which presents a popular masculine theme of the period usually called "the imperfect enjoyment" (impotence at the crucial moment). She wrote erotic poems exactly in the manner of contemporary men, only reversing the sexes, as she is torn between two lovers, or praises a man's beauty, or toys with homosexuality.

24. Behn, *Works*, IV, 74-75. For discussion of the hostile treat-
    ment of intellectual women in the drama, see Jean Elisa-
    beth Gagen, *The New Woman: Her Emergence in English
    Drama 1600-1730* (New York: Twayne, 1954), pp. 48-65.
    Onahal, the superannuated but still attractive wife of the
    African King in Behn's *Oroonoko* (1688), is another exam-
    ple of an older woman presented with unusual sympathy.
    Though her beauty has decayed, she retains her wit, and
    thus can still attract a young man; his courtship to her is
    not altogether feigned; *Oroonoko* is found in *Shorter Nov-
    els: Seventeenth Century*, ed. Philip Henderson (London:
    J. M. Dent, 1962), pp. 165, 167. Often writing in the first
    person, Behn made some use of a female persona, but did
    not develop it to a meaningful extent.
25. E.g., in *The Wonder* and *Marplot in Lisbon*, in *The Works
    of the Celebrated Mrs. Centlivre* (London: John Pearson,
    1872), II, 143; III, 11, 13. However, like Behn, Centlivre
    complained of antifeminist prejudice against her plays, for
    instance in the Dedication to *The Platonick Lady* (1707).
26. *Ibid.*, I, 210.
27. John J. Richetti, *Popular Fiction before Richardson* (Oxford:
    Clarendon, 1969), p. 179.
28. Quoted in Robert Adams Day, *Told in Letters: Epistolary
    Fiction before Richardson* (Ann Arbor: University of Michi-
    gan Press, 1966), p. 81.
29. See Richetti's analysis in *Popular Fiction*, pp. 124, 130-35,
    143-48. These stories support the denigrating antifeminist
    assumption of Richardson's villain Lovelace, that a woman
    once subdued is always subdued.
30. *Memoirs of Europe* (1710-11), quoted in Gwendolyn B.
    Needham, "Mrs. Manley: An Eighteenth Century Wife of
    Bath," *Huntington Library Quarterly*, LIV (1950-51), 270.
    For Manley's defense of women's right and capacity to be
    authors, see her prologue to *The Lost Lover* and her poem
    honoring Catherine Trotter Cockburn for *Agnes de Castro*.
31. Penelope Aubin's romances, strongly contrasting with Man-
    ley's and Haywood's in their insistent morality, show no
    greater insight into woman's nature or position. Although
    Aubin's good men treat women with infinite consideration,
    they assume them to be property that would be disastrously
    damaged by rape. The most ludicrous example involves
    Violetta, a Venetian lady enslaved by the Turks and raped
    by her owner, Osmyn. On her return to Europe, a kindly
    priest tells her she need not retire to a convent, since her
    crime was mitigated by her not belonging to a husband;
    but she should not marry the man she loves until Osmyn

dies and she has mourned for him six months (*The Strange Adventures of the Count de Vinevil*, 1721). Aubin's good female characters, who conform to every detail of traditional feminine morality, are no closer to human beings than are Haywood's and Manley's sexual objects.

32. Jane Barker, *A Patch-Work Screen for the Ladies* (1723, the sequel to *Love Intrigues*; New York: Garland, 1973), pp. 14, 57.

33. *Ibid.*, pp. 78-79.

34. *Ibid.*, p. 79.

35. My analysis has drawn somewhat from Josephine Grieder's introduction to *A Patch-Work Screen*, p. 9, and from Patricia Meyer Spacks's *Imagining a Self: Autobiography and Novel in Eighteenth Century England* (Cambridge: Harvard University Press, 1976), pp. 67, 70. Barker's *Exilius* (1715), her first written though not first published tale, is a conventional heroic romance, though unlike Manley's and Haywood's in its rigorous enforcement of chastity.

36. Mary Davys, *The Accomplished Rake*, in *Four before Richardson: Selected English Novels, 1720-1727*, ed. W. M. McBurney (Lincoln: University of Nebraska Press, 1963), p. 357.

37. Davys's *Reform'd Coquet* (1724) draws the development of a female counterpart of Galliard—equally selfish and wrong in her values, though not of course equally harmful, since women had less power than men. Davys has more sympathy for the coquette than for the rake, reforming rather than punishing her. She also humanizes her by trying to show how a basically intelligent and virtuous woman could attach so much importance to worthless flattery.

38. In the interim Haywood produced a moderately feminist periodical called *The Female Spectator* (1744-46), which decorously insists on filial obedience and wifely patience, but also shows original thought about the problems of marriage. In one paper she reminds women that it is just as important to know their own feelings for a man they are thinking of marrying as to know his for them, and in another, she perceptively analyzes a marriage that went wrong because the husband took an unnecessarily dictatorial tone in restraining his wife's social life; see *The Female Spectator* (Dublin: George and Alexander Ewing, 1747), I, 12; II, 149-53. In her second novel, *The History of Jemmy and Jenny Jessamy* (1753), Haywood explicitly repudiated the blind romantic passion she had extolled in her earlier tales. Jenny demonstrates common sense and self-control, as well as love.

39. Eliza Haywood, *The History of Miss Betsy Thoughtless* (London: T. Gardner, 1751), IV, 59-60.
40. *Ibid.*, IV, 252.
41. Charlotte Lennox, *The Female Quixote*, ed. Margaret Dalziel (London: Oxford University Press, 1970), pp. 27, 149.
42. *Ibid.*, p. 327.
43. *Ibid.*, p. 31.
44. *Ibid.*, pp. 83-84, 91.
45. *Ibid.*, p. 383.
46. Sarah Fielding, *The Adventures of David Simple . . . in the Search for a True Friend* (London: A. Millar, 1754), I, 188-89, 192, 194-96, 201-2.
47. *Ibid.*, I, 204-6, 210. Toadeating, or servile flattery, was often the major function of unfortunate women who had to support themselves as companions. Burney's Juliet in *The Wanderer* (1814) was to be subjected to the same fate.
48. *Ibid.*, I, 187; II, 46, 212. A virtuous couple in Sarah Fielding's *History of the Countess of Dellwyn* (1759) devote their fortune to establishing a home for poor gentlewomen (something like Astell's Protestant monastery), to save them from the miseries of dependence on rich people. A clergyman's widow rejoices that two of her daughters are servants to this couple, as that is so much easier a lot than being unpaid lady dependents. Charlotte Lennox's Henrietta (1758), though an earl's granddaughter, would rather work as a lady's maid than depend as a companion; for she can find satisfaction in the relative independence of honest self-support. Jane Collier's *An Essay on the Art of Ingeniously Tormenting* (1753) is particularly eloquent on the miseries of the paid companion, who is less well off than a servant.
49. Fielding, *David Simple*, II, 221, Last Vol., 34. The relationship between Cynthia and Camilla may be an idealized rendition of the actual relationship between Henry Fielding's intellectual sister and his adorable but conventional wife.
50. Sarah Fielding, *The History of the Countess of Dellwyn* (New York: Garland, 1974), I, 42. Sarah Fielding's *Ophelia* (1760) is an interesting attempt to present a female noble savage, though it is not convincingly worked out. Ophelia rejects stays as unnatural, enjoys men's company as friends rather than lovers, and in general insists on acting as a human being independent of her sexuality. Abducted by the hero-villain, Lord Dorchester, she escapes undamaged, perhaps because (unlike Clarissa) she is not thinking all the time about sexual violation.

❦❧ [4] ❦❧

THE LIBERATING EFFECT
OF SENTIMENTALISM

To that half of the world which goes through life in a vegetative state, says Arabella Fermor in Frances Brooke's *Emily Montague* (1769), "love and sentiment are entirely unnecessary." But those who "are something awakened" know, "whatever tall maiden aunts . . . may say of the indecency of a young woman's distinguishing one man from another, and of love coming after marriage," that marrying "on sober prudent principles, a man one dislikes, [is] the most deliberate and shameful degree of vice of which the human mind is capable."[1] Arabella's belief that love and sentiment are essential to a superior person and that repression of feeling is positively sinful, springs from the sentimentalism that increasingly came to dominate literature and morality during the eighteenth century: an assertion of the value of emotion in reaction to the tough, matter-of-fact rationalism of the Restoration. Earlier women writers might have agreed with these views, but would not have expressed them with such assurance.

At its best, sentimentalism humanized and enriched the picture of sexual relationships that seems so cold in Swift and Astell, so mercenary in Defoe, and refined the feelings they dealt with so bluntly. It glorified the possibilities of sexual and domestic love and gave respect to feelings that are real even if less definable than rational principles and laws. At its worst, sentimentalism dissolved reason, law, and fact into emotion, and reduced emotion to softness and quivering sensitivity.

Sentimentalism has traditionally been associated with women because they are supposed to be the more emotional sex. As interpreted by playwrights contriving sentimental appeals to "the ladies," it meant tearful pictures of virtue in distress, edifying pictures of virtue conquering through self-abnegation, and a world in which benevolent feeling was stronger than moral law or physical fact. But sentimentalism did not have to be narrow and false. It could justly assert the value of personal feeling as opposed to abstract law, as Thomas Otway did in *Venice Preserved* (1682). Otway appropriately used a woman to represent the value of affection and family ties and their tragic destruction in a male-dominated world of abstract idealism and masculine bonding. For women have always been identified with private feelings and the emotional life of the family. In the eighteenth century, when women were excluded from public life and discouraged from abstract interests, they had to seek fulfillment in familial love and social interaction within a narrow domestic circle. Therefore, to belittle tenderness, consideration, and nuances of taste was to strip women's lives of meaning and satisfaction.

Sentimental literature focused on emotional ties and problems that were of particular interest to women, and prominently featured a moral ideal considered feminine, one of gentleness, passivity, and self-abnegation. All its writers professed a new concern for women; Steele at least was sincere in calling himself a "Friend to Women" and a "Guardian to the Fair."[2] Whether sentimentalism was feminist as well as feminine depended on whether the author genuinely identified with women or merely dealt in attitudes conventionally associated with them. Generally speaking, therefore, it was women writers who made use of sentimental values to improve the position of women.

Shallow sentimentalism is particularly evident in drama, the form most responsive to popular taste. Instead of heroines like Harriet and Millamant, we find in comedy such women as Steele's Indiana (*The Conscious Lovers*, 1722) and Colley Cibber's Lady Easy (*The Careless Husband*, 1715), who are distinguished solely by beauty and devotion to their men. Indiana, who started life as an "infant captive," has no resource but sweet dependency upon the hero. If he should marry her, her "purpose of life is only to please him"; if not, she will "have nothing to do but to learn to die."[3] Lady Easy would not think of retaliating against her callously unfaithful husband. She refrains even from reproaching him, constrained partly by duty but mostly by fervent love. In the end he is reformed by her virtue and offers her his "conquer'd heart," a gift that overwhelms her with joy and gratitude.[4] The most shining example of this type of feminine virtue is Mrs. Beverley in Edward Moore's *The Gamester* (1753). Though Mr. Beverley has reduced her and their child from affluence to destitution by incorrigible gambling, she declares, "I live but to oblige him. She who can love, and is beloved like Me, will do as much."[5]

Such characters might evoke warmer sympathy or higher admiration than their Restoration predecessors, but they do so at the expense of their human equality. Indiana requires protection because she is obviously inadequate to look after herself. Of course it gratified men to glory in their helpfulness to such creatures and their compassion for them. Lady Easy and Mrs. Beverley gain angelic status by giving up their right to decent treatment. They demonstrate their moral superiority through a total devotion and self-sacrifice that would never be expected of men. Sentimentalism longed for figures to illustrate an unlimited human capacity for love and patience, and laid the burden of illustrating it on women. Since these characters represented an ideal that was too attractive to repudiate, they served to press restrictive moral standards on women. Moreover, sentimental admiration for long-suffering virtue could lead to gratification at the heroine's sufferings (disguised as pity). Her distress made her so beautiful and appealing that it seemed a shame to alleviate it.

Occasionally, however, sentimental drama such as Nicholas Rowe's "she-tragedies" revealed genuine sympathy with women. Focus upon an erring woman's distress in *The Fair Penitent* (1703) led to sympathetic insight into her situation. Calista has been seduced by Lothario and is still in love with him, but her father forces her to marry Altamont, who loves her. Altamont discovers her with Lothario and kills him, and Calista ultimately kills herself from remorse. *The Fair Penitent* is weakened by sentimental orgies provoked by Calista's abject repentance for her sin, which is defined as violating her father's honor and (in an interesting reflection of Robert Filmer's linking of patriarchy in the family and the state) is associated with civil disorder.

Nevertheless, the play powerfully expresses the desperation of a passionate woman forced into passive submission. Calista is surrounded by virtuous well-meaning men who will do anything for a woman other than find out what she wants. Her father dismisses her misery at her approaching marriage as typical feminine coyness, and when she plainly tells Altamont that she cannot love him, he assures her the marriage will be good because he loves her. Reproached by her father for looking unhappy at her wedding, Calista exclaims against the perpetual subjection of woman to male relatives who groundlessly claim to possess "superior reason."[6] Calista's feminist argument is undercut by the unchastity that disgraced her in eighteenth-century eyes, but she remains a figure to command respect as well as sympathy. Rowe used her to pit feminine feeling against masculine law and order.

Unlike the attractive, cold-hearted rakes of the Restoration, Lothario is condemned for his betrayal of Calista, as well as his cynical denigration of woman's virtue. The sentimentalists recognized the cruelty of men who "embrace without love" and "make vows without conscience of obligation."[7] Steele systematically campaigned against callousness toward women, from tyranny over wives to sexual exploitation of tradeswomen.[8]

Since women were seen primarily as wives, Steele's campaign to enhance this role was especially useful. "I have very long entertained an ambition to make the Word *Wife* the most agreeable and delightful Name in Nature," he declared.

> Marriage is an institution calculated for a constant Scene of as much Delight as our Being is capable of. Two Persons who have chosen each other out of all the Species, with Design to be each other's mutual Comfort and Entertainment, have in that Action bound themselves to be good-humour'd, affable, discreet, forgiving, patient, and joyful, with Respect to each other's Frailties and Perfections, to the

End of their Lives. . . . the most indifferent Circumstance administers Delight. . . . The marry'd Man can say, If I am unacceptable to all the World beside, there is one, whom I entirely Love, that will receive me with Joy and Transport, and think her self obliged to double her Kindness and Caresses of me from the Gloom with which she sees me overcast. I need not dissemble the Sorrow of my Heart to be agreeable there.[9]

Like his predecessors, Steele noted that a married couple should make mutual concessions and expected a wife to console her husband for setbacks in the outside world; but he gave it all a positive turn. Love suffuses the relationship, mitigating sorrow and enhancing joy. The wife is dear and important, and she helps her husband not from coerced submission but spontaneous love. The couple do not merely live together without squabbling, but take the keenest pleasure in each other's society.

These high expectations cannot be met with a partner who is merely suitable; marriage can be what it should be only with the one right person. Though he spoke in terms of love rather than rights, Steele implied that a woman is entitled to a loving partner, rather than one who merely refrains from mistreating her. He condemned a husband who "robbed" his wife "of all the endearments of life," giving "her only common civility, instead of . . . that constant assemblage of soft desires and affections which all feel who love."[10]

Yet Steele's exclusive emphasis on sentiment in marriage could lead him to ignore important facts and conceal exploitation of the wife. He disregarded the practical injustice of depriving wives of power over money and thought it distasteful and inappropriate to make a wife a settled allowance. When financial agreements are made before marriage, "tenderness is thrown out of the question . . . the good offices, the pleasures and graces of life, are not put into the balance," he wrote in the *Tatler.* Self-interest peeps out from under the sentiment when he explains that "supplying a Man's Wife with *Pin-money* is furnishing her with Arms against himself, and . . . becoming accessary to his own Dishonour." There is no legitimate need for such an allowance, since a properly affectionate husband will give her whatever she ought to have. And there are positive

advantages to this economic dependence, Steele blandly proceeds: "There is no greater Incitement to Love in the Mind of
Man, than the Sense of a Person's depending upon him for her
Ease and Happiness; as a Woman uses all her Endeavours to
please the Person whom she looks upon as her Honour, her
Comfort, and her Support." Steele refused to see the inevitable
divergence of interest between even people who love each other
and the tendency of power to corrupt even the well-meaning. He
assumed that a husband was dishonored by not maintaining
control over his wife. With all his concern for women's feelings,
he had no concept of equal rights. His ideal wife's description
of her role shows that he expected a woman to give her husband far more than he gives her: "I ... have no other Concern
but to please the Man I love: he's the End of every Care I have;
if I dress 'tis for him, if I read a Poem or a Play 'tis to qualify
my self for a Conversation agreeable to his Taste: He's almost the
End of my Devotions, half my Prayers are for his Happiness."[11]

Henry Fielding shared Steele's sentimental appreciation of
women and marriage, and his one-sidedness. His picture of the
Booth marriage in Amelia (1751) warmly evokes the couple's
intense concern about each other, their delight in each other's
company, their enjoyment of their children. Amelia is in every
way a blessing to her husband, contriving to make a comfortable home with the inadequate means he provides and constantly encouraging him after his failures in the outside world.
But William Booth contributes to the relationship only by loving her dearly. He has a life outside, but she is not "capable of
any sensation worthy the name of pleasure" when neither her
husband nor children are present. While she constantly worries about preserving her chastity for Booth and finds the liking
of any other man "highly disagreeable," he enjoys an affair with
Miss Matthews. Yet when he indulges in jealous outbursts
against her, she falls on her knees and pleads. Amelia gives her
husband the ultimate gratification of depending totally on him
for her happiness while making no reciprocal demands. She
persists in looking up to him; despite his constantly demonstrated incompetence, she "would not presume to advise him"
on financial matters.[12] Fielding did not share Amelia's blindness

to her husband's faults, though he did consider it a virtue; but his sentimental overemphasis on good intentions caused him to treat them overindulgently. For such writers, love made a good husband faithful and affectionate, while it made a good wife totally self-sacrificing. Their sentimentalism reinforced the usual eighteenth-century double standard, by obscuring the actual conditions in relationships and imposing a falsely exalted ideal on women.

It might seem, then, that whatever women gained from sentimentalism in terms of consideration for their feelings and appreciation of their role as wives, they lost in terms of patronage and exploitation. Yet without sentimentalism, we would not have the novels of Samuel Richardson. (His masterpiece, *Clarissa*, is an infinitely more subtle improvement on *The Fair Penitent*.) And Richardson's work was enormously helpful to women—affirming the worth of their feelings and their interests, developing a form that women writers could follow.

Richardson was essentially a sentimental writer. His heroines are virtuous in the approved mode—delicate, modest, and dutiful. They constantly faint, they cannot express their feelings directly, they are exasperatingly submissive to constituted authority. They exhaustively analyze their feelings and motives, psychologically and morally. Richardson dwelt lovingly upon their sufferings—the trials of Pamela (1740), the imprisonment and dying of Clarissa (1747-48), the romantic frustration of Harriet and Clementina in *Sir Charles Grandison* (1753-54).

But Richardson put this sentimental material to feminist use. His heroines shine in the conventional womanly virtues, but they have intelligence, strength, and integrity as well. Chastity, a virtue enforced by patriarchy and usually implying men's property right in women, becomes an assertion of feminine integrity for his Clarissa when she refuses to capitulate to her own sexual attraction to Lovelace or the world's pressure to marry him.[13] Moreover, Richardson did not merely present her suffering as a beautiful object for contemplation, but used it to provoke indignation at the oppression of women. He replaced self-indulgent compassion with genuine empathy, putting himself in a woman's place and seeing through her eyes. Because of this total involvement, he applied sense as well as sensibility to his presentation of women. Clarissa and the others are distinguished by and suffer from exceptional sensitivity, but they also suffer objectively from oppressive social attitudes and institutions. Morality in the novels is determined by rational law and responsibility as well as emotion, and thus provides a basis for arguing women's rights. Though Richardson had all three of his heroines censure Swift for coarse views of women, he shared Swift's respect for women's minds and his disenchantment with conventional sexual roles.

Also like Swift, he delighted in the society of intelligent young women. He was equally interested in developing their minds and more respectful of their distinctively feminine perceptions. Surrounding himself with women friends, he drew out their views on moral and social issues, started subjects to be discussed with them in lengthy correspondence, and developed his third novel in terms of their advice. It is true that he could be stuffily conventional when dealing with his own wife and daughters, but his novels display a genuinely radical advocacy of women.[14] The release of imagination in creating fiction seems to have freed Richardson from conventional moral inhibitions, as it did Defoe. Where the imagination is most in control, as in *Clarissa*, the feminism is bolder; where it is least, as when Sir Charles Grandison is expounding his views, conventional inhibitions set in.

In *Clarissa*, Richardson set up a situation which powerfully dramatized the oppression of women: Clarissa, a person of virtue, intelligence, and integrity, struggles to determine the course of her own life—and is doomed to fail, since her society will not allow a woman to live independently. Driven from her home by her need to protect her freedom from an odious marriage, she is then subjected by Lovelace to relentless pressure—culminating in rape—to acknowledge dependence on him.[15] Although she does manage to defeat him morally, she does so at the price of dying.

Clarissa's story derives its enormous impact from her sensitivity—her sensibilities offended by masculine arrogance, her constant scrupulous examination of behavior and motivation. Neither Lovelace nor her relatives can understand, much less respect, her feelings. Her family cannot see what impels her to refuse the man they are pressing on her, since she is not in love with anyone else. Mrs. Howe, mother of her best friend, agrees that too much bustle is being made about her feelings: "Is it such a mighty matter for a young woman to give up her inclinations to oblige her friends?" Astell and Swift, accepting marriage as a practical but intrinsically imperfect arrangement, might have been equally unsympathetic to Clarissa's fastidiousness.

Lovelace is confident that he can do what he likes with Clarissa, not only because of his masculine forcefulness and her fascination with him, but because he cannot accept her scruples or her outraged dignity as significant. A typical Restoration rake, he feels no guilt for deceiving, attempting to seduce, and even raping Clarissa. Like other sentimental writers, Richardson brought out the hostility and unfairness of the rake, who makes a game of what was deadly serious for the woman, since her place in society generally depended upon her reputation. In the case of rigidly idealistic Clarissa, the game is even more cruel because she must keep her chastity if she is to continue respecting herself. With the rake's glib assumption that marriage means defeat and confinement for a man, Lovelace would prefer what he fatuously calls the life of honor: that is, a free-love relationship in which the man is free to leave and the woman is bound to him by love (and, though he does not mention it, by the ruined reputation which leaves her no other option).

But Richardson saw what his contemporaries did not, that Lovelace's selfishness was shared by most men in his society, including sentimentally devoted husbands. He put into the mouth of this sadistic libertine a vision of ideal marriage that sounds very much like those of Steele and Fielding. Lovelace would like his wife to be "governed in her behavior to me by Love," not "by Generosity merely, or by blind Duty":

> I would have her look after me when I go out, as far as she can see me . . . and meet me at my return with rapture. I would be the subject of her dreams, as well as of her waking thoughts. I would have her think every moment lost, that

is not passed with me ... When I should be inclined to
Love, overwhelm me with it; when to be serious or solitary
... retireing at a nod ... Be a *Lady Easy* to all my pleasures,
and valuing those most who most contributed to them;
only sighing in private, that it was not *herself* at the
time.[16]

He would have a wife persuade only through "expostulatory
meekness, and gentle reasoning, mingled with sighs as gentle,
and graced with bent knees, supplicating hands, and eyes lifted
up to your imperial countenance." By dutifully submitting to
her man, especially when he is wrong, a woman will come to
deserve his "high opinion ... of her prudence and obligingness—
And so, by degrees, she will become her master's master." Take
away the sadistic phrasing, and both advice and rationalization
could have come from a standard guide to wifely duty.

A man can unblushingly present such a view if he assumes
that the woman he loves is his property, who exists as the object of his desire, rather than as a human being like himself,
and who can find fulfillment only through him. Lovelace constantly uses expressions like "this prime gift, WOMAN" and
minimizes his guilt on the grounds that he has invaded no
one's property in raping Clarissa: "Have not those who have a
right in her, renounced that right? ... is she not a *Single
woman?*" Besides, he can always wipe out his crime by marrying her, since if she becomes his wife, "whom but myself shall
I have injured?" That a woman could be her own property or
have her own honor, simply does not occur to him.

Considering Clarissa only as a sexual object, Lovelace never
does understand what he has done to her. He cannot see that his
violation of her will and self-respect was more significant than
that of her body; therefore he cannot see why she rejects a marriage that would cover up the physical violation while laying
her under mental subjection for life. Since it never occurs to
him that women are entitled to the rights of men, he cannot see
that a woman has a *right* to be treated decently, and he thus
expects Clarissa to be grateful for his offer of marriage.

Richardson demonstrated with indignation that such vil-
lainous selfishness was acceptable in Lovelace's society. The

honorable Colonel Morden praises his generosity in offering to marry Clarissa in exchange for having deceived, bullied, and (as he thinks) seduced her. Richardson portrays Lovelace as continuing to be accepted by people who know he has ruined Clarissa's life; he would have escaped all punishment but for the chance that she had a cousin who was a better swordsman. Most telling point of all, everything he did to her—including imprisonment and rape—would have been legally and, in conventional eyes, morally justified had she been his wife.[17] Though Lovelace states his possessiveness with unusual openness, it was implicit in his culture and quite compatible with the outwardly benign attitudes of writers like Henry Fielding, who could conceive no higher happiness than "the possession of such a woman as Sophia" and who described adultery as "robbing" a man "of that property, which, if he is a good man, he values above all others."[18]

While Fielding's heroines are objects of interest because the heroes love them, Richardson constantly affirmed that women exist as independent beings. He insisted as strongly as Astell that they could find fulfillment outside of marriage, that they need not center their lives on a man. He gave to the villain Lovelace the conviction that woman is a feminine earth, dreary and desolate unless shone upon by a male sun. Lovelace is sure that friendship between women lasts only until "a *man* comes in between the pretended *inseparables*," and never holds "to the endangering of life, limb, or estate, as it often does in our nobler Sex." Thus Richardson exposed the contempt for women which underlies the traditional claim, often advanced without ostensible hostility, that female friendship is at best a stopgap until marriage; at worst, a thin disguise for petty rivalry over men.

With equal conviction and more influence than Astell, Richardson demonstrated his confidence in women's capacity for friendship and in the quality of their minds. The noble friendship in *Clarissa* is that of the women, not the men; Part II of *Pamela* and all of *Sir Charles Grandison* are filled with similar friendships between women attracted by each other's minds and uninfluenced by sexual jealousy. The friendship between Clarissa and Anna is the most significant and satisfying relationship in their lives. Anna admires Clarissa without envy and illustrates in her friend's troubles the reckless generosity that Lovelace restricted to the "nobler Sex." Disproving his sneer, she is ready for Clarissa's sake to jeopardize her all-important reputation, by going to London with her disgraced friend.

Richardson's women can think of fulfilling themselves without men because they have the same capacities for independent development. While his views on women's education represent enlightened opinion of his time, his emphasis on the intellectual capacity of women shows unusual commitment. He populated his novels with articulate women who are equal or superior to their male counterparts: Pamela excels both Parson Williams and Mr. B. in ready wit and sound judgment; Clarissa holds her own with the brilliant Lovelace; Anna Howe and Charlotte Grandison are more intelligent than their suitors.

In addition to criticizing education that did all it could to restrict feminine intellectual development, Richardson, like Astell, challenged the entrenched contemporary assumption that knowledge of Latin and Greek was essential to make a person educated. Anna points out the narrowness of men who glory in their superior knowledge of the classics, which they have only because of educational opportunities closed to women, and satirizes the university graduate who disdainfully smiles "at a mistaken or ill-pronounced *word* from a Lady, when her *sense* has been clear, and her sentiments just; and when he could not himself utter a single sentence fit to be repeated, but what he borrowed from the authors he had been obliged to study."[19]

But the most impressive evidence of Richardson's respect for women's minds appears indirectly in the amount of space he devoted to reporting their discussions of general questions. Clearly he wanted to make the point that women were qualified to consider any topic and that their ideas were worth hearing. He explicitly justified women's voicing opinions by the rule which Harriet's grandfather gave her: "Not impertinently to start subjects, as if I would make an ostentation of knowledge; or as if I were fond of indulging a talking humour," but to respond frankly when called upon to give her "sentiments upon any subject."[20] Fielding, in contrast, singled out as a particular excellence Sophia's refusal to express an opinion, even when pressed to do so by Allworthy, Thwackum, and Square. There is no indication in his novels that women can or that good women want to participate in anything like intellectual conversation. Fielding's intellectual women are ignorant, conceited, objectionably self-assertive, and unchaste.

Recognizing the intellectual equality of women, Richardson did not condemn them as presumptuous or unfeminine for criticizing men who deserved criticism. His intelligent women are free of that awe of the masculine mind which Fielding considered appropriate. In contrast to his Mr. Allworthy, who asserts that "the highest deference to the understandings of men" is "a quality, absolutely essential to the making a good wife," Sir Charles Grandison says such submission is necessary to the happiness only "of common minds." A good woman in *Pamela* declares that she would oppose the wrong-headed actions of a stupid husband and be mortified when he made a fool of himself in company.[21] Even saintly Clarissa would have to make heroic efforts to avoid despising a husband intellectually inferior to herself.

Richardson's intelligent women are keenly aware of masculine conceit and enjoy puncturing it. While Sir Hargrave displays his witty gallantry before Harriet and Mr. Walden repeats lines of Tibullus at her "in an heroic accent," she coolly evaluates both of them. She enjoys sniping at "the Lords of the *creation*" and can even criticize the peerless Sir Charles for his patronizing attitude. Charlotte Grandison openly deflates his chivalry when he pompously claims that "we men should have power and right given us to protect and serve your Sex . . . and, at last, lay all our trophies . . . at your feet." She tartly rejoins: "you have concluded with some magnificent intimations of superiority over us—Power and right to protect, travel, toil, for us, and lay your trophies at our feet. . . . Surely, surely, this is diminishing us, and exalting yourselves, by laying us under high obligations to your generosity."[22]

Charlotte and Anna Howe carry their free criticism of men to the point of open hostility. Yet Richardson presented them sympathetically, not as the unruly monsters they would have appeared to his contemporaries. Anna, though less perfect than Clarissa, is not castigated for her plain-speaking, her insubordination to her narrow-minded mother, her reluctance to marry her fiancé, Hickman, or her declaration that she will not blindly obey him after marriage. The judgment on her is not that she is presumptuous and selfish, but that her failings, if such they are, are "much more lovely . . . than the virtues of many of her Sex!" Though meekness and gentleness like Clarissa's make Richardson's ideal woman, an active, self-willed person like Anna is superior to a meek domestic animal. In the end Anna makes a good wife, and without changing her character. Lovelace would not have believed this possible, for he is sure that "a directing wife" will not stop until she makes her husband despicable and herself "a plague to all about her."[23]

Richardson saw warfare and domination in all sexual relationships, in contrast with sentimental writers who would smother the conflict of interests and the oppression with romance. Indeed, his most conspicuous romantic lover is the rake Lovelace, whose raptures are shown to be utterly self-centered. When Richardson described good marriages, he talked about money (Lord and Lady L. in *Grandison* pool their income and spend it on an equal basis), freedom to criticize (Sir Charles exhorts Harriet to blame him if she thinks him wrong), and shared decision-making (Anna and Hickman follow the lead of whichever one speaks first). He did not emphasize romantic love, which he realized could not refine away the problems of married life. He was as aware of a wife's disadvantages as Defoe or Astell, though his heroines express themselves less bluntly.

Clarissa longs to settle in a single life, in which she could "defy the Sex. For I see nothing but trouble and vexation that they bring upon ours." Like Millamant, she worries about loss of identity in marriage; but, existing in realistic novel rather than high comedy, she sees no way to avoid it: the wife's lot is "To give up her very Name, as a mark of becoming his absolute and dependent property; To be obliged to prefer this strange man['s] . . . humours to all her own—Or to contend perhaps, in breach of a vowed duty, for every innocent instance of free-will— to go nowhither; To make acquaintance; To give up acquaintance; To renounce even the strictest friendships perhaps; all at his pleasure, whether she think it reasonable to do so or not." As for the argument that women gain needful protection through marriage, Clarissa says it is their "way of training-up" rather than their natural weakness which makes them "need the protection of the brave"; and Anna adds that in marriage "this brave man will free us from all insults but . . . His own!" Finally, Anna exposes the fundamental flaw in traditional patriarchal marriage by pointing out that there is not one man in a hundred "whom a woman of sense and spirit can either *honour* or *obey*, tho' you make us promise *both*, in that solemn form of words which unites or rather *binds* us to you in marriage." Both characters note that this formula was devised by men.[24]

Marriage even to a paragon like Sir Charles Grandison involves some sacrifice of a woman's interests, as his sister explains: "Her name sunk, and lost! The property, person and will, of another, excellent as the man is."[25] In Fielding it is only the whorish Lady Bellaston and the adulterous peer who cast aspersions upon "the matrimonial institution itself, and at the unjust powers given by it to man over the more sensible, and more meritorious part of the species."[26]

Richardson recognized that stress is intrinsic to the best of marriages and is aggravated by the disproportionate power of the husband. As Anna says, "*Men*, no more than *women*, know how to make a moderate use of power. . . . All the animals in the creation are more or less in a state of hostility with each other." It would be nice to think that love could dissolve this hostility, but it can do so only by suppressing the interests of one partner. The only solution is a system of mutual concessions and obligations similar to Millamant's: the couple should agree on boundaries "beyond which neither should go: and each should hold the other to it; or there would probably be encroachments in both."[27]

In Richardson, then, sentimentalism is always stiffened by rational emphasis on rights and regulated by practical reality. Though his material is emotional distress, ranging from the sufferings of Clarissa through everyday social frictions or anxieties, the heroines who suffer also think. Though they are properly feminine, they do not blindly love or obey. Both Clarissa and Harriet recognize that their difficulty in resisting other people's demands is a weakness, resulting from the compliance trained into women. It occurs to Clarissa that women might do well to make the world respect them by asserting themselves, even at the price of "being the *less* beloved."[28]

Richardson was never carried away by the romantic or sentimental view that only emotions matter, and he could see women as people like himself rather than projections of his emotions. Holding this attitude may have been easier for him than for other men because his personal relations with women were based on rational friendship rather than romantic passion. The morbid fantasies that contributed so much to his inspiration may also, by increasing his awareness of the negative elements in men's attitudes toward women, have led him to question conventional roles; certainly they would not reinforce complacency about the sexual status quo.

Richardson actively encouraged women to write for publication; he actually blamed them for hiding "their talents in a napkin" because they were "afraid, lovely dastards, of showing themselves capable of the perfections they are mistresses of."[29] More important, he created a form of novel useful to them, one in which they could use what they knew—their thoughts about family relationships and the genteel social scene, their feelings in romantic and social situations. There was little room for such things in the picaresque world of action and violent passion, most of which was out of bounds to any woman more respectable than Moll Flanders. Sophia Western could not be the center of interest in *Tom Jones,* and her emotional problems—separation from the man she loves and pressure to marry one she absolutely hates—are too broadly conceived to sustain attention. Largely debarred from external action, women characters had to arrest interest through their subtle responses to others or their examination of motives or private moral questions.

By studying women's consciousness in detail, Richardson gave it status as a subject worth considering and laid out a field in which women novelists were qualified to write. His identification with a female protagonist in *Pamela*, in *Clarissa*, and to a large extent in *Sir Charles Grandison* led him to consider questions of interest to women from a woman's point of view: What does marriage mean to a woman in a patriarchal society? How should men and women talk to each other? How does a conventional romantic work like Otway's *The Orphan* look to a woman? By letting female characters express well-considered views on such questions and by making a hero like Grandison, his ideal of manly excellence, participate with interest, Richardson effectively dramatized not only the importance of women's concerns but the value of their thoughts; in so doing he gave women writers confidence to develop their own ideas.

While Richardson departed from convention in giving his heroines far more intellect and mental independence than was usual in sentimental literature, he accepted the convention that they must be examples to their sex by illustrating virtue beyond reproach. Clarissa can be a disheartening ideal if we think of her meticulousness in fulfilling her duties to others regardless of how they treat her, her readiness to die because she cannot meet impossible moral standards, and even her ability to die because her feelings have been outraged. Fortunately, Richardson presented alternatives in the form of women like Anna Howe and Charlotte Grandison, who are attractive and virtuous even though they do not conform to the conventional ideal. By pairing his admirable characters in this way, Richardson provided real women with a positive role model who was not a martyr and opened more varied and interesting possibilities for novels focusing on women.

Frances Brooke is a good example of a woman whose talent might well have remained undeveloped had it not been for Richardson's achievement. A clergyman's daughter who shared Mary Astell's conservatism in Church and State, she had none of Astell's combativeness and boldly unconventional views on women. Her first novel, *Lady Julia Mandeville* (1763), is thoroughly sentimental, constructed entirely of refined emotions. But her later novels happily combine sentiment with rational control. *The History of Emily Montague* (1769) balances sentimental characters with sensible ones, and in *The Excursion* (1777), adventures that could easily become sentimental agonies are recounted in an agreeably dry, worldly tone that puts them into proportion. The characters in these two novels inhabit a realistic world with problems that are not exclusively emotional. *The Excursion* is sentimental in the tradition of Fielding, setting warm spontaneity over prudential self-control; but Brooke sharply diverges from the masculine tradition by applying this standard to a female character, her heroine.

Emily Montague develops directly from the Richardsonian novel, though Brooke shifted the balance from pathos to comedy. The sentiment appears sometimes as excessive regard for emotional susceptibility, but also as respect for subtle but important feelings—feelings that in the real world were habitually overruled in favor of order or family convenience. Without much thinking about it, Emily has agreed to marry the man her uncle has selected for her—a good-looking, respectable, wealthy and well-born man who is outwardly suitable, but is, she now realizes, hopelessly uncongenial. It is clear that he will be a civil but inattentive husband, oblivious to her need for reciprocal sympathy and lively affection.

Recognizing that her feelings for her fiancé are "languid," Emily asks herself whether it is "romantic" to wish for ideal love and companionship in marriage. Her problem is to extricate herself from her engagement in a world that discounts such wishes as fanciful and self-indulgent, where "timidity, decorum, or false honor," compliance with one's family, "and weak fear of the censures of the world" all combined to force a woman to stifle her feelings and personal preferences.[30] Her predicament is more realistic than Clarissa's since her fiancé has no blatant shortcomings. (It is hard to believe that even the Harlowes would force Solmes upon their daughter, but Richardson had to make him dreadful in order to maintain Clarissa's impeccable character by absolutely justifying her refusal to obey them.)

Although Emily is a perfect sentimental heroine in her intense sensitivity, she does not have the passivity usually associated with the type: she has strong feelings and is prepared to brave convention in order to follow them. It is the strength, as well as the refinement, of her feelings which makes the hero, Colonel Rivers, fall in love with her. Preferring sincere warmth to propriety, he does not want a woman who merely responds to his courtship: "the eyes, the air, the voice of the woman I love, a thousand little indiscretions dear to the heart must convince me I am beloved, before I confess I love."

One would expect a sentimental hero to be appreciative of women's refinement, punctiliously considerate of their feelings, and rarefied in his ideal of love. What distinguishes Brooke's Rivers from the stereotype is that he not only loves women but respects them as independent beings; he sees them as people rather than sexual objects, and even notices that they were unjustly treated under the law. Rivers enjoys only a mixed society in which women and men converse rationally; he deplores the frequent domination of such society by the sexual fears of the prude or the sexual vanity of the coquette, and he declares that "those tremendous men, who have designs on the whole sex, are, and ever were, characters as fabulous as the giants of romance. Women after twenty begin to know this, and therefore converse with us on the footing of rational creatures, without either fearing or expecting to find every man a lover." Unlike men who see women purely as sexual objects, Rivers prefers mature women over girls, whose only advantage, he says, is "freshness of complexion." (Emily is twenty-four.) He points out how unfair it is to value women only as romantic partners and then arbitrarily limit their exercise of that role to early youth.

His insistence that women can converse intelligently with men recalls Sir Charles Grandison, but Rivers embodies values more congenial to women. More dependent on women than Grandison, he is not so impeccably—and implausibly—chaste. He has enlivened his bachelor state with affairs, but he has taken care to choose experienced widows, women who would not be harmed. Rivers is not so awesomely superior as Grandison, nor so fond of instructing and dominating. Although he can be patronizing—he delights in women's conversation because he loves "their sweet prattle beyond all the sense and learning in the world"—he is not egotistical or domineering. Like Grandison, he brings together two women who love him; unlike Grandison, he acknowledges that the situation degrades both women and that he was culpably vain to set it up.

Far from wanting to direct his wife, Rivers maintains that "whatever conveys the idea of subjection necessarily destroys that of love." (Here he is closer to Defoe than to a typical sentimental lover, who would assume that a good wife's love naturally includes submission.) After marriage, he makes a point of giving Emily a room of her own, where he will never intrude; for he recognizes from his own experience that everyone values "some place which we can say is peculiarly our own . . . whither we can retire even from those most dear to us."

Rivers's empathy with women carries him even further, into considering their political position. Through him Brooke expressed the typically feminine insight that England, the paradise of wives, actually treated women worse than supposedly less enlightened cultures. Rivers explains that the Huron Indians allowed the unhappily married to divorce, and he goes on to observe that they allotted a significant share in government to "The sex we have so unjustly excluded from power in Europe": "In the true sense of the word, we are the savages, who so impolitely deprive you [i.e., women] of the common rights of citizenship . . . I don't think you are obliged in conscience to obey laws you have had no share in making; your plea would certainly be at least as good as that of the Americans, about which we every day hear so much."[31]

Just as Englishmen smugly overvalued the gallantry which set them above the Indians, they dwelt on the cruelty of Roman Catholic convents for demanding of women life-long vows that were not always voluntary. Brooke exposed this hypocrisy through Emily's friend Arabella Fermor. Once, when Arabella was inveighing "against the cruelty of forcing girls to commit themselves as nuns *for life*," a French woman silenced her by saying marriage is also for life, and "without a year of probation." Arabella now admits that French parents who push their daughters into the convent are no worse than English ones who push them into marriage, and indeed that a nun's "situation is . . . paradise to that of a married woman, of sensibility and honor, who dislikes her husband."

Arabella is not, however, a dedicated feminist, for she is too immersed in social gaiety to think about serious questions and sufficiently young and attractive to get anything she wants from men by charming them. But she does offer a bracing contrast to the delicate, sentimental, dependent Emily (as Anna does to Clarissa). She is presented as virtuous and amiable even though she is self-willed, flippant, and flirtatious. She often ridicules Emily's finer feelings, does not depend entirely on the man she loves, and frankly admits that she delights in general admiration, which, "without coquetry 'tis in vain to expect." By naming her character after Arabella Fermor, the real-life original of Alexander Pope's Belinda in "The Rape of the Lock," Brooke invites a comparison between them. Though both are ravishingly attractive coquettes, only Brooke's Arabella is seen from the inside as a thinking human being. Belinda escapes moral censure because she is so silly that she cannot be held humanly responsible; Arabella, because Brooke makes the reader understand and sympathize with her motives, as she intelligently asserts her individuality within the situation of romantic courtship.

Arabella does not fall helplessly in love: rather, deciding it is time to get married, she picks out the man she wants and easily secures him. While Emily, the proper romance heroine, can enjoy nothing without her lover, Arabella contrives sometimes to pass the hours of Fitzgerald's absence "pleasantly enough, if any other agreeable man is in the way." Nor is she alarmed if she sees "him flirt a little with others." Remarking that Emily "loves like a foolish woman" and herself "like a sensible man," Arabella wishes that women were not brought up to be more emotional than men; she regrets that "Every possible means is used, even from infancy, to soften the minds of women, and to harden those of men."[32] Brooke realized that women were brought up to be sentimental, presumably because men wanted them that way.

The very form of *Emily Montague*, letters expressing the thoughts and feelings of a group of young people who are forming into couples, focuses attention on the normal emotional life of women. Thinking about women naturally leads to feminist issues, from social pressure to marry without love, to the possibility of nonsexual friendships between the sexes, to the denial to women of any voice in the government.

In *The Excursion*, more explicitly than in *Emily Montague*, Brooke uses sentimentalism to justify a woman's right to express herself, both emotionally and creatively. Its heroine, Maria, is enthusiastic and imprudent; she loves injudiciously and risks sexual "ruin." However, Brooke demonstrates that her warmth and generosity outweigh her faults, and she allows her to recover from her errors as a young man might do.

Maria, a sanguine, impulsive girl of eighteen, falls in love with a worldly young lord. Because of her inexperience and his jaded selfishness, they misunderstand each other completely: she counts on becoming his wife, while he assumes she will be his mistress. While Brooke keeps a proper awareness of the moral values—the pathos of Maria's situation and the cold exploitativeness of the young aristocrat—she does not dissolve into the maudlin laments or denunciations this situation would have inspired in most of her contemporaries. Instead, she shows how the misunderstanding could arise between two intelligent people without conscious malice.

Brooke's characterization of young Lord Melvile is perceptive, almost sympathetic. Though he plays the same role as Lovelace, he is a naturally humane man, corrupted by the cynical principles inculcated by his Chesterfield-like father. He is so remarkably attracted to Maria that he would have lost his heart to her, had he still a heart to lose. But years of fashionable dissipation have reduced him to a state where his only passion with respect to women is vanity. The interplay between this cool creature of fashion and the romantic ardent Maria is presented with sufficient detachment to have its comic side; certainly it is far from the conventional melodrama of rake plotting against innocent lamb.

Brooke had a more relaxed and realistic attitude toward sex than Richardson did. She poked gentle fun at his picture of a world infested by predatory males and could regard sexual sins with equanimity: Colonel Rivers has had affairs, and the doings of Lord Melvile and his father are described as immoral but not monstrous. Moreover, she integrated respect for women's personalities with acceptance of their sexual role and therefore presented sexual experience as pleasurable rather than frightening, even for women. Richardson's Anna shows her independence by putting men off; Brooke's Arabella, by flirting with them on her own terms. Maria recognizes and expresses her love as no Richardsonian heroine would have felt free to do.

Wishing to approximate the normal experience of women, Brooke pointedly avoided the melodramatic clichés that were used to make the sentimental heroine's situation more poignant. When Maria set off for London, her uncle "cautioned her, not against the giants of modern novel, who carry off young ladies by force in post-chaises and six with the blinds up, and confine free-born English women in their country-houses, under the guardianship of monsters in the shape of fat housekeepers, from which durance they are happily released by the compassion of Robert the butler [see *Pamela*]; but against worthless acquaintance, unmerited calumny, and ruinous expence."[33]

The conventional heroine would have been too virtuous—that is, too impeccably correct—to fall victim to any such realistic perils; but warm, imprudent Maria leaves herself open to scandal and lets herself be misled into extravagance. She unintentionally offends people by neglecting small civilities and "those trifling forms, which mask vice, and protect virtue"; and "Conscious of her own integrity," she disdains "every species of disguise" and expresses her feelings without regard to the reserve expected of women. She publicly shows her affection for Lord Melvile and even invites him to a tête-à-tête supper when she expects him to propose. Her willfulness and indiscretion make Maria partly responsible for her troubles. The effect may be less pathetic than that of unmerited distresses heaped on an innocent victim, but it is considerably more realistic and interesting.

At the same time, contrary to convention, Brooke suggests that indiscretion, even in a woman, is a minor failing that is far outweighed by love and sincerity. Maria suffers anxiety and embarrassment, but no permanent harm; and in fact the man she eventually marries likes her the better for frankly acknowledging that she had loved the man who abandoned her.

Only a sentimental feminist could pardon Maria for loving Lord Melvile before he had been approved by her family, and even before he had proposed marriage. The rationalists—and here Richardson would agree—believed an unmarried lady should confine herself to passively accepting a man's attentions, and they thus denied women emotional expression. Brooke, on the contrary, presents Maria's spontaneous passion as generous, and her admission that she loved a man who did not appreciate her as casting shame on him, not her. Brooke's implication that women can and should feel passion on their own, not merely in response to men—that they had a right to emotional as well as intellectual fulfillment—was a radical one, anticipating the claims that were to shock readers of Mary Wollstonecraft and the Brontës.

Not only is Maria emotionally self-assertive, but she longs to be recognized as an author. Such an urge toward ego gratification was considered almost as immodest in a woman as loving without sanction, and often condemned in similar terms. Maria does not assert that she was reluctantly forced to publish by financial need or by an imperative mission to reform the public; rather, "that enthusiasm inseparable from true genius" makes her aware of her ability and eager for public recognition.

Maria's passionate vocation for authorship does, unfortunately, drop out of sight; the last we hear about it is her maidenly fear lest it be revealed to her family. But in her preface Brooke unequivocally defended women's right to publish novels, and not merely for the purpose of financial sustenance. It is true that some terms of her defense are too sentimental to appeal to the modern feminist: women are qualified to write novels because of their "quick sensibility, native delicacy of mind, facility of expression"; although they are rightly debarred from government, science, and formal education, they may exert influence in "the softer empire of private life . . . as well by writing as by conversation." Nevertheless, she does assert that a woman with literary talent has a right to exercise it, to intermix with her domestic duties "such studies as become her station in the scale of rational beings," and even to desire "public approbation."[34]

What Brooke used in the sentimental tradition was not its invitation to luxuriate in artificially contrived feelings, but its respect for legitimate ones. This respect was particularly valuable in a time of patriarchal attitudes and institutions, when women were pressured to conform to others' wishes, not to pay attention to their own. Emily Montague's rejection of her unexceptionable fiancé for no flagrant cause would have been condemned in actual society or in a novel by Tobias Smollett, yet in the world of sentiment her feelings of vague disappointment and unease, her hopes for romantic fulfillment are important enough to justify breaking her engagement. Rivers's exhortation to a rakish friend about to marry, that he must always remember that "the heart of woman is not less delicate than tender,"[35] must be seen against a background of social opinion that recognized nothing more subtle than physical abuse as a legitimate grievance in a wife.

Moreover, interest in women's feelings led to identification with their point of view, and this in turn promoted an articulation of feminist opinions which would not have been thought of in a male-oriented tradition. The subjective nature of the sentimental novel well adapted it to the expression of feminist resentments and hopes that had no chance for realization in the external world. Finally, because sentimental literature dealt with sexual feelings, it brought a needed emotional dimension to the starkly intellectual approach of such earlier feminists as Mary Astell.

While sentimentalism might undermine the cause of women's rights by glorifying female martyrdom or exaggerating female helplessness, the movement as a whole provided an essential impetus toward feminism. By asserting the worth of feminine perceptions and values, it gave women confidence to express themselves and to claim emotional fulfillment. When stiffened by reason, as it was in Richardson and Brooke, it could promote analysis of women's unfair situation. Even the radical Mary Wollstonecraft, late in the century, valued "sensibility" and used it, as much as abstract rights, as the basis of her claims in her last feminist work, *Maria* (1798).

In fact, sentimental feeling did more than rational argument to improve the position of women. For sentimentalism persuaded by appealing to the emotions, but without shocking, because it stayed within the bounds of convention, accepting traditional definitions of masculine and feminine. Working within this tradition, a person like Brooke could develop feminist sentiments without outraging propriety and thus could gently influence people to respect women's desire for expression and fulfillment. As the century progressed, men felt more obligated to consider women, to respect them as people, to marry for love rather than convenience, to treat wives as friends rather than housekeepers; and women were able to integrate intellectual development with their traditional role and to develop a literary expression of their own.

NOTES

1. Frances Brooke, *The History of Emily Montague* (New York: Garland, 1974), III, 32-33.
2. Richard Steele, *The Spectator*, Everyman edition (London: J. M. Dent, 1950), II, 91; III, 312.
3. Richard Steele, *The Conscious Lovers* (Lincoln: University of Nebraska Press, 1968), p. 40.
4. Colley Cibber, *The Dramatic Works* (London: J. Rivington, 1777), II, 82.
5. Edward Moore, *The Gamester* (Ann Arbor: Augustan Reprint Society, 1948), p. 455.
6. Nicholas Rowe, *The Fair Penitent*, in *Six Eighteenth-Century Plays*, ed. John Harold Wilson (Boston: Houghton Mifflin, 1963), pp. 9-10, 20, 27. There are glints of feminism in other plays by Rowe, but these are even less satisfactorily developed: two women characters in his *Jane Shore* protest against the unfairness of the sexual double standard; see Rowe, *Three Plays*, ed. J. R. Sutherland (London: Scholartis Press, 1929), pp. 267-68, 308-9. In performance, Calista's grand defiance was more apparent: W. R. Chetwood said that Anne Oldfield as Calista seemed to put her monitor Horatio, Altamont's virtuous male friend, "into a Mousehole (quoted in *Three Plays*, p. 344).
7. Steele, *Conscious Lovers*, p. 39.
8. Steele, *Spectator*, I, 468-69. Steele defended milliners and coffeehouse proprietors against men who regarded them as fair game for lewd remarks and perpetual flirtation, pointing out that it is not gallant, but rather grossly inconsiderate, to impair the reputation and waste the time of a woman helpless to resist.
9. *Ibid.*, IV, 50-51.

10. Richard Steele, *The Tatler*, No. 53.

11. *Ibid.*, No. 199; *Spectator*, II, 256, 380-81.

12. Henry Fielding, *Amelia*, Shakespeare Head edition (Oxford: Basil Blackwell, 1926), I, 1, 109, 224; II, 65; III, 102-3, 158, 161, 242. Cf. Moore's more contemptible Mr. Beverley, who is also supposed to be a good man, presumably because he expresses affection for his wife (*Gamester*, p. 502). Both Hester Thrale and Mary Wortley Montagu testify to Fielding's lack of consideration for his own wife, despite his ardent love for her: see *Thraliana: The Diary of Mrs. Hester Lynch Thrale (later Mrs. Piozzi) 1776-1809*, ed. Katharine C. Balderston (Oxford: Clarendon, 1951), I, 14; and Lady Louisa Stuart's "Introductory Anecdotes" to Lady Mary Wortley Montagu, *The Letters and Works*, ed. Lord Wharncliffe (New York: AMS Press, 1970), I, 106.

13. John J. Richetti, "The Portrayal of Women in Restoration and Eighteenth Century Literature," in *What Manner of Woman: Essays on English and American Life and Literature*, ed. Marlene Springer (New York: New York University Press, 1977), p. 94.

14. Richardson actually opposed a settled allowance for his daughter on her marriage, on the grounds that he disapproved of "making a Wife in the least manner independent of her Husband"; and he thought girls could not be trusted to attend schools away from home; see T. C. Duncan Eaves and Ben D. Kimpel, *Samuel Richardson: A Biography* (Oxford: Clarendon, 1971), pp. 478, 564.

15. Ian Watt, *The Rise of the Novel* (Berkeley: University of California Press, 1957), p. 224.

16. Samuel Richardson, *Clarissa*, Shakespeare Head edition (Oxford: Basil Blackwell, 1929-31), II, 79; IV, 264. With Clarissa's refusal to marry Solmes even though she has no other attachment, contrast Fielding's Sophia, who can resist her father's pressure to marry Blifil only by the aid of her word of honor given to Tom and her love for him, in *Tom Jones*, Shakespeare Head edition (Oxford: Basil Blackwell, 1926), IV, 230.

17. Richardson, *Clarissa*, III, 241; IV, 217, 235-36, 377; VI, 68; VII, 355-57.

18. Henry Fielding, *Tom Jones*, IV, 306; *Amelia*, III, 75 (Dr. Harrison, the right-minded clergyman, is speaking).

19. Richardson, *Clarissa*, IV, 245; V, 274-75; VIII, 240. Contrast Anna's comment with the scene in *Amelia* where Dr. Harrison gleefully puts down Mrs. Atkinson for a small error in Latin (III, 67-70). Pamela echoes Astell when she laments

that when a girl manages to rise above her narrow education, "her Genius is immediately tamed by trifling Imploy-
ments, lest, perhaps, she should become the Envy of one
sex, and the Equal of the other." Men condemn women for
their addiction to "common Tea-table Prattle, while they
do all they can to make them fit for nothing else" (Samuel
Richardson, Pamela, Shakespeare Head edition, IV, 320,
363). In Sir Charles Grandison, Richardson suggested a system of "Protestant nunneries" which, like Astell's scheme,
would relieve ladies from economic pressure to marry
(Shakespeare Head edition, III, 382-83).

20. Richardson, Grandison, I, 20.
21. Fielding, Tom Jones, IV, 182; Richardson, Grandison, VI,
    143; Pamela, IV, 261-62.
22. Richardson, Grandison, I, 65; III, 252-53; V, 415-18.
23. Richardson, Clarissa, V, 280; VIII, 204, 301. Actually, Rich-
    ardson verged on overindulgence to Anna's and Charlotte's
    persistent teasing of the men who love them. Probably he
    excused it as the expression of generalized hostility toward
    men developing from their half-conscious anger against a
    society that exploited women.
24. Ibid., I, 192, 223; II, 150, 314; VIII, 198. Clarissa's objection
    to marriage is very similar to that expressed in real life by
    Elizabeth Carter: "what might I not have suffered from a
    husband! Perhaps be needlessly thwarted and contradicted
    in every innocent enjoyment of life: involved in all his
    schemes, right or wrong, and perhaps not allowed the lib-
    erty of even silently seeming to disapprove them!" See
    A Series of Letters between Mrs. Elizabeth Carter and Miss
    Catherine Talbot . . . 1741 to 1770, ed. Montagu Pennington
    (London: F. C. and J. Rivington, 1819), I, 334.
25. Richardson, Grandison, V, 393.
26. Fielding, Tom Jones, III, 105; IV, 102-3.
27. Richardson, Clarissa, II, 149; III, 230.
28. Ibid., I, 33, 48; Grandison, I, 131.
29. Eaves and Kimpel, Richardson, p. 205.
30. Brooke, Emily Montague, I, 87; II, 113-14. There is an in-
    teresting real-life confirmation of Emily's predicament in a
    conduct manual, The Female Aegis (1798). This work is
    largely plagiarized from Thomas Gisborne's An Enquiry
    into the Duties of the Female Sex (1797), but the anony-
    mous author did add one passage explaining how a girl
    might find herself engaged to a man she did not care for.
    Secluded from experience and trained to be unassertive,
    many a girl mistook "indistinct partiality" for "rivetted

attachment," simply because she rather liked a man, was flattered by his attentions, and was not attached to anyone else; *The Female Aegis; or, The Duties of Women* (New York: Garland, 1974), pp. 90-91.

31. Brooke, *Emily Montague,* I, 15-17, 67-69, 175-78, 228; II, 186, 195; IV, 42, 47. The Americans' plea did not, of course, include women. Seven years later, Abigail Adams made the same point as Rivers, in a letter to her husband: "in the new code of laws" for a newly independent America, "I desire you would remember the ladies and be more generous and favorable to them than your ancestors. . . . If particular care and attention is not paid to the ladies, we are determined to foment a rebellion, and will not hold ourselves bound by any laws in which we have no voice or representation." John Adams facetiously dismissed her argument. See *Familiar Letters of John Adams and His Wife Abigail Adams,* ed. Charles Francis Adams (Freeport, N.Y.: Books for Libraries, 1970), pp. 149-50.

32. Brooke, *Emily Montague,* I, 144; II, 161-63, 178-79; III, 29-30. Brooke consistently used Richardson's device of paired heroines: Emily and Arabella in *Emily Montague,* proper Louisa and impulsive Maria in *The Excursion,* hypersensitive Julia and sensible Anne Wilmot in *Lady Julia Mandeville.* Anne stipulates like Millamant that her husband is to continue courting her after marriage; see *Lady Julia Mandeville,* ed. E. Phillips Poole (London: Eric Partridge, 1930), p. 188.

33. Frances Brooke, *The Excursion* (London: T. Cadell, 1785), I, 22.

34. *Ibid.,* I, vi, x-xi, 39, 96; II, 230.

35. Brooke, *Emily Montague,* II, 198.

~~~ [5] ~~~

THE FEMININE NOVEL

The sentimentalists' insistence on the primacy of a woman's feelings threatened the whole pious structure that would sacrifice her emotional fulfillment to social or familial convenience. Their novels repeatedly disprove the comfortable assumption that a woman ought to be able to adjust happily to an uncongenial marriage. The tragic error of Elizabeth Griffith's Lady Barton (1771) is marrying Sir William without love, not falling in love with a more congenial man. (She married because of Sir William's obtuse persistence and her own vanity and ignorance, for, flattered by his vigorous pursuit and not realizing what she was getting into, she accepted him instead of waiting for a compatible match.) She comes to grief not for harboring feelings that oppose the convenience of her family and society, but for suppressing them.[1] The mother of Charlotte Lennox's Euphemia (1790), blandly assumes that Euphemia is too "reserved and delicate," as well as too reasonable, to be capable of passion, and therefore can love any man who seems suitable.[2] She pressures her dutiful daughter into marriage, and the result is disastrous. It turns out that Euphemia's feelings were a better guide to her husband's character than was her mother's pragmatic judgment.

It is easy to see why these novels appealed to women. In a world where their preferences and sensitivities were habitually disregarded, it was gratifying to see "sensibility" exalted as an essential virtue for women and men. At times this could be taken to extreme lengths, as in Sophia Lee's "The Young Lady's

Tale—The Two Emilys," in which the heroine, incapable of assertion and tremblingly sensitive, is wounded by the thoughtlessness of men until she ultimately educates those around her to
respond to her every modestly unexpressed wish. In the end,
"Virtue and sweetness, personified in Emily, formed the center
of a wide circle" of males, who looked up to her as an example
and never were "tempted, through the course of her long life,
to diverge from the sphere of so dear an attraction."[3]

Few of these novels indulged in such fantastic wish fulfillment, but all gratified women readers by making a woman the
center of attention. The heroines might suffer from abduction,
but never from "indifference and neglect."[4] Moreover, women in
fiction usually enjoyed freedom real women never had. Typically the heroines had yet to choose their marriage partners,
so that their consent had to be won to a course of life still open.
And they had far more opportunity for choice. They were usually orphans, so they had no obligation to observe parents'
wishes; and they were provided with several men to choose
from. Charlotte Smith's Emmeline (1788) has three desirable
and three undesirable suitors for her hand. A real woman would
more likely have to choose, as Burney did, between a man she
did not like and penurious spinsterhood. How pleasant it must
have been to immerse oneself in fictional situations where a
woman could refuse to marry for a livelihood or could decide
between a dashing impetuous suitor and a sedate responsible
one. A heroine in fiction could successfully reject the dictum
that "it is her business to endeavour to procure an establishment,
instead of affecting these fine romantic airs."[5]

The "fine romantic airs" were not only accepted but glorified in the women's novels. All the heroines, as well as the
sympathetic male characters, were richly endowed with a sensibility that made them value emotions over practical consid-
erations and be alert to the finer points of compatibility, love,
and consideration. In this context, Cecilia could reject with
horror her guardian's dictum, generally accepted in their day,
that she need not know her prospective husband since, "where
the connexion [proposed] is a proper one, a young lady of
delicacy has only to accede to it."[6] The fictitious heroine had the

opportunity not only to reject a man who did not meet her expectations, but also to examine the right one to make sure he did. Ann Radcliffe's Emily St. Aubert (*The Mysteries of Udolpho*, 1794) was attracted to Valancourt and knew her father approved of him, but did not immediately commit herself. "She feared to trust the preference her heart acknowledged . . . on so short an acquaintance"; her own and her father's first observations "were not sufficient testimonies of his general worth to determine her upon a subject so infinitely important to her future happiness."[7]

The lengthy delays before the ultimate happy marriage is reached in these novels, which result from external obstacles such as differences in rank and misunderstandings, as well as from the heroine's modest or prudent scruples, serve not merely to prolong the tale but also to express a resistance to man's dominion such as that openly declared by Millamant and Betsy Thoughtless. However tedious or frivolous the heroine's objections may seem to the modern reader, they expressed a real, and generally frustrated, need of the eighteenth-century woman: to prolong the period when she had a choice and was courted for her consent, to put off the time when her position would be permanently determined and her compliance with a man's wishes expected as a matter of course.

The heroines of these novels were gratifying illustrations of female worth. While few were as emotionally liberated as Frances Brooke's Maria, all had keenly sensitive feelings, which the author idealized. They also shared her intelligence: an "understanding" which does not merely know its place (like Sophia Western's), but which thinks and judges for itself, even if it may not dare to put that judgment into action. As the narrator or central consciousness of her novel, the heroine constantly demonstrated her capacity to perceive and evaluate the world around her. Moreover, even notably conservative women authors made a point of affirming women's intellectual capacity. Frances Sheridan's Sidney Bidulph (1761), a depressingly submissive heroine, has learned Latin from her brother; and it is a mark of her future husband's incompatibility that he suggests she would do better to embroider a rose than to read Horace.[8] Sophia Lee's

Mrs. Marlow (*The Recess,* 1785), physically a dreary example of feminine delicacy ("the soft symmetry of her person united every common idea of beauty and elegance to a feminine helplessness, which is . . . the most interesting of all charms"), has an understanding "enriched by a most extensive knowledge, to which she was every day adding by perpetual study."[9] Emily St. Aubert's father has taught her Latin, and even while escaping from Udolpho she does not forget to bring along the books that are her constant solace in her vicissitudes. Mary Walker's *Letters from the Duchess of Crui* (1776) conventionally advocates wifely obedience and dependence, but its declared purpose was to make women "conscious of their capacity for attaining any knowledge to which they may aspire."[10]

Charlotte Smith's heroines are particularly capable of thinking for themselves. Althea (*Marchmont,* 1796) easily saw through the "Blind servility, wilful misrepresentation, or the rhodomontade of declamation" in the political pamphlets she dutifully read to her father.[11] Celestina's (1791) "active mind was perpetually in search of new ideas." Her awareness of her mental superiority "to almost every body she conversed with" did not show unwomanly conceit, for "Nobody was ever yet eminently handsome in person, or eminently brilliant in intellect, who did not feel from self-evidence that they possessed these advantages."[12]

Intelligence and education did not conflict with the sentimental ideal of womanhood. Strength did, so much so that girls' schools encouraged fragility by rigid corseting and inadequate exercise. Though they feared to make their heroines physically robust lest they seem unfeminine, most of the women novelists tried to reconcile sensibility with courage and spirit. Committed to a sentimental ideal of delicacy, the authors still wanted to create female characters who could be respected as human beings. Obviously, these heroines are timid, fragile, and submissive by modern standards; but they must be evaluated in terms of the social and literary tradition from which they came. Women authors made a point of endowing their heroines with presence of mind and strength to withhold compliance or control their own impulses. In the context of a society that forced women into passivity, such resistance was genuine evidence of independence and integrity.

In giving her heroines more independence of mind than most, Smith also particularly insisted on their fortitude, often in contrast to heroes who have less rational control. Though young and inexperienced, without friends or position, Emmeline is able to hold her own in arguments with wealthy aristocrats accustomed to domination. Lord Montreville is aghast to find "that a little weak girl should pretend to a sense of rectitude, and a force of understanding greater than his own."[13] Monimia (*The Old Manor House*, 1793), though "so slight as not to be able to do any kind of household work," has the enterprise to find needlework to support herself and her husband; she does not tell him because it would shock his sensibility to see his wife engaged in gainful employment.[14] Corisande (*Letters of a Solitary Wanderer*, 1800) habitually displays "that firmness which, wholly different from masculine fierceness, is the highest attribute of a female mind." When she is abducted, she does not weep or faint, but defies the villain, mustering "a degree of firmness, that more abashed her persecutor than any expressions of womanish resentment could have done."[15]

Radcliffe's heroines display "the strength of fortitude" as well as "the grace of sensibility,"[16] and they value strength more. Emily in *The Mysteries of Udolpho* resolutely controls her tendencies toward over-emotionalism, despondency, and superstitious fears. She stands up to Montoni when he tries to bully her into ceding him her estates, despite his virile forcefulness and despotic power in the castle. Though she cannot gain her point, she outargues him and emerges with her dignity intact—just as a woman in real life might do when bullied by a husband or father. Ellena in *The Italian* (1797) is consistently firm and rational, in control of her feelings regardless of her horrifying surroundings. Vivaldi is not capable of her self-knowledge and control, nor is Valancourt able to afford Emily masculine support. On one trying occasion he reproaches himself: "I! who ought to have supported you, I! have increased your sufferings by the conduct of a child!"[17] Nor is it he who rescues her from Udolpho. Ellena and Emily, with their color-

less but distinct personalities, their conventional but firm characters, are different indeed from the passive female objects of
men's Gothic fiction.[18]

Women sometimes redefined courage to suit their sex, and
this could be a genuine reassessment of values rather than a
mere evasion. Burney's Juliet (*The Wanderer*, 1814) can always
find the necessary courage to support her prolonged trials, though
it is "the effect of secret reasoning, and cool calculation of consequences," rather "than of fearless temperament, or inborn
bravery."[19] Radcliffe disparages such typically virile courage
when she dismisses that of the villain Montoni as "a sort of
animal ferocity; not the noble impulse of a principle, such as
inspirits the mind against the oppressor, in the cause of the
oppressed [and such as women in her novels frequently dis-
play]; but a constitutional hardiness of nerve, that cannot feel,
and that, therefore, cannot fear."[20] Heroines such as Smith's and
Radcliffe's, irrefutably feminine and virtuous and yet strong
enough to make their presence felt and to win at least moral
victories, provided a satisfying ideal for women to identify with.

Often the novelists rewarded their heroines' merit with external success as well as approval. They showed their feminine,
properly conducted heroines triumphing over men through
superior self-command.[21] In this way the greater self-control
imposed upon women became a source of strength and superiority rather than a mere deprivation. When Smith's Delamere
falls in love with Emmeline, he pursues her relentlessly, exploiting all his advantages of sex, social position, and wealth,
brushing aside her justified concern for her reputation, and not
bothering to inquire whether *she* loves *him*. Meanwhile she
conducts herself irreproachably, as she agrees to an engagement
to soothe his tantrums and represses her subsequent attraction
to a more congenial man, though refusing a clandestine marriage to Delamere. And she is ultimately rewarded, as rash
Delamere gets himself killed in a pointless duel and leaves her
free to marry the man she prefers.

In Helen Maria Williams' *Julia* (1790), a young man engaged to a sweet and deserving girl falls in love with her mentally superior cousin, Julia, but conscientiously marries his original fiancée. Julia loves him but controls her passion and sur-

vives quite happily; however the young man, though well-intentioned, cannot. As a result he dies of a brain fever: "Such was the fate of this unfortunate young man, who fell the victim of that fatal passion, which he at first unhappily indulged, and which he was at length unable to subdue."[22]

Lennox's Euphemia married Mr. Neville to please her mother and soon found him to be foolish and inconsiderate. When he cannot have in England "a fortune that will enable him to live in a style to which he has annexed ideas of respect," he drags her to America, without even deigning to consult her beforehand. Though she has far more sense than he, she must always take care to avoid giving her persuasion "the air of advice"; for he considers this "a liberty not to be endured in a woman and a wife" and "never heartily approves of any thing that he is not the first mover of himself." Even when Neville means well, he manages to be troublesome, as when his raging and storming at a woman who has disturbed his wife after childbirth makes the inconvenience worse. Neville is not all bad: he is capable of humanity and competence, and he is not abusive or unfaithful. But his thoughtlessness and overassertion of masculine prerogative make him a constant trial.

Though she accepts obedience as a wife's "indispensable duty" and resolutely fulfills "the duties of my station," Euphemia clearly feels her superiority as she tells a woman friend: "with some persons it is not safe to be reasonable. Whenever it happens that my arguments press home upon [Mr. Neville], he . . . falls into a passion—I say not a word more—happy if silence will shelter me; but that is seldom the case, for he pursues me even to this last retreat, and nothing will serve him but my confession that he has convinced me I am in the wrong. For the sake of peace I submit to this." Euphemia practices obedience as punctiliously as Henry Fielding's Amelia does, but the effect is entirely different: since Euphemia is doing her duty rather than following her natural leader, she can maintain her superiority while obeying. She may owe him obedience, but it is not his due.

Euphemia's moral superiority is ultimately ratified by external triumph and rewarded by relief from her husband. She regains her adolescent son, lost as a child in the American

woods; he worships her and is disconcerted by Neville's habit-
ual contempt for her ideas. The family returns to England, where
Neville's rich uncle, whom he has fecklessly antagonized, leaves
fifteen thousand pounds to Euphemia, "for her sole use and benefit, not subject to the controul of her husband . . . that she may
have it in her power . . . to reward her children, according to the
measure of duty and affection she receives from them." Neville's
portion is carefully restricted so that it will pass in good shape
to his heirs. In the end Euphemia has everything she wants—
devoted children, financial independence, effective freedom from
Neville, and a serene consciousness of having at all times done
her duty.[23]

The only thing she lacks is sexual fulfillment, and that is
not presented as important.[24] Clara Reeve's Mrs. Strictland and
Mrs. Darnford (*The School for Widows*, 1791) are similarly rewarded for obedience and fortitude in unhappy marriages: their
husbands, a boor and a spendthrift, die in their prime and leave
the widows free to capably manage their own lives. In Sarah
Scott's *Millenium Hall* (1762), five ladies create a manless heaven
of culture and philanthropy. All have been happily released
from wretched marriages or have refused to marry at all. They
now study and paint, teach girls, and save poor gentlewomen
from the misery of going out as companions—and they manage
everything much better than men could do.

In Agnes Maria Bennett's *De Valcourt* (1800), women create
a satisfactory world by converting men rather than excluding
them. Here three women use their superiority of mind and
character to reform or defeat the evil men who oppose them.
Lady Mountshannon, unable to blind herself to her husband's
unworthiness, revolts at "meanly" submitting to his authority
but has to recognize that "the laws of society admit of no
remedy." Left to herself, she raises her boy and girl according
to enlightened principles, educating them exactly alike in independence, fearlessness, and love of knowledge. She manages her
husband's estate but, disdaining to accept support from a man
she no longer loves, lives on her own fortune (how she can do
this under contemporary law is not explained). Conflict develops when Lord Mountshannon tries to force his daughter, Ma-

tilda, to abandon De Valcourt, whom she loves and her mother approves, and marry a man of his choice; he has promised her to each of two young aristocrats in return for money he owes them. Convinced of woman's vanity and cowardice, he has no doubt he can persuade or browbeat her into accepting any man of title and fortune.

Matilda, however, has rational principles and plenty of resolution. She resists oppression with firmness, not tears or pleading. She remains calm and dignified during the usual lovers' misunderstandings, unlike the amiable but weaker De Valcourt, who once yields to a jealous tantrum. Though Matilda "loved too well to withhold her forgiveness . . . she resolved at some future period to correct that violence of temper, and erase from his mind that aptitude to suspicion his commerce with evil had created." Meanwhile, she and her mother persuade Ormond, one of her unwanted suitors, to leave her alone; but the other, abetted by her father, continues to pursue her. In the course of her troubles, Matilda meets Jannette, a highly intelligent French peasant girl who has been educated and seduced by Ormond. She convinces Jannette not to live any longer as his mistress; Ormond is torn between love and pride, but finally agrees to a secret marriage.

In the end, Lady Mountshannon is restored to the guardianship of her children and the management of her husband's property. He occupies a solitary corner of the castle, where he devotes himself to superstitious penance for his life of crime. Ormond remains delighted with his Jannette. Matilda marries De Valcourt, but does not depend on romantic love or a family for her total fulfillment: "they constantly spent their mornings in pursuing, separately, some useful employment or improving study; while the communication of their progress in knowledge or utility furnished their evenings wtih rational delight, and prevented that yawning indifference, and stupid insipidity, which too often, in the married life, succeeds to the first months of rapture." She develops improvements in agriculture which are copied all around the country, while he applies himself to the idealistic but less practical aim of devising a perfect system of government.[25]

Another indirect challenge to the limitations of the sentimental ideal appears in the female novelists' surprisingly sympathetic presentation of nonconforming women. Even in Burney's depressingly restrictive *Camilla* (1796), Camilla's dangerous friend Mrs. Arlbery is neither vicious, unattractive, nor wholeheartedly discredited. Burney could not resist making Mrs. Arlbery entertaining and letting her present a good case for her way of life. Her spirit does enchant men, and her defiance of public opinion does not bring the ruin women were assured it would, or even any harm at all. Events prove her quite right in claiming, "You are made a slave in a moment by the world, if you don't begin life by defying it. Take your own way, follow your own humour, and you and the world will both go on just as well, as if you ask its will and pleasure for everything you do and want and think."[26] Camilla is enslaved at the end of the book, while her friend remains free. Mrs. Arlbery is even given the opportunity to expose the hero, Edgar Mandlebert, for the selfish prig he is, though Burney's development of the plot aims to prove her stinging analysis to be wrong.[27]

Charlotte Smith's Miss Newenden, in *Ethelinde* (1789), lives alone, cares nothing for public opinion, spends her time hunting with men, and jeers at feminine delicacy and sentimental distress. She is criticized for mannishness, but is presented much more favorably than her sister-in-law, the pretty, insipid Lady Newenden. When the heroine is almost drowned, and the other ladies occupy themselves with expressing their terror in the most becoming manner, only Miss Newenden helps her. Miss Newenden's "usual careless kindness" is not exalted virtue, but it is by no means usual among the fashionable conforming ladies in the book. In the end she makes a foolish marriage, but the author allows her to be extricated with little pain.

Lady Newenden, on the other hand, is seduced, simply because her mind is too feeble to resist the flattery of a rake, and she dies in disgrace. At first Smith seems to be presenting the two characters as equally objectionable extremes—the one showing too much "masculine" hardness; the other, too much "feminine" softness of mind and character. We might expect the second to be treated more gently, as merely carrying to an extreme the sensibility and softness of temper which Smith commends in her heroine. But it turns out that Miss Newenden is neither made contemptible nor severely punished.[28]

Those whom these novelists do pillory are female fools—characters who are satisfied with themselves because they meet the conventional standards for women, although in fact they lack significant good qualities. Like Winchilsea's, this satire produces a different effect from men's because it emphasizes the gap between these standards and genuine human excellence and because the characters' failings do not necessarily inconvenience men. Lennox's Mrs. Bellenden in *Euphemia* is a conventionally good woman—"an obedient wife, a tender mother, and an easy companion . . . gentle in her censures of her acquaintance, except when they offend against the laws of modesty, or the rules of ceremony, and then . . . she is very severe." She is well-bred and fashionably educated, for she sings, dances, and plays the harpsichord skillfully, draws and embroiders prettily, and "can carry on the small talk of a tea-table in French." Yet Lennox shows that her trivial mind and narrow sympathies make her inadequate as a human being: she "has a great contempt for what she calls book-learning in women; and thinks chastity and good breeding, for so she pairs them, the highest of female virtues."[29]

The total immersion in domestic concerns of Smith's Lady Ellesmere (*The Banished Man*, 1794) is presented as contemptible rather than appropriately womanly. She is simply uninterested in the greatest public event of her time, concerned with kings and politicians only because "of the places they had to give; she wished her son Ellesmere, the great object of her ambition, had one of them; but of despotic government, of limited monarchy, or republicanism, she had not a single idea; and never knew from whence originated the revolution in France, of which . . . she had been hearing for four years." Though an affectionate mother, she was not distressed when her son left for battle, for she had no idea of its danger: "She had not a mind capable of figuring what she never saw."[30]

Burney's Indiana in *Camilla*, who appears to be enchantingly feminine, is revealed to be an empty-headed, cold-hearted coquette. She is beautiful enough to attract universal attention in public places, but too insipid to hold a man's interest, for all intellectual subjects bore her. Only a soft man who is blindly in love with her can remain captivated by her prolonged "starts, little shrieks, and palpitations" after running away from a harmless bull. This male sentimentalist is burlesqued as he incites her to renewed efforts by exclaiming, "What lovely timidity!—What bewitching softness!—What feminine, what beautiful delicacy!"[31]

Setting a woman at the center of the novel necessarily modified the presentation of male characters, who now appear in terms of their relationship to women. The heroes are considerate and thoughtful to an extent unimaginable even in such an amiable character as Tom Jones, who would generously respond to what women's wishes he was aware of, but would be oblivious to subtle needs. Burney's Lord Orville, on the other hand, distinguishes himself by "sweetness, politeness, and diffidence" and constant thoughtful attention to Evelina's peace of mind.[32] The women's heroes are as gentle and as mindful of family responsibilities as women were expected to be (e.g., Orlando in *The Old Manor House*, Marchmont in *Marchmont*), and their relationship with the woman they love is and will remain all-important, transcending worldly ambition or friendship with men (Montgomery in *Ethelinde*, the Marquis of Lenox in "The Young Lady's Tale"). Men like Fielding's Booth or Moore's Gamester Beverley, who exploit their female relatives, are never represented as amiable by these women. They sternly disparage good nature unsupported by responsibility, because that was so often used to palliate a man's failure to look after wife and children.[33]

Just as the heroes value and consider women, the villains sneer at their capacity, threaten and exploit them, and brutally override their wishes. Radcliffe's Montoni (*The Mysteries of Udolpho*) and Schedoni (*The Italian*) make clear their contempt for women's minds and characters. Smith's Mohun (*Marchmont*) is confident he can seduce Althea because "women, whatever slight difference of character may arise from understanding or education, are really alike in weakness and vanity, and to be won by the same means."[34]

Over and over, a man like Jane Austen's Mr. Collins assumes that any woman would be delighted to have him, regardless of his personal disadvantages, and interprets gentle refusals as duly modest encouragement. Because they see an unmarried woman as unclaimed property, they assume their right to court her and be accepted. Smith's Celestina is pursued by two equally selfish suitors, one aggressive and one gentle and clinging. The first man tries to bully her into accepting him, demanding how she can refuse, since she is not engaged and admits she can find no objections to his person, family, or fortune. Her refusal "piqued his pride, without destroying what he called love." When the second man fights a duel for her (against her wishes), he argues that she should reward him for risking his life. When she protests that she does not love him, his friend assures her: "he is content . . . with your esteem, with your friendship; and knows that, in such a heart as yours, love will follow his attachment to you." This man would lay down his life for Celestina, but he will not consent to her simple request that he let her go to London without him.[35]

The novelists anatomize antifeminist prejudice, from the outright boorishness of Burney's Captain Mirvan to patronage disguised as chivalry. When Lord Orville makes a point of including young ladies in a conversation, Mirvan roars that "girls" have no opinions worth mentioning: "Ask 'em after any thing that's called diversion, and you're sure they'll say it's vastly fine—they are a set of parrots, and speak by rote . . . but ask 'em how they like making puddings and pies, and I'll warrant you'll pose 'em."[36]

An old Admiral in *The Wanderer* is more subtly satirized, as he combines well-meaning chivalry with foolish prejudices. Though he is kind to the destitute Juliet, he assumes that she has been abandoned after seduction; for he is convinced that no man, nor the world, would leave a woman desolate "who has kept tight to her own duty, and taken a modest care of herself." This comfortable assumption is systematically belied by the novel's plot, in which Juliet, a model of virtue and decorum, is exposed to calumny, threats, and poverty. The Admiral would not think of hurting a woman, since she cannot fight back, but condemns out of hand one who runs from a dreadful husband: "God forbid I should uphold a wife in running away from her lawful spouse, even though he be a Frenchman! . . . A man, being the higher vessel, may marry all over the globe, and take his wife to his home; but a woman, as she is only given him for his helpmate, must tack after him, and come to the same anchorage."[37]

Elizabeth Hamilton exposed the spurious courtesy of a conceited male scholar by making an intelligent female character complain, "it is when he *descends,* that he offends me most . . . I could bear the most pompous display of his learning far better than the arrogance of his stupid and affected reserve, or the conceited air with which he lets himself down to the level of a female understanding."[38] And Harriet Lee dryly surveyed the whole picture when she noted men's inability to evaluate women rationally: "The [female] sex is indeed one of those unlucky topics that generally distances a man's head from his heart: for where is the phoenix that calls both into the council when he speaks of it?"[39]

Contempt for women is a salient feature of the bad husbands who figure prominently in this fiction. The deficiencies emphasized by women authors are strikingly different from those cited by men—they are more practically damaging and more usual. The women make little of unfaithfulness (the most serious sin for men, who liked to think women lived for love) and much of failure to support the family, irresponsibility or poor judgment that mocked the official position that man was qualified by his superior wisdom to rule the household. To lament a bad husband's unfaithfulness gave him more status than these women were prepared to grant. They show wives exasperated by their husbands' inadequacies rather than wounded by their sins. Smith's Leonora (*Letters of a Solitary Wanderer*) is "Personally indifferent" to her worthless husband and objects to his affairs simply because of the expense.[40]

The novelists describe not physical brutality, but the pettish complaints, snubs, and put-downs that must have been much more common. As Amelia Opie says of her heroine's husband in *Adeline Mowbray* (1804), his faults were "almost too trivial to be mentioned . . . [by] a biographer. But . . . many a conjugal union which has never been assailed by the battery of crime, has fallen a victim to the slowly undermining power of petty quarrels, trivial unkindnesses and thoughtless neglect." This man "knew not that opportunities of conferring large benefits, like bank bills for 1000£, rarely come into use; but little attentions, friendly participations and kindnesses, are wanted daily."[41]

Charlotte Smith created a portrait gallery of bad husbands, generally modeled on Mr. Smith. In each case, an intelligent woman finds herself and her children under the power of a foolish, irresponsible man, who considers himself entitled by his sex to do as he likes. The woman could run the family competently—and in fact does, so far as his mismanagement permits—but the man constantly puts her down. Poor Mrs. Stafford in *Emmeline* is tied to a man who pursues one silly scheme after another. She fears for the fate of her children, but has to realize she has no influence over his actions. Though he rudely rebuffs her attempts to advise him as long as he mistakenly thinks all is well, he expects her to pull him out of any difficulty. Though he "had neither relish for her conversation nor respect for her virtues," though he criticized her constantly whenever they were together, he grumbled whenever she was not with him.[42] Leonora explicitly repudiates her deference to the conventional code that a wife must not correct her husband: "I have since severely repented the pusillanimity which made me abandon the interests of my children, in the hope of temporary tranquility which I did not obtain."[43]

Elizabeth Griffith's Sir William Barton is not evil, merely insensitive. He stops his wife from giving ten pounds to a distressed family in order to proclaim that she has no right to take such a step independently (afterwards he helps the family without telling her). He objects to her corresponding with her sister as wasteful (women "who are fond of scribbling, are never good for anything else") and pointless: "female friendship is a jest," and women only converse with their own sex "for the sake of indulging" themselves "in talking of the other." Lady Barton and her sister agree that it is rash for a man to reveal "such illiberal sentiments, to one who has been so lately prevailed upon to pronounce those awful words, 'love, honour, and obey!' " since "we can neither love those we despise, nor those who seem to despise us."[44] And events are to prove them right. She will meet a congenial man who respects her and will form an adulterous passion. She will be duly punished, but the real guilt, Griffith implies, is Sir William's.

The happy endings in these novels express women's wish-fulfilling fantasies; what is more convincing is their vivid representation of women's difficulties—shown realistically in the recurrent bad husbands, symbolically in the persecutions and imprisonments of Gothic fiction. The sufferings of these heroines, struggling to maintain dignity and happiness against overwhelming forces, were not mere sentimental exploitation, but reflected the helplessness that was forced upon women in real life. In Sophia Lee's historical novel *The Recess*, two fictitious daughters of Mary Queen of Scots, both exquisitely beautiful and feminine, have been brought up in a secret underground apartment, safely closed in from the world. Once they emerge, they are put through a harrowing series of abductions, imprisonments, and bouts of madness—a melodramatic rendition of the manipulation and exploitation of actual women in sixteenth-century power politics and even of women in Lee's own time. They can do nothing to control their own fate, and their sufferings are intensified because they cannot, like men, escape from emotional distress through other interests or active life.[45]

The same enforced passivity is represented on a realistic domestic level in *Evelina*. Evelina is piqued by the gentlemen at a ball, who "as they passed and repassed, looked as if they thought we were quite at their disposal, and only waiting for the honour of their commands; and they sauntered about, in a careless indolent manner, as if with a view to keep us in suspense." She is repeatedly embarrassed by the social custom that required a woman to accept any man who asked her to dance, unless she was prepared to withdraw altogether and not dance at all. Finally, she suffers prolonged suspense as she longs for Lord Orville to propose but cannot take any initiative to encourage him, or even find out his sentiments.[46]

The novelists noted that ladies could not control even their own time, despite their freedom from real work, because of pointless obligations or a restrictive environment. They protested, as Winchilsea had, against the pressure on women to waste their lives on trivia. Lady Barton complains that her mornings are consumed in formal visits and that she has been "interrupted ten times in the filling of a page" of a letter.[47] Rosalie in Smith's *Montalbert* (1795), the eighteen-year-old daughter of a country clergyman, can do nothing to enliven her dreary life. She loves to read, but her mother has few books, and her father only sermons and sectarian pamphlets. She is forbidden to converse with the only intellectual in the neighborhood, an old priest. She can only mope around her home, sketching as much as she can, but constantly interrupted to make tea for people she is not interested in seeing. She early "became conscious, that such sort of people as she was usually thrown among... who only escape from dullness by flying to defamation, were extremely tiresome to her, though she saw that nobody else thought so, and suspected herself of being fastidious and perverse."[48] Rosalie's modest doubts were to be expected in a woman brought up to think she should fit into any situation in which she is placed, but Smith recognizes her right as an intelligent person to chafe at dullness. When Harriet Fitzpatrick in *Tom Jones* is similarly impatient with the social life afforded by Fitzpatrick's neighbors, Fielding implies that she is motivated merely by unhappiness with her husband and her usual over-eagerness for self-gratification.

Money problems, which might be thought too crude for sentimental fiction, actually got much attention from women novelists. Smith, in particular, emphasized the plight of wives who could neither restrain their husband's improvidence nor improve their family's situation themselves. She also dealt indirectly with the injustice of women's position by attacking primogeniture, a system that sacrificed not only the younger sons in the family but also, of course, all the daughters. It appears at its most odious in *The Old Manor House*, where Philip Somerive casually squanders a scanty inheritance that should be shared with his brother and sisters. As a result, one sister is pushed into marriage with a man she hardly knows, another almost marries a superannuated roué, and the brother is pressured to marry an odious heiress.[49]

Burney dealt increasingly with money in her novels, though at first indirectly. Her Cecilia (1782) naïvely thinks that because she is an heiress she can use her money to make a satisfying life for herself. But she discovers that she can direct her life no more than any other woman, and in the end she loses her fortune because her uncle's will had left it to her on condition that her husband adopt her surname, and the man she loves is not willing to do so. It is an ingenious allegory of the state of all women, who had to give up both name and control of their money at marriage.[50] Camilla is subjected to embarrassment, anxiety, and finally delirium as a result of debts for which she is nominally responsible but which in fact result from the limited income, inexperience, and exploitation by a male relative that were a normal part of woman's lot. (Her older brother, who spends money as he likes without criticism, has forced a loan from her.)

But it is in her last novel, The Wanderer; or, Female Difficulties, that Burney deals explicitly with the helplessness of women in her society, either to resist sexual encroachment or to support themselves. Once we accept the heroine's total isolation from her family (sufficiently plausible since she is a refugee from revolutionary France), we can see her trials as a realistic picture of a woman's—or at least a lady's—lot. Juliet must support herself, but despite her superior talents, the best education afforded to young ladies, and a resolution to work and endure, her every attempt fails. She does her best to follow the advice of her mentor to "learn to suffice to" herself. But no efforts are efficacious. She tries giving private harp lessons, but cannot collect payment; indeed, none of her occupations yields a living wage. She loses her music students when her reputation is impugned by her apparent lack of family connections. She rejects the idea of performing in public with a horror that seems ridiculous until we learn that the reputations of public performers do not matter—because they are already lost. The virtuous hero explicitly warns her that a public appearance would disgrace her own family and any into which she might marry.

Juliet tries doing fine needlework for private customers, but again finds she cannot collect payment. She takes a regular position in a milliner's shop, but it is constantly frequented by men who regard the workwomen as "their natural prey." She works as a lady's companion, but finds her job of entertaining a disagreeable woman as difficult as it is unpleasant: she must "be always at hand, early or late. . . . Success . . . was unacknowledged, though failure was resented. There was no relaxation to her toil, no rest for her person, no recruit for her spirits." She has to steal a few minutes from her sleep in order to write to her only friend in England. The humiliations of her position are truthfully detailed by Mr. Arbe, when he hopes Juliet has "not turned what they call 'toad-eater' and . . . let yourself out, at so much a year, to say nothing that you think; and to do nothing that you like; and to beg pardon when you are not in fault."[51] Burney appropriately gives this sentiment to a man, who, never having to choose such a life himself, would not recognize that women were often forced into it. Leaving this intolerable situation, Juliet tries to find peace in the country, but continues to be insulted and molested, and even almost raped, because men see a lone woman as legitimate prey. She also observes that a farmer treats his wife and daughters as servants, while sharing money and power with his sons.

The book relentlessly dramatizes woman's helpless situation, in terms Burney explicitly provides six times. Loss of her music students prompts Juliet to think: "how insufficient . . . is a FEMALE to herself! How utterly dependant upon situation—connexions—circumstance! how nameless, how for ever fresh springing are her DIFFICULTIES, when she would owe her existence to her own exertions! Her conduct is criticised, not scrutinized; her character is censured, not examined; her labours are unhonoured, and her qualifications are but lures to ill will!" In the last paragraphs of the book, Burney laments "the DIFFICULTIES with which a FEMALE has to struggle! Her honour always in danger of being assailed, her delicacy of being offended, her strength of being exhausted, and her virtue of being calumniated!" though she points out that Juliet's "mental courage" has surmounted them.[52]

Burney's phrasing might suggest that Juliet's difficulties were merely the factitious ones of the stereotypical sentimental heroine. But in fact they have been very real—threatened sexual violation, social ostracism, destitution with no prospects of relief. The wrongheaded Elinor Joddrell exhorts her, "Put aside your prejudices, and forget that you are a dawdling woman, to remember that you are an active human being, and your FEMALE DIFFICULTIES will vanish into the vapour of which they are formed." But in fact it was impossible for a lady to throw off the internal and external shackles put on her by society. (Elinor considers herself liberated, but in fact has no difficulties to contend with.) Juliet does everything that could possibly be expected, but keeps getting frustrated in her efforts to support herself and to win the respect which her virtue deserves. Her unaided "mental courage" could achieve nothing; only fortunate circumstances in the end give her the happiness she has deserved all along. Burney significantly compares her to Robinson Crusoe, "as unaided and unprotected, though in the midst of the world," as he was on his uninhabited island.[53] Alike in not receiving help from others, they are shockingly different in their resources for helping themselves; for while Crusoe has been trained to self-reliance and enterprise, Juliet must go against everything she has been taught. Unequipped with useful skills or practical experience, she has also been actually trained to be passive, retiring, and incompetent in practical affairs. Like Burney herself, she is ashamed to take money for her work.

It is easy to ridicule Juliet's inefficacy, as she demonstrates her outstanding education by correct spelling or faints on her way to the stage when she is supposed to give a concert. But it is more to the point to recognize that she is suffering from crippling limitations imposed by society. In fact, her female difficulties are melodramatic projections of everywoman's situation. Very few ladies could support themselves more effectually than Juliet does, and reputation was vital not only to preserve a woman's self-respect but to qualify her for employment and to ward off insult. And reputation did not depend on her own innocence or exertions, but on what others thought of her, which in turn depended on who was backing her. Juliet's miseries as a professional companion—the endless hours, the absence of salary, the lack of appreciation—have much in common with women's normally expected service in their own families, though Burney does not draw the connection. She shows Juliet welcoming dependence on Harleigh, when she marries him at the end; but earlier Burney has let her express gratification at supporting herself, because "The hope of self-dependence" is "ever cheering to an upright mind." Respectable ladies were not yet prepared to admit that dependency upon duly constituted protectors, even tolerably conscientious ones, might not be the happiest situation for an adult.[54]

Though Burney does imply that women are best off protected by their families, she raises the question of whether they should be enabled to function without them. Certainly the book exposes the fallacy of training women to be weak on the theory that men will protect them, since the heroine is insulted, maligned, exploited, and threatened throughout. She should have been provided with means of defense instead of being systematically deprived of them.

It is easy to deride these novels, if we think of the maudlin emphasis on "female difficulties" in *The Wanderer*, the absurd ideal of helpless, irrational femininity that is held up for admiration in "The Young Lady's Tale," the contrived sentimental agonies that keep true lovers apart for volume after volume, and the fussy propriety of heroines obsessed with preserving their reputations.[55] The chastity, self-control, dutifulness, and delicacy enjoined on women in real life were doubly enjoined on the fictitious woman who was not worthy to be a heroine if she could not serve as a model. Because the morality enforced on women in both fact and fiction was essentially negative, the emphasis tends to fall on the errors the heroine avoids rather than the good qualities she has.[56] The novelists' presentation is further strained by the need to preserve their heroine's moral perfection through all the compromising positions demanded if the plot was to thrill. She had to maintain flawless innocence while being sophisticated enough to deal with the dangerous situations in which—somehow—she found herself involved.

The differing expectations for women and men, in fiction as in fact, are revealed in a contemporary reviewer's justified longing "to see a female character drawn with faults and virtues, to see her feel the effects of misconduct, which does not proceed from a bad heart or corrupted inclinations, and to see her in the end happy, in consequence of her reformation; in short to see a female Jones, or another Evelina, with faults equally embarrassing, yet as venial."[57] Tom Jones's faults are plain to see. But where are Evelina's? Burney claimed that Evelina was not a "faultless Monster that the world ne'er saw," but "the offspring ... of Nature in her simplest attire." But actually only Mr. Villars or Lord Orville could find "heedless indiscretion" in her temper, and she is far too well trained in the courtesy-book virtues to be a product of simple nature.[58] No doubt the intention of Burney and other novelists who professed to create imperfect heroines was to liberate women by showing spirit and spontaneity as attractive and by representing female characters who were human beings rather than flat ideals; but the effect of the actual finished characters is repressive.

Moreover, the form of the feminine novel, which released the creativity of writers like Brooke and Jane Austen, could hamper those whose talents did not happen to fit it. Burney subordinated her gift for vivid rendition of life's surface and humorous social satire in order to portray the sentimental distresses of an exemplary young lady, though she lacked the psychological and emotional depth to render these moving. The Wanderer, which takes its solitary heroine through society, could have been a fascinating female picaresque, but instead has the appearance of an uninspired manual of proper female conduct.[59]

Women were now established and accepted as novelists—but they were expected to write in a "feminine" way, demonstrating delicacy of feeling, dealing with emotional distress rather than practical problems, abstaining from radical social criticism or political discussion. Men looked to women novelists for "that ideal world of the affections, which they hoped was inhabited by their woman-kind."[60] Thus the feminine novel could have the unfortunate effect of reinforcing the concept of a separate woman's world, removed from the world of reason and reality, the world that counts.

Yet with all its obvious limitations, the feminine novel helped women to express themselves and established the worth of their perceptions, interests, and values. The delicate distresses of this fiction are less significant than its presentation of women's feelings about their acquaintances, from suitors to neighbors, and its consideration of women's problems, from social boredom to finding the right mate, to dealing with an unsatisfactory husband, to supporting themselves. The persistent charge that novels were dangerously inflammatory—hard to understand in terms of the actual works—may reflect the justified suspicion that they were, however covertly, a form of female self-assertion. In any case, by formulating women's wishes and complaints, they helped to develop feminine awareness, if not feminism.

As vehicles for the expression of woman's sensibility, the novels are filled with insights, small in themselves but together significantly broadening the range of the novel. For example, Sophia Lee, who seems to be conforming to the worst conventions of ladies' fiction in "The Young Lady's Tale," breaks through the fantasy to notice one way in which social custom weakened women's ability to deal with life: "It is among the many advantages which men possess over women, that they may, if they will, know themselves; and perhaps to that alone may be ascribed their superiority of judgment in all the great contingencies of life. Women breathe, as it were, in an artificial atmosphere; and what hot-house rose can bear without shrinking even the genial gales which bring the garden plants to perfection?"[61] Thus Lee recognized that it was the evasions of polite social life, not innate deficiency, that prevented women from developing objective judgement, especially about themselves. Thus weakened, women found it difficult to assert themselves realistically or to withstand the criticism which everyone must meet who functions in the world.

Even where there is no evidence of feminism, the feminine point of view necessarily asserts itself through the consciousness of the young woman who is at the center of the story. Necessarily, she must be an independent entity, not existing merely in relationship to men. Cecilia forms for herself "A scheme of happiness at once rational and refined," which does not even mention marriage: she will drop "all idle and uninteresting acquaintance" and select only friends who can improve or enter-tain her, will devote her leisure to reading and practicing music, and will use her fortune to help the needy.[62] Even when the heroine is a model of conventional virtue, her motive is to live up to her own moral standards rather than to make herself agreeable to men. And in descriptions of marriages, the empha-sis often shifts from what wives should do for husbands to what husbands should do for wives.

Since we must see through the heroine's eyes, we are con-stantly aware of her feelings; what is emphasized is what is important to her, for example, male conceit and aggression. We also know at first hand that, modest and quiet as a heroine like Evelina appears, she is capable of shrewd and severe judgment of those she sees. Without overtly asserting feminism, a novel like *Evelina* inescapably makes the point that woman is no mere helpmate to man, but an independent entity who often has a sharp mind. With Radcliffe's heroines we are always aware of a mind at work—not an interesting one, perhaps, but an in-telligent one worthy of respect. As Emily constantly strives to discount the effects of superstition, to find logical explanations of events and motives, to evaluate methodically what she has to fear in any given situation, we believe in her as a rational human being. She exists independently of her love for Valan-court and the perils she is placed in, as we see when, despite her alarm over a forced trip to Italy, she can take pleasure in visualizing Hannibal's passage over the Alps.

The effect of telling a story from a woman's point of view is dramatically shown by comparing the last sentence of Smith's *Celestina* with the ending of *Tom Jones*. Contrast Fielding's "Mr. Jones appears to be the happiest of all human kind: For what happiness this world affords equal to the possession of such a woman as Sophia, I sincerely own I have never yet dis-covered," with Smith's ending: "Celestina beheld in Willoughby, the best and most affectionate of husbands—whose whole life was dedicated to the purpose of making her happy—and whose only apprehension seemed to be, that with all he could do, he must fall infinitely short of that degree of merit towards either heaven or earth, which that fortunate being ought to possess, who was blessed with so lovely and perfect a creature as Celestina."[63]

NOTES

1. Elizabeth Griffith, *The History of Lady Barton* (London: T. Davies and T. Cadell, 1773), II, 75, 108-9. Harriet Lee presented a similar situation in "The Wife's Tale" in *Canterbury Tales*, in which a sixteen-year-old girl is pressured to accept a man she does not love because she is too young and unformed to resist; her subsequent elopement is more his fault than hers.
2. Charlotte Lennox, *Euphemia* (London: T. Cadell and J. Evans, 1790), I, 143.
3. Harriet Lee and Sophia Lee, *Canterbury Tales* (New York: Mason Brothers, 1857), III, 431. Silly as it was, this story appealed to at least one intelligent woman, Hester Thrale, who, in dealing with Henry Thrale and Samuel Johnson, knew what it was like to have one's wishes ignored; see *The Intimate Letters of Hester Piozzi and Penelope Pennington, 1788-1821*, ed. Oswald G. Knapp (London: John Lane, 1914), pp. 159-60.
4. Anna Laetitia Barbauld, prefatory essay to her edition of *The British Novelists* (London: F. C. and J. Rivington, 1810), I, 54.
5. Charlotte Smith, *Montalbert* (London: E. Booker, 1795), I, 57.
6. Frances Burney, *Cecilia, or Memoirs of an Heiress* (London: J. M. Dent, 1893), I, 309.
7. Ann Radcliffe, *The Mysteries of Udolpho*, ed. Bonamy Dobrée (London: Oxford University Press, 1970), pp. 106-7.
8. Frances Sheridan, *Memoirs of Miss Sidney Bidulph, Extracted from Her Own Journal* (London: Harrison and Co., 1786: *Novelist's Magazine*, XXII, 1787), p. 43.
9. Sophia Lee, *The Recess: or, A Tale of Other Times* (New York: Arno Press, 1972), I, 5.
10. Mary Walker, *Letters from the Duchess of Crui and Others, on Subjects Moral and Entertaining* (London: Robson, Wal-

ter, and Robinson, 1776), I, iii. Lacking a real plot, the book consists largely of a discussion of education for women, conducted by three intelligent women who agree that women have more potential than is usually developed and explain how they are discouraged from learning. Lady Filmer wants women to have "the education of a man," while Mrs. Pierpont suggests that their minds can develop better without the systems which "prevail in colleges and schools" to warp the thinking of men (I, 100-1; II, 30).

11. Charlotte Smith, *Marchmont* (London: Sampson Low, 1796), III, 104.

12. Charlotte Smith, *Celestina* (London: T. Cadell, 1791), III, 81, 186.

13. Charlotte Smith, *Emmeline: The Orphan of the Castle*, ed. Anne H. Ehrenpreis (London: Oxford University Press, 1971), pp. 122-23.

14. Charlotte Smith, *The Old Manor House*, ed. Anne H. Ehrenpreis (London: Oxford University Press, 1969), pp. 486, 494.

15. Charlotte Smith, *Letters of a Solitary Wanderer* (London: Sampson Low, 1800), III, 235, 334.

16. Radcliffe, *Mysteries of Udolpho*, pp. 79-80.

17. *Ibid.*, p. 159.

18. For further affirmations of woman's courage, see Lee, *Recess*, III, 243; Walker, *Duchess of Crui*, I, 95; and Frances Burney, *Evelina: or The History of a Young Lady's Entrance into the World* (New York: W. W. Norton, 1965), p. 202.

19. Frances Burney d'Arblay, *The Wanderer; or, Female Difficulties* (London: Longman, Hurst, 1814), II, 83.

20. Radcliffe, *Mysteries of Udolpho*, p. 358. Cf. Agnes Maria Bennett, *De Valcourt; A Novel* (Dublin: P. Wogan, 1800), p. 166: Lady Mountshannon thought "the opposers of injustice, should ... be mild, firm, and courageous; uninfluenced by passion, or selfish feeling; unbiassed by resentment, and actuated only by the wish of preserving their own happiness, or the happiness of others, from the encroachments of public or domestic tyranny."

21. Frances Sheridan's *Sidney Bidulph* portrays a gratifying influence of woman over man, but hardly provides a satisfactory wish fulfillment, since the heroine's insistence on a single sexual standard ruins her own life as well as the hero's.

22. Helen Maria Williams, *Julia, A Novel* (London: T. Cadell, 1790), II, 237.

23. Lennox, *Euphemia*, I, 58, 148, 162, 165; II, 38-39, 121-23; IV, 4-5, 254-55, 263-64. Smith's long-suffering Mrs. Stafford in *Emmeline* is rewarded in a similar manner, as Mr. Stafford is packed off to a lucrative appointment in the West Indies, leaving her and the children in peaceful affluence in England.

24. Patricia Meyer Spacks, *Imagining a Self: Autobiography and Novel in Eighteenth Century England* (Cambridge: Harvard University Press, 1976), pp. 65-66.

25. Bennett, *De Valcourt*, pp. 7, 128, 265. I am grateful to Ellen Messer-Davidow for drawing my attention to this novel.

26. Frances Burney d'Arblay, *Camilla, or A Picture of Youth*, ed. Edward and Lillian Bloom (London: Oxford University Press, 1972), p 246.

27. *Ibid.*, pp. 367, 455, 482-84. The masculine Mrs. Selwyn in *Evelina* is likewise criticized for satirizing her acquaintance and taking the offensive in social conflict. Yet Burney seems to enjoy showing her effectively putting down men and uses Mrs. Selwyn's no-nonsense directness to cut through the over-delicacy that is keeping Evelina and Lord Orville apart. Gerard A. Barker strengthens the case for Burney's favorable attitude toward Mrs. Selwyn in "The Two Mrs. Selwyns: *Evelina* and *The Man of the World*," *Papers on Language and Literature*, XIII (1977), 80-84.

28. Charlotte Smith, *Ethelinde, or The Recluse of the Lake* (London: T. Cadell, 1789), I, 83; V, 279. Elinor Joddrell of *The Wanderer* and other nonconformists directly influenced by Wollstonecraft will be discussed in Chapter 7.

29. Lennox, *Euphemia*, I, 189-90.

30. Charlotte Smith, *The Banished Man* (London: T. Cadell and W. Davies, 1794), II, 110-12; III, 46-47. In Smith's "The Story of Henrietta," Henrietta causes much unnecessary misery for herself and the fiancé she loves by foolish "apprehensions of censure" she has imbibed from the aunt on whom she has been raised to depend blindly; and a wife elopes because an education designed to repress her will and reasoning capacity has left her without principles to resist temptation (*Letters of a Solitary Wanderer*, II, 27, 213-15).

31. Burney, *Camilla*, pp. 134-35. Cf. the affected fears of Miss Mushroom in Elizabeth Hamilton's *Memoirs of Modern Philosophers*, which provoke wonder "that any creature, ranking in the list of rationals, could form a wish of being distinguished for pre-eminence in weakness" (New York: Garland, 1974), I, 278-79. Though only one novelist, ap-

parently, dared to create a plain heroine (the female author of *The Mental Triumph*, 1789, cited by J. M. S. Tompkins, *The Popular Novel in England, 1770-1800* [Lincoln: University of Nebraska Press, 1961], p. 151), the women generally emphasized physical beauty as little as possible. Burney originally intended Cecilia to be an "unbeautiful, clever heroine"; see *Diary and Letters of Madame d'Arblay*, ed. Charlotte Barrett (London: Swan Sonnenschein, 1893), I, 233. See also the hostile characterizations of the beautiful Marianne (Jane West's *A Gossip's Story*, 1797) and Miss Bellenden (Lennox's *Euphemia*).

32. Burney, *Evelina*, p. 61.
33. E.g., Charlotte Smith, *Minor Morals* (London: A. K. Newman, 1817), pp. 93-94.
34. Smith, *Marchmont*, IV, 379-80. Verney, the abominable husband in her *Desmond*, adds contempt for women's intellect to his other despicable qualities; and Smith's recurrent dishonest lawyers try to conceal their chicanery from women by putting down their intelligence—a tactic with which she herself probably was painfully familiar.
35. Smith, *Celestina*, IV, 26-29, 108, 162, 165. Cf. the scene in *Cecilia* where, motivated by simple humanity, she tries to prevent a duel, and thereby convinces everyone that she must be in love with one of the two men.
36. Burney, *Evelina*, pp. 97-98. Lord Merton's fashionable manners and philandering, less obviously offensive than Mirvan's bullying, cover an equal contempt for women (pp. 257, 343-44).
37. Burney, *The Wanderer*, I, 64-65; V, 319-20. The Admiral may have been modeled on a conceited old retired general whom Burney ridiculed in her diary. He was outraged to learn that a "fair female should presume to study Greek," but equally outraged by a man who physically abused his wife and daughter: "What! cruel to a fair female! Oh fie! fie! fie!—a fellow who can be cruel to females and children, or animals, must be a pitiful fellow indeed" (*Diary and Letters*, ed. Barrett, I, 202-4).
38. Hamilton, *Modern Philosophers*, II, 350-51.
39. Lee and Lee, *Canterbury Tales*, I, 106.
40. Smith, *Letters of a Solitary Wanderer*, V, 250-51.
41. Amelia Opie, *Adeline Mowbray, or The Mother and Daughter* (New York: Garland, 1974), III, 57-58, 67.
42. Smith, *Emmeline*, pp. 177, 443.
43. Smith, *Letters of a Solitary Wanderer*, V, 121.
44. Griffith, *Lady Barton*, I, 2-3, 34.

45. Lee, *Recess*, III, 27-28.
46. Burney, *Evelina*, pp. 17-18. The depth of Burney's feelings is revealed by her retort to a male friend who reproached her for talking unnecessarily long to another man: "what choice has a poor female with whom she may converse? Must she not, in company as in dancing, take up with those who choose to take up with her?...No man...has any cause to be flattered that a woman talks with him, while it is only in reply; for though *he* may come, go, address or neglect...she, let her think and wish what she may, must only follow as he leads" (*Diary and Letters*, ed. Barrett, II, 324). While appearing to accept this male dominance, she gets back at men by making clear that her acquiescence does not involve liking or respect. See Spacks's analysis of Burney's passivity and how she used it, in *Imagining a Self*, pp. 160-91.
47. Griffith, *Lady Barton*, I, 53, 75. Burney never had the temerity to develop this point openly in connection with a fictional heroine, but she confided it to her diary, where she complained of having to spend an evening with a woman she disliked, merely because she called: "O! how I hate this vile custom which obliges us to make slaves of ourselves!— to sell the most precious property we boast, our time;—and to sacrifice it to every prattling impertinent who chooses to demand it." She went on to praise, though with some ambivalence, women who dared to defy convention. On another occasion she first condemned Miss Allen's tendency to ridicule fools and then admitted her own impulse to do the same. See Fanny Burney, *Early Diary: 1768-1778*, ed. Annie Raine Ellis (London: George Bell, 1907), I, 54, 134.
48. Smith, *Montalbert*, II, 137. Smith's Althea (*Marchmont*) realizes "that in her father's family even her time would not be her own" (I, 63).
49. Delmont in Smith's *Young Philosopher* is in the same situation, and in *Desmond* two sisters are persistently sacrificed to their brother's interest, with the result that he has become self-indulgent to the point of self-destructiveness.
50. See Rose Marie Cutting, "Defiant Women: The Growth of Feminism in Fanny Burney's Novels," *Studies in English Literature*, XVII (1977), 521.
51. Burney, *The Wanderer*, II, 62; III, 110, 266, 338. Burney was not always so understanding of the dependent companion's lot; contrast her totally unsympathetic portrayal of Miss Bennet in *Cecilia*.
52. *Ibid.*, II, 197; V, 395. Cf. II, 230, 367; III, 36; IV, 318.

53. *Ibid.*, III, 36; V, 394.
54. *Ibid.*, II, 63. Cf. Charlotte Lennox's Henrietta, who rejoiced at being freed from dependence as a servant or companion, but was happy to be "under the care of a brother, whom she tenderly loved"; *Henrietta* (London: A. Millar, 1758), II, 255. Only the disreputable Manley openly protested against the economic dependence of wives *per se*; see Chapter 3.
55. Both Emily and her creator, Sophia Lee, glory in a sensibility which "knows not how to qualify—descends not to contention—disdains to be soothed" (*Canterbury Tales*, III, 346); the villain of the story is a competent woman. Robert Palfrey Utter and Gwendolyn Bridges Needham cleverly reduce the sentimental heroine to absurdity in *Pamela's Daughters* (New York: Macmillan, 1937), pp. 41-42.
56. Cf. Burney, "A fear of doing wrong has always been the leading principle of my internal guidance" (*Diary and Letters*, ed. Barrett, IV, 475).
57. *Critical Review* (June, 1788), quoted in Tompkins, *Popular Novel*, p. 168.
58. Burney, *Evelina*, preface, p. 323. Nevertheless, Burney should get credit for realistically giving her adolescent heroine the awkwardness of adolescence. Smith's Emmeline, in contrast, only fifteen years old and brought up in an isolated castle by servants, is endowed with "a kind of intuitive knowledge" which enables her to acquire all a lady's accomplishments, as well as to demonstrate flawless poise in the most trying social situations. Burney's Camilla, named after a legendary woman warrior and perpetually being warned about her excessive freedom and liveliness, is a more pathetic imitation of a spirited woman.
59. The contrast between her passive suffering in these situations and the more active role of the picaro, who can prove himself, while she must wait to be certified by the discovery of her family, could have been developed into a devastating social comment. Unfortunately, Burney preferred to lay emphasis on her heroine's ladylike virtues and correct reactions to her trials, so that this uninteresting material seems to be the *raison d'être* of the book. In the same way, *Cecilia* suffers from overemphasis on the perfect propriety of the heroine, who cannot be implicated in the social follies that constitute the best part of the book, and cannot even shrewdly comment on them. The lack of connection between Cecilia's sentimental distresses and the comic turns of the social nuisances causes the latter to become tedious

and makes it necessary to introduce an otherwise irrelevant character, Mr. Gosport, to provide the necessary witty analysis of what is going on.

60. Tompkins, *Popular Novel*, p. 125.
61. Lee and Lee, *Canterbury Tales*, III, 172.
62. Burney, *Cecilia*, I, 61-62.
63. Henry Fielding, *Tom Jones*, Shakespeare Head edition (Oxford: Basil Blackwell, 1926), IV, 306; Smith, *Celestina*, IV, 353. Cf. the ending of Radcliffe's *Mysteries of Udolpho*, where Emily is left enjoying domestic retirement with Valancourt and together with him "aspiring to moral and labouring for intellectual improvement."

৩৫৯ [6] ৯৯৯

RADICALISM AND FEMINISM

Late eighteenth-century radicalism, nominally dedicated to sweeping aside prejudice to bring liberty and equality for all, might have been expected to furnish intellectual support for the feminist insights that had been developing in the novel. It certainly called into question patriarchal assumptions used to rationalize oppression of women. Interpreting subordination as a self-serving invention of the dominant class, radicalism undermined the hierarchy of the family; arguing that goodness is achieved through freedom rather than restraint, it removed the justification for restricting women to preserve their innocence; denying that the inheritance of property was a sacred right, it nullified a traditional reason for damning adulterous wives.

Unfortunately, however, radical theory was eagerly applied to women's rights only by those who were already disposed to be feminist, while others ignored this application, just as the implications of Enlightenment rationalism and sentimental respect for feeling could be ignored earlier in the century. Most of the radical reformers, English and French, were as indifferent to the rights of women as certain of their successors in the 1960s.[1] Mary Wollstonecraft sorrowfully noted in her *Vindication of the Rights of Woman* (1792) that the report of the French Revolutionary leader Talleyrand calling for free public education did not include girls.

The eminent philosopher William Godwin showed no sensitivity to women's oppression even though he was married to

181

Wollstonecraft. Considering the depth and exhaustiveness of his criticism of society in *An Enquiry Concerning Political Justice* (1792, revised 1796), it is remarkable that Godwin never thought to question the irrational assumptions that restricted women. He dealt with women and marriage as an aspect of property, attacking contemporary marriage not because it oppressed woman but because it restricted proprietorship in her to one man.[2] Thomas Paine referred to the oppression of women by law and public opinion, and Jeremy Bentham argued the rationality of woman suffrage; but neither demonstrated persistent concern with women's rights. Bentham soon dropped the subject because he felt an attempt to give women the vote would arouse more controversy than it was worth.[3] Even a radical woman might be oblivious to feminist issues: Catharine Macaulay, who campaigned tirelessly for universal manhood suffrage, never claimed the vote for women.[4]

The radicals' main contribution was in the area of sexual liberation, as they all challenged the disproportionate emphasis on chastity which kept women inhibited by dread of irrevocable ruin. One of Robert Bage's characters hesitates to accept a marriage proposal on the grounds that she has read in novels that women who have suffered rape, as she has, "must die, or be immured for ever," since "all crimes but this may be expiated"; but she is assured that, though such enthusiastic honor may be found in books, one hopes, "for the sake of the human intellect, little of it will be found anywhere else."[5] Bage's Kitty Ross, seduced at sixteen, not only survives but makes a good marriage; moreover, she has developed "a certain Amazonian goodness, so very much unlike the feeble, gasping, dying virtue of the generality of the sex."[6]

Bage's novels are filled with delightfully spirited young women (who are never, however, the heroine) and perfectly rational young men who demolish the conventional assumptions about sexual character. Miss Fluart of *Hermsprong* (1796) admonishes her friend Caroline, who persists in sacrificing herself for her selfish father, that all duties are reciprocal. Hermsprong calls Caroline's submission to her abominable father a weakness and refuses to call it an amiable one, as no weaknesses are amiable. An admirer of Wollstonecraft, he argues for the potential equality of women and for an education that would promote that equality; women should develop their minds, not their charms.[7]

What probably stimulated Wollstonecraft to write of the rights of women was her radical indignation at Edmund Burke's *Reflections on the Revolution in France*, which she answered with *A Vindication of the Rights of Men* (1790). She was particularly outraged by his chivalric denunciation of those who insulted Queen Marie Antoinette, in which he concluded that, without chivalry, "a queen *is* but a woman; a woman *is* but an animal, and . . . not of the highest order." Wollstonecraft wanted genuine respect to replace such chivalry; this would encourage the "fine lady" to "become a rational woman," who would "fulfill her part of the social compact" by superintending her family and suckling her children. The homage Burke is so proud of offering women "vitiates them, prevents their endeavouring to obtain solid personal merit, and . . . makes those beings vain inconsiderate dolls, who ought to be prudent mothers and useful members of society."[8]

Though inspired by revolutionary principles, her *Vindication of the Rights of Woman* carries on the earlier rational feminist tradition that a woman should be strong and reasonable and not allow herself to be reduced to a mere sexual object. Like Astell, Wollstonecraft insisted that a woman's primary endeavor must be to develop herself as a rational moral being; like Swift, she pointed out that weak, narrow-minded women cannot be adequate mothers; like Defoe, she showed why women must be capable of functioning independent of men. Wollstonecraft was as opposed to sentimentality as they were, seeing sensibility as a weakness and men's sentimental effusions over women as mere cloaks for disparagement and exploitation.[9]

Under the influence of radical theory, Wollstonecraft was more explicit in condemning the idea of a sexual character and readier to discard patriarchal assumptions of church and state. She did not hesitate to dismiss as a "poetical story" (or rather as an invention by man to justify his subjugation of woman) the Biblical account that describes woman created for man.[10] More aware than her predecessors of societal influences, she attributed woman's weaknesses to defects in institutions, insisting that these must change if woman is to reach her potential.

Liberated by the radical questioning of predestined social roles, Wollstonecraft denied, with unprecedented explicitness, that there is a "sexual character"; that is, a difference in the qualities desirable in women and in men. "There is but one way appointed by Providence to lead *mankind* [including women] to either virtue or happiness." To prescribe a different moral ideal for women cannot help but make them inferior: "to speak explicitly, women are not allowed to have sufficient strength of mind to acquire what really deserves the name of virtue." Gentleness is a virtue in both sexes, but not when carried to the extreme enjoined on women: "when forbearance confounds right and wrong, it ceases to be a virtue; and, however convenient it may be found in a companion—that companion will ever be considered as an inferior, and only inspire a vapid tenderness, which easily degenerates into contempt."

Weakness of mind or body incapacitates a woman for marriage and motherhood just as it incapacitates a man for his profession. Women should influence others the same way men should, through candid reasoning, not through wiles and manipulation. Far from serving as an appropriate guard to women's innocence, ignorance deprives them of the opportunity to form reasoned principles, which are the only basis for virtue. Wollstonecraft strenuously objected to the double standard that allowed men to develop good qualities according to their various natural dispositions, but leveled all women to "one character of yielding softness and gentle compliance."[11]

Most strikingly of all, she insisted that women must be independent: independence is "the grand blessing of life, the basis of every virtue." She recognized, as women had before, that dependence is intrinsically degrading, but differed from them by including dependence on a husband. She would correct this situation by defining independence as fulfilling one's duties in society. Thus a husband and wife are "equally necessary and independent of each other" when each fulfills "the respective duties of their station." A wife can be just as independent as a husband if she follows her own reason, aims at achieving virtue rather than pleasing men, and makes herself a useful member of society.[12]

Wollstonecraft was as keen a critic of the frivolity, affected sensibility, and deviousness of conventional women as Swift was, and of course with the same object of inspiring them to a higher ideal. But, with the heightened social awareness of her time, she recognized that these failings were produced by social conditioning and could not be corrected without social reform. She illuminated the condition of women by comparing them with male groups subject to similar limitations—soldiers, who were equally ill-educated; noblemen, who equally lacked useful social function; and Protestant Dissenters, who were equally forced by lack of power into deviousness and narrow loyalties.

She saw that women could not be expected to be large-minded if they were confined to trivia, nor be honest if they were taught to conceal their feelings. They would naturally think too much about attracting men if they were valued primarily as sexual objects and would naturally seek power by devious means if they were deprived of their legitimate rights and influence. Women's tendency to repeat "a set of phrases learnt by rote" follows naturally from an education that tells them that their " 'highest praise is to obey, unargued' the will of man." Wollstonecraft joined with Swift in deploring women's obsession with dress, but traced this preoccupation to their lack of larger interests: they have no business nor intellectual involvement, "and they find politics dry, because they have not acquired a love for mankind by turning their thoughts to the grand pursuits that exalt the human race, and promote general happiness."[13]

To eliminate this distortion of women by miseducation, she proposed a national system of coeducational schools, in which every child would be educated up to her or his capacity. Her plan for organized schooling is particularly significant because most people, including even feminists like Mary Hays, still maintained that girls could be adequately educated through private study at home.[14] Wollstonecraft concentrated on education as the means of reforming women, and men's attitudes toward them, as was typical of her period; but she also thought about legal and economic changes and perhaps would have campaigned for them had she lived to complete her work. She condemned laws that "make an absurd unit of a man and his wife," suggested that women have representatives in government (this hesitantly, for she recognized that the idea of woman suffrage would probably "excite laughter"), and lamented that superior women "have not a road open by which they can pursue more extensive plans of usefulness and independence" than domestic life affords. She went on to suggest that women "be physicians as well as nurses" and manage farms or shops so as not to be dependent on men for support.[15]

Mary Hays, a close friend of Godwin and Wollstonecraft, derived support from the same circle of political and religious radicals. All her life she argued for women's rights and celebrated their achievements, in *Letters and Essays, Moral and Miscellaneous* (1793), *An Appeal to the Men of Great Britain in Behalf of Women* (1798), *Female Biography* (1803), *and Memoirs of Queens* (1821).[16] In the third of her *Letters*, "On the Influence of Authority and Custom on the Female Mind and Character," she dramatized the disastrous limitations of narrowly conventional motherhood through the story of Sempronia, a conscientious woman who exacted passive obedience from her daughters and ruled out liberal education as a waste of time: "The sole accomplishments . . . [she] deemed necessary to constitute a good wife and mother, were to scold and half starve her servants, to oblige her children to say their prayers, and go stately to church, and to make clothes and household furniture from morning to night." The eldest daughter, Serena, attracted a cultured merchant, who deluded himself that her inert silence resulted from "delicate timidity" and looked forward to the delight of teaching her. He soon discovered that it was too late to form her mind: as he read sublime literature to her, she would interrupt "to observe upon a phaeton that passed the window." She had not the spirit to oppose him, but her insipid compliance bored him to the point that he sought entertainment outside the home, fell into dissipation, and became bankrupt.

Martha, the second daughter in Hays's story, was more fortunate in marrying a man who did not look for intellect or cultivation; but she lacked Serena's naturally gentle disposition. Her passions, uncontrolled by rational principles and exacerbated by her mother's tyrannical restraint, made her so intolerable a companion that her husband had to move her to a remote country house, where she took to drink and died. The two younger daughters lacked the others' good looks and, having nothing else to offer, remained unmarried. Ann was converted to fanatical religion by accidentally hearing a Methodist sermon and sank into superstitious terrors and melancholy madness. Charlotte had more mental ability than the others, but, kept from books and intelligent company, she had nothing to apply it to but ornamental busywork. In youth she was happy "forming many little plans ... for the disposition of the nuptial finery, the furnishing of her house, and the style of her equipage"; but middle age could offer nothing but envy and disappointment, until she too declined into depression.[17]

Writing in a period of conservative reaction, Hays began her *Appeal to the Men of Great Britain* in an apologetic tone, but went on to argue as vigorously as Wollstonecraft against the stereotyping of sexual character. A desire to excel is natural and therefore justified in every human being, she pointed out; but what is called laudable ambition in men, is condemned as vanity in women. Ambition is considered too sublime for women, but it is used "to varnish over the passions, and crimes of men." Men's ideal for women—requiring passive compliance most of the time but strength available "upon all convenient occasions" —is both absurdly inconsistent and outrageously exploitative. "There are no vices to which a man addicts himself, no follies he can take it into his head to commit, but his wife and his nearest female relations are expected ... to look upon, if not with admiration, at least with respectful silence, and at awful distance. Any other conduct is looked upon, as a breach of that fanciful system of arbitrary authority, which men have so assiduously erected in their own favor; and ... is accordingly resisted with the most acrimonious severity." Any protest, however reasonable, enrages men; for they cannot bear to see the face they "consider as formed only to suggest ideas of pleasure, delight, or submission" to them, expressing any other feelings.[18]

Men say, "with as much earnestness and gravity as if it were true," that their authority over women was established for the mutual good, especially since women may exert power through sweet dependency. Experience as well as reason shows this to be absurd, though men may actually believe, when the images of young and beautiful women "work them up to a temporary sentiment of love and tenderness for the whole sex," that women "have no need of law or right on their side, and have only to be seen to be obeyed." Actually, men "do not upon the whole like [women] the better, or at least they do not treat them the better—which is the only true test of love—for their forced humility and submission." Women's only security can come from a clear definition of rights and limits even in the love relationship of marriage: setting due bounds to authority both prevents abuse and ensures reasonable obedience. "These truths are simple and obvious enough, and are now very readily acknowledged, in all matters except where women are concerned," because men have power to enforce justice from each other and women do not. A husband, like a king, is universally tempted to extend "his prerogative a *little* too far."[19]

Like Wollstonecraft, Hays aimed to improve social attitudes by which lower-class wives were considered as drudges and upper-class wives as ornaments, and the "maternal character ... which cannot be taken from them ... is reduced to as low a pitch of consequence as possible." Her approach, however, was more sentimental, perhaps because she was never married. She believed dependence on a man one loves is neither disagreeable nor degrading: "where is the woman who has ever experienced ... a true and virtuous attachment, who would not rather a thousand times owe her happiness to the indulgence of an amiable man whom she loves, than to any other circumstance that imagination can suggest?" Furthermore, "a woman of sense and virtue" will not for a moment hesitate between intellectual pursuits and attentiveness to a father or other relative.[20]

Perhaps this downgrading of professional self-fulfillment for women limited her views on what occupations were appropriate.

She shared Wollstonecraft's concern that women had practically no way of supporting themselves, but she found that "Nature dictates with a force not to be misunderstood, that women are not formed for warlike enterprises," nor for manual trades. While they have the natural capacity for practicing law, "delicacy as well as common sense, points out objections . . . to women taking any active part in popular assemblies." While delicacy does permit women to be doctors to their own sex, the idea of their doing so is, for some unspecified reason, revolting. The only woman physician Hays ever saw "acted upon me like an emetic; and she had nearly the same effect, upon most of her female acquaintance."[21]

Priscilla Wakefield's more enlightened plea for expanding opportunities for women is firmly based on the radicals' concept of human responsibility. Like Hays and Wollstonecraft, she believed that women should be useful—and valued for their usefulness. She opened her *Reflections on the Present Condition of the Female Sex* (1798) by extending to women Adam Smith's dictum "that every individual is a burthen upon the society to which he belongs, who does not contribute his share of productive labour for the good of the whole": "since the female sex is included in the idea of the species, and as women possess the same qualities as men, though perhaps in a different degree, their sex cannot free them from the claim of the public for their proportion of usefulness." But most ladies do not contribute their share, because "a contracted education, custom, false pride, and idolizing adulation" have "concealed, not only from others, but from themselves, the energies of which they are capable." Rather than wasting her days in frivolous needlework or minute supervision of the household, a mother should devote her time to "forming the minds of her children." In particular, since the best talisman for preserving conjugal fidelity is interesting business, "mothers of all degrees cannot too earnestly habituate their daughters to daily application to some object of real utility."[22]

An upper-class married woman should make herself useful supervising charities that she understands better than men would, such as the care of infants in poorhouses and decent treatment for parish apprentices; a tradesman's wife should understand her husband's business so as to help him and, if necessary, carry it on after his death. But especially Wakefield was concerned with the lady who has no man to support her, who, "Unaccustomed to struggle with difficulty, unacquainted with any resource to supply an independent maintenance," may have no resource but prostitution.

Yet prejudice "rises like an insurmountable barrier against a woman, of any degree above the vulgar, employing her time and her abilities, towards the maintenance of herself and her family." A country that respects the character of the merchant looks down on the woman "whose good sense and resolution enable her to support herself" in commerce; young men actually feel they demean themselves by marrying girls who have "been trained up to any profitable employment," instead of giving "them a preference on account of this mark of their superior judgment." Yet surely, "that which is a moral excellence in one rational being, deserves the same estimation in another," so that it is as honorable in a woman as in a man to exert her utmost abilities to support herself and those who have a natural claim to her protection.[23]

As its subtitle indicates, Mary Ann Radcliffe's *The Female Advocate; or, An Attempt to Recover the Rights of Women from Male Usurpation* (1799) also argues woman's right to, as well as need for, economic opportunities. Although most women "are so perfectly tamed, either through custom or compulsive submission" that they would be only too happy to be subordinate dependents, men do not always accept this responsibility. And, Radcliffe goes on, if men "refuse to protect [women], they have no right whatever to govern." Raised to look to men for support, unprotected women naturally fall into prostitution—and then they are reviled for idleness and profligacy. Society deprives women of useful education or encouragement to be independent—yet "what statute is there, which grants that man alone shall live, and women scarcely exist?"[24]

Although Wollstonecraft was strongly emotional, she took a severely rational stance in *A Vindication*, rightly suspecting that sentiment was often used as Jean-Jacques Rousseau used it, to cloak patronage and exploitation of women. Believing that Reason was the only dependable basis for women's rights, she exhorted women to cultivate strength rather than sensibility, warned them against courtship and chivalry, implied that they should be able to do without love from men, and assured them that a good marriage is based on friendship.[25] But later her own passionate affairs with Gilbert Imlay and William Godwin made her realize that women needed emotional fulfillment as well as respect.[26]

Maria; or, The Wrongs of Woman (1798), a novel that remained unfinished at her death, expresses this newfound emotional freedom, as well as illustrating the oppression of women which she protested in *A Vindication*. Maria marries to escape an unhappy home but comes to regret her decision when she perceives her husband's failings and meets superior men. Her disgust with her husband increases when he will not allow her to spend money, even to help her sisters, who, being ladies, cannot support themselves. The crisis, however, does not come from his selfishness, but from the trite melodramatic device of his attempt to sell her to another man, which provokes her to leave him. As the novel opens, he has pursued and caught her and, with perfect legality, imprisoned her in an insane asylum.

Wrongs such as these had appeared before in women's novels, but Wollstonecraft focuses more explicitly on the oppression of women and traces it to an unjust legal system, which, she implies, must be changed. Toward the end of the book, Maria makes an eloquent and reasoned plea in court for her right to a divorce, with retention of her own property, so that she can marry the man she loves. The judge's summing up offers a devastating indictment of the conservative social system that justified oppression by denying there was a problem: "if women were allowed to plead their feelings, as an excuse or palliation of infidelity, it was opening a floodgate for immorality. What virtuous woman thought of her feelings?" Maria's imprisonment in the madhouse might perhaps entitle her to a sentence of separation from bed and board, but, "Too many restrictions could not be thrown in the way of divorces, if we wished to maintain the sanctity of marriage; and, though they might bear a little hard on a few, very few individuals, it was evidently for the good of the whole."[27]

Both Maria's claim and the narrow-minded judge's charge show the connection between women's feelings and their rights. The radicals' demand for emotional liberation took strength from the respect for women's feelings which had already been developed by the cult of sensibility. From mid-century, writers like Frances Brooke, who had no interest in politics, had been defending a woman's right to refuse a suitor merely because she did not like him, and idealizing generous, enthusiastic women even though they might violate strict prudence and propriety.

But Wollstonecraft, emboldened by radical theory, actually renounced law in the name of feeling. Maria shows a newly assertive confidence in her right to leave her vicious husband: "The magnitude of a sacrifice ought always to bear some proportion to the utility in view; and for a woman to live with a man, for whom she can cherish neither affection nor esteem . . . is an abjectness of condition" that can never be "a duty in the sight of God or just men." Wollstonecraft's most striking innovation was to introduce Maria's sexuality into the discussion. She declares that sexual relations should never be forced by duty: "we cannot, without depraving our minds, endeavour to please a lover or husband, but in proportion as he pleases us." Even more radically, she denies that a woman bound for life to a husband she cannot love should be "obliged to renounce all the humanizing affections."[28] In other words, she should be freed to live with another man.

As she explicitly rejects the conventional view of chastity, Wollstonecraft refuses "to praise as a virtue, a woman's coldness of constitution, and want of passion; and make her yield to the ardour of her lover out of sheer compassion, or to promote a plan of frigid comfort." Such "may be good women, in the ordinary acceptation of the phrase . . . but they want that fire of the imagination, which produces *active* sensibility, and *positive* virtue." The sentimentalists had already associated warm feelings with imagination, and the radicals added independence of thought.[29] Maria was to develop from "a woman of sensibility, with an improving mind" into a person of sufficient wisdom and confidence to challenge and repudiate conventional repressive morality; it was her shocking treatment by her husband and her subsequent fulfillment with another man that would educate her "to discern the fallacy of prejudices at war with nature and reason" and fortify her to defy them. Thus Maria was to illustrate the idea suggested in the *Vindication*, that judgment and fortitude develop from giving scope to the passions even when they lead one astray. For moral as well as aesthetic reasons, Wollstonecraft flouted the contemporary convention that allowed the hero of a novel "to be mortal, and to become wise and virtuous as well as happy," but required heroines "to be born immaculate, and to act like goddesses of wisdom, just come forth highly finished Minervas from the head of Jove."[30]

Maria's lower-class counterpart, the asylum maid Jemima, is matured by even harsher methods. (Even in this radical novel, the idealized heroine is less convincing than this secondary character, cynical and hardened, yet not dead to sympathy.) Orphaned and penniless because her unwed mother was cast out by her employer (while her father, a fellow servant, was only reprimanded), Jemima is soon forced into hard service. Her employer does not bother to seduce, but bullies her into sexual relations; his wife discovers the affair and throws her out of the house. Though Jemima is revolted by sexual abuse, she is forced into prostitution as her only possible means of support. She has a brief period of happiness as the mistress of an intelligent man, enjoying his mind though she loathes his sexual demands; but on his death his relatives virtuously drive her from the house. As a woman, and one of blasted reputation, she can just barely earn her living by slaving as a laundress, though a man of half her industry and ability could earn a decent livelihood. She is injured on the job, forced into thievery, then prison and the workhouse, from which she can escape only into her present odious employment in the asylum.

It was natural for Mary Hays to adapt the sentimental novel to radical teaching, since she had seen herself as a heroine of sensibility before she became a feminist.[31] Her Emma Courtney (*Memoirs of Emma Courtney*, 1796) shares Hays's sensibility but is also frankly described as passionate. Only a radical author would have dared to represent a heroine "enslaved by passion," even though her actions were strictly virtuous and even though she was explicitly offered as a warning rather than an example. Despite this nominal disapproval, Emma's passionateness is clearly related to her awesome superiority, as her strong passions stimulate her strong mind to overpowering love for the hero, resolution in fulfilling her duties, and that "Free thinking, and free speaking, [which] are the virtue and the characteristics of a rational being."[32] Unfortunately, Hays was not able to make Emma's nobility convincing, so that her principles appear to be rationalizations of her wishes; her warm passions and exquisite sensibility, self-centered indulgence of her feelings.

This weakness in characterization undermines the important feminist assertion Hays makes by having Emma choose the man she wants to marry and propose to him. While most women novelists had satirized the arrogance of men who expected women to accept proposals automatically, they assumed women might do no more than decline or respond gracefully to a man they could love. Hays boldly asserted that a woman is entitled to take the initiative in the matter most important to her future life, but unfortunately she made Emma as overbearing as any self-centered male. Emma falls in love with Augustus before even seeing him and becomes ever more attached on acquaintance. By and by she proposes to him and, when he fails to respond, persists: "My heart obstinately refuses to renounce the man, to whose mind my own seems akin!" In fact, she doubts that he has a right to refuse her, since her mental health, and hence her usefulness to society, depends upon fulfilling herself through marrying him.[33] Hays avoids resolving this issue by having Augustus secretly married to another woman, thus depriving him of the power to marry Emma, even though he loves her. But in any case, Emma's clamorous, self-righteous persistence discredits the justified assertion of woman's right to express her needs.

Hays likewise failed to establish her major point that Emma is, like Wollstonecraft's Maria, the victim of social oppression. For Emma's troubles seem to be largely self-created; her dependence on Augustus is her own fault, not society's. Hays also fails to demonstrate the culpability of society in *The Victim of Prejudice* (1799), since it is not social institutions that embitter the life of the innocent heroine, but a fiendish baronet who martyrs her "by unrelenting persecution."[34]

Eliza Fenwick, a friend of Hays and Wollstonecraft, made her protest against repressive feminine morality in *Secresy* (1795). Her heroine, Sibella, is a female Noble Savage, whose natural reason resists a traditionally restrictive upbringing to claim equality and emotional freedom. She would rather devote her mind to architecture or navigation than the minutiae of dress; she wants to be the companion of man and declares she cannot be unless she is his equal. She enters such a relationship with the man she loves, too beautifully innocent to marry him first: for "Custom has not placed its sordid restraints upon her feelings."[35]

As legally enforced chastity is a sordid restraint on love, the other traditional feminine virtues are a useful device to further men's exploitation of women, and, in fact, are actually opposed to virtue: "The perpetual hue and cry after obedience and obedience has almost driven virtue out of the world, for be it unlimited unexamined obedience to a sovereign, to a parent, or husband, the mind, yielding itself to implicit unexamined obedience, loses its individual dignity, and you can expect no more of a man than a brute."[36]

However pure and justified she may be, Sibella comes to a sad end because her lover cannot see the sacredness of their free union. The only happy and successful liberated woman in eighteenth-century fiction appears to be Mary Ann Hanway's Lady John Dareall in *Ellinor* (1798). Though she introduces Lady John conventionally, as a bad example of repudiating one's sexual role, Hanway soon lets her develop into a total ideal. Lady John's boisterous health does not detract from her beauty, nor her lack of sensibility from her good feelings; and her freedom from "feminine" timidity makes her appear impressive rather than brazen. She is not criticized for scorning the world's opinion and conventional women, or even for having left her delicate, bookish husband because he bored her and then associating freely with a congenial man. (It is not specified whether they are having an affair.) She eloquently preaches the doctrines of Wollstonecraft's *Vindication*, insisting on woman's natural equality with man and deploring the conditioning that makes her dependent; she goes so far as to maintain that "freedom of will was the sovereign good and restraint the greatest evil."[37] Not only does Lady John get away with living just as she likes, but Hanway exempts her from any charge of selfishness, making her virtuous in every significant way. What is most remarkable, Lady John's son, whose father she has contemptuously abandoned, is as devoted and respectful as if she were the most dutiful of women.

Lady John is, obviously, a wishful fantasy. Apart from the fact that few women had the money necessary to live as they liked, her freedom from guilt, her acceptance by society, and her son's uncritical devotion are blatantly unrealistic. The convention-defying heroines of Wollstonecraft, Hays, and Fenwick—it is significant that Lady John is not a heroine—are all destroyed, although the authors make clear that the blame lies on society rather than on the nonconforming women.

Though Elizabeth Inchbald was a friend of Godwin and Charlotte Smith was a sympathizer with the French Revolution, their radicalism did not lead them to systematic feminism. Inchbald's *Nature and Art* (1796) sardonically exposes social lies, pretensions, and complacency; but the book's only feminist concern is an attack on the overemphasis on female chastity through its portrayal of Agnes Primrose. Agnes, an essentially virtuous cottager's daughter, lets herself be seduced by a prelate's son, William. Because she refuses to part with the resulting illegitimate child, she is forced to work as a kitchen slavey, then as a servant in a brothel, and finally as a prostitute. As such, she loses all self-respect: "Degraded in her own judgment, she doubted her own understanding when it sometimes told her she had deserved better treatment." She is the victim of the belief inculcated in her that a woman who has lost chastity has lost all worth, but she suspects the truth that society makes the prostitute a scapegoat—the same society that respects and promotes her cold-blooded seducer. In a dramatic final scene, Agnes, who has been convicted of felony, is sentenced by William, who has risen to a judgeship by sacrificing personal loyalty and love; and Inchbald points the irony: "these very persons had passed together the most blissful moments that either ever tasted."[38]

Miss Milner of *A Simple Story* (1791) is closer to the conventional heroine of eighteenth-century fiction, but she too is a superior human being destroyed by society's overemphasis on narrow virtue in women, as well as its misguided system of feminine education. She carries on the tradition of the generous, imprudent sentimental heroine; the radical influence appears in Inchbald's recognition that her failings are socially caused and clear definition of the patriarchal authority against which her rebellion has some justification.

Miss Milner is a beautiful heiress who falls in love with her guardian, Dorriforth, an upright but rigid Roman Catholic priest. After he is released from his vows (in order to perpetuate a Catholic earldom), he realizes that he loves her. But even in the courtship period there is trouble, since she insists on having her own way and he insists on exerting judicious control over her. Far indeed from the conventional feminine ideal, Miss Milner is thoughtless, defiant of authority, fond of power and admiration, impulsive and imprudent. And yet Inchbald shows her to be a lovable as well as attractive woman. Lacking the negative virtues of feminine propriety, she has all the outgoing ones that transcend that ideal—passionate love, generosity, warm reckless sympathy. She defies her stern guardian by bringing into his home the young nephew whom he has unjustly repudiated. She loves her guardian—before he has even proposed to her—"with all the passion of a mistress," as well as "all the tenderness of a wife."

Miss Milner is often irritating. She cannot stop flirting; she runs compulsively to social events she does not care for; she wastes money on trifles she does not want; though she loves her fiancé passionately, she insists on testing his love by seeing how much he will sacrifice to it: "I will do something that any prudent man ought *not* to forgive; and yet, with that vast share of prudence he possesses, I will force him still to yield to his love."[39]

Her follies, however, are not so much her fault as that of

eighteenth-century society. As Wollstonecraft had demonstrated, they were fostered by the deficient education of women and by the way men treated them. Without making this feminist point explicitly, Inchbald shows how a person who has never been taught to reason or to discipline herself will lack serious interests and be unable to see the consequences of her actions. Living in a society that overemphasized sexual attractiveness in women, covering its essential lack of respect by treating women with gallant indulgence as long as they were young, beautiful, and unmarried, Miss Milner naturally thinks she can get away with anything. Since sexual success is her only means of ego gratification, she coquets to gain male admiration and makes the most of the courtship period by trying her power over the man who loves her. She is not restrained by reason because she has been encouraged to believe that frivolity and caprice are attractive in women. She unthinkingly accepts the views of fashionable society, but she can hardly be blamed, since she has had no opportunity to develop sounder standards.

Miss Milner is the victim of Dorriforth's conventional thinking as well as her own, since he insists on judging her by the narrowest feminine ideal of the time. His conception of feminine propriety causes him to exaggerate her faults and undervalue her virtues. Once he is free to marry, he turns first to Miss Fenton, a model of obedience and correct behavior—who is so, Inchbald makes clear, because she lacks ideas or strong feelings of any kind. Soon, however, he realizes his passion for the better and more lovable woman, even though she is far from his preconceived ideal and in fact he cannot understand her. He is simply baffled by her normal egotism—her enjoyment of male admiration, her wish to marry for pleasure rather than duty, and her resentment of peremptory commands. By profession and character, he expects passive submission from women.

For, although Dorriforth is a high-principled man, and his corrections of Miss Milner are usually rational and just, he is also unsympathetic, rigid, and self-righteous. He had "an obstinacy; such as he himself, and his friends termed firmness of mind; but had not religion and some opposite virtues weighed heavy in the balance, it would frequently have degenerated into implacable stubbornness."[40] Here as elsewhere, Inchbald delicately exposes the drive for dominance that male authority figures like to call zeal for virtue. Miss Milner is faulty, but Dorriforth is frighteningly inflexible.

Unfortunately, Inchbald let convention prevent her from developing this study of incompatibility between two people who love each other but cannot accept each other's values. Instead, she had Miss Milner slip weakly into adultery and then die of remorse, while Dorriforth behaves with an arrogant vindictiveness that is scarcely criticized though it seems much worse than the adultery that provoked it.[41]

Charlotte Smith never created so interesting a heroine, but her novels are peppered with assertions of women's right to think and criticize, and with protests against antifeminist restrictions. Writing under relentless financial pressure, she had to attend to what was acceptable in ladies' fiction, so she kept to the usual pattern with more or less grace, although at the same time she protested against it. Her novels characteristically focus upon the sentimental distresses of a faultless young girl, but they constantly reveal that Smith's true interest and inspiration lay in social criticism. The books come alive when she exposes the inferiority of someone puffed up by high social position or excoriates the callousness of government by the privileged. For this reason, *The Old Manor House* (1793) is much her best novel, because it centers on a young man, whom she can send to fight in the American Revolutionary War and make horrified comments on it.

Smith flouted convention when she discussed politics, for even though many moderates agreed with her attack upon English abuses during the American Revolution, they considered the subject out of place in a woman's work. Her irony at the expense of "this dear England of ours ... the very best of all possible countries ... [with plenty of] fine places for those who have great talents, and admirable sinecures for others who have only great interest—excellent laws to defend the property of those who can pay to be so defended" is more inflammatory.[42] But her defense of the French Revolution, in *Desmond* (1792), was truly shocking. She went so far as to call Burke's *Reflections on the Revolution in France* "an elaborate treatise in favor of despotism." In her preface she justified her presentation of current politics on the grounds that women have a natural "interest in the scenes that are acting around them, in which they see fathers, brothers, husbands, sons, or friends engaged." She went on to protest against a system that despised women "as insignificant triflers" if they were ignorant, but censured them "as affecting masculine knowledge if they happen[ed] to have any understanding."

What life the book has is in its political satire; the nominal main plot is drearily conventional, dripping with sentimental distress and tied to narrow morality. The virtuous heroine, married to a worthless husband, blindly sacrifices everything for him; we are supposed to admire her resolve "to be a complete martyr to [her conjugal] duty." Geraldine recognizes that she is as miserable "a slave as the French were before the Revolution," that in rejoining her husband she is putting "on the most dreadful of all fetters—Fetters that would even destroy the freedom of my mind"; nevertheless, she does not hesitate to put them on.[43]

On the other hand, Smith did represent her virtuous hero in love with this married woman and showed her, though strictly faithful, appreciating him. And Smith took a liberal view of lapses from conventional morality in women who were not her heroines. In several of her novels, kept mistresses were represented as kind and generous, and wives were shown as committing adultery not because they were vicious but because they were pushed into marriages before they knew men or themselves, because their education had provided them with no inner resources, or because their husband neglected and exploited them while another man showed tender consideration. To the disapproval of contemporary reviewers (including the young Wollstonecraft!), she even let one adulteress look forward, after much suffering, to marrying her lover.[44]

Smith's interest in large social and political questions made her realize the limitations of the feminine novel. Although this form had helped so many women to express themselves, it also confirmed their place in a private world of refined sentiments, safely insulated from the usefulness and influence in society which the radicals sought for women. Though forced by economic necessity to follow this convention, Smith repeatedly protested against its restrictions. In the preface to *The Banished Man* (1794), she raised (but then rejected) the possibility that she would make "the experiment that has often been talked of, but has never . . . yet been hazarded"—"to make a novel without love in it." After exciting opening chapters set in Revolutionary France, she brought in the usual romance.

Then, through a clearly autobiographical character, she commented on this proceeding. Charlotte Denzil, who has to support her family as a novelist, humorously contrasts the sentimental refinements she must write about with the sordid realities she must live with. Mrs. Denzil goes to her writing desk after listening to Mr. Tough's importunate demands that she pay his bill—"precious recipe to animate the imagination and exalt the fancy!" Here "she must write a tender dialogue" between some damsel of innumerable perfections "and her hero, who, to the bravery and talents of Caesar, adds the gentleness of Sir Charles Grandison, and the wit of Lovelace. But Mr. Tough's . . . rude threats . . . have totally sunk her spirits; nor are they elevated by hearing that the small beer is almost out" and "the pigs of . . . her next neighbour, have broke into the garden."[45]

Smith chafed particularly at the requirements that prevented a heroine in ladies' fiction from having enough mind and character to command interest or even genuine respect. In *Marchmont* (1796) she protested that the limitations on the heroine made her long to stop writing fiction. First, "very young women [Althea is sixteen] have no striking traits of character to distinguish them, till some circumstance in their lives either calls forth their understanding, or decides that they have none." Second, "any very marked feature" is considered to disfigure a heroine. "Too much reason and self-command destroy the interest we take in her distresses. It has even been observed, that Clarissa is so equal to every trial as to diminish our pity." So the novelist is not free to give a heroine "other virtues than gentleness, pity, filial obedience, or faithful attachment." Smith tried to make the heroine of this novel a more forceful and interesting character. She tells us that Althea's unusual misfortunes produced "that fortitude and strength of mind which gave energy to an understanding, naturally of the first class." But unfortunately she failed to demonstrate Althea's unusual energy or intelligence in the action of the book.[46]

None of the radical novelists were able to turn the conventional feminine novel into an effective vehicle for feminism. As Smith subordinated her social satire to routine tales of blameless afflicted young women, Fenwick incongruously kept her Sibella an innocent sentimental heroine while she flouted the law of marriage. Amelia Opie's *Adeline Mowbray* (1804) slips from a penetrating but sympathetic analysis of Wollstonecraft's ideas on marriage into maudlin sentimental fiction, as Opie twists the characters of Adeline's mother and husband to drive her onto the traditional tear-drenched deathbed. Even Wollstonecraft created a flat heroine in Maria, whose ideas are far more interesting than her character.

The radicals' more extreme opinions—their approval of sexual passion in women and their rejection of all sexual distinctions in conduct and values—were too shocking to most people to have widespread influence. Sometimes radical writers went out of their way to outrage conventional opinion: when virtuous Mary Hays made virtuous Emma Courtney define chastity as simple constancy,[47] she provided ammunition for those who identified radicalism and feminism with sexual laxity. Moreover, in preaching emotional liberation, these authors too often let passion slip into loose emotionality, self-assertion into self-indulgence. Emma Courtney, devastated because she cannot have her Augustus, is not an edifying example of liberated womanhood. Conservative critics, of course, made the most of such characters.

On the other hand, radical theory must have strengthened the liberalizing tendencies already present in the feminine novel. Miss Milner carries on the spontaneity and independence of Brooke's and Richardson's nonconformists, but Inchbald's radicalism heightened her emotional freedom and increased our sympathy for her rebelliousness. Smith's assertions that women might and should have opinions on politics is a natural extension of the insistence found even in conservative female novelists that women should develop their minds. As it was accepted that women should have intellectual interests of some kind, Smith was simply broadening their scope.

It is probable that the radical movement had important indirect effects on women who would never have thought of justifying adultery or asserting their right to seek a husband by themselves. It must have sharpened women's recognition of the miseries of their dependent state, strengthened their belief that they deserved better education and more intellectual respect, and made them wonder about the double standard, with its insistence on the all-importance of modesty and propriety. Radical writers gave women confidence to venture out of their traditional sphere—personal relationships among a small social group—into the larger area of moral and political ideas. Even though Elizabeth Hamilton wrote *Memoirs of Modern Philosophers* (1800) to ridicule the radicals' theorizing, it is as much a novel of ideas as Inchbald's *Nature and Art* or Smith's *Desmond*. Most important, by forcefully articulating the complaints and aspirations that had already been suggested in women's sentimental fiction, the radical feminists helped to make women's rights an issue that had to be seriously discussed.

NOTES

1. David Williams has surveyed French thinking on the subject in "The Politics of Feminism in the French Enlightenment," *The Varied Pattern: Studies in the 18th Century* (Toronto: A. M. Hakkert, 1971), pp. 333-51. People who really cared about women's rights, such as Condorcet and Olympe de Gouges, were in the minority; the antifeminism of the Napoleonic Code (1804) ratified the Revolutionary government's rejection of women's claims for equality in 1793.
2. William Godwin, *An Enquiry Concerning Political Justice and Its Influence on Morals and Happiness*, ed. F. E. L. Priestley (Toronto: University of Toronto Press, 1946), II, 507-8. The heroines of the novels Godwin wrote after he knew Wollstonecraft are still entirely conventional in character and role.
3. Paine's article in the *Pennsylvania Magazine*, 1775, quoted

in Hazel Mews, *Frail Vessels: Woman's Role in Women's Novels from Fanny Burney to George Eliot* (London: University of London, 1969), p. 12; Jeremy Bentham, "Plan of Parliamentary Reform," in *The Constitutional Code,* from *The Works,* ed. John Bowring (New York: Russell and Russell, 1962), III, 463-64; IX, 108-9.

4. Catharine Macaulay was important for the position she held rather than for her achievements. Her eight-volume *History of England from the Accession of James I to That of the Brunswick Line* (1763-83), inspired by her enthusiasm for liberty, does not rank with the great histories of her century but did demonstrate that a woman could produce a large-scale professional history. References to Macaulay in the *Life of Johnson* and elsewhere prove that she established herself as a prominent liberal thinker. However, her writings on women are disappointing. Although Wollstonecraft enthusiastically praised her *Letters on Education* (1790), I suspect she was responding more to Macaulay's position as a conspicuous female liberal than to any feminist insights. Macaulay did deny the existence of a sexual character ("there is but one rule of right for the conduct of all rational beings"), attributed all the imperfections charged to women to situation and education, and recommended the same "sports and studies" for girls and boys (*Letters on Education* [New York: Garland, 1974], pp. 201, 202). But she devoted as much space to banal religious discussion and conventional moralizing as did Hannah More.

5. Robert Bage, *Mount Henneth,* Ballantyne's Novelist's Library (London: Hurst, Robinson, 1824), IX, 132. However, Elizabeth Griffith, no radical, had equally mitigated the crime of unchastity. A virtuous character in *The Delicate Distress* (1769) could have pitied or even loved a woman who let herself be seduced by an agreeable young man: "I am not such an Amazon in ethics, as to consider a breach of chastity, as the highest crime, that a woman can be guilty of; though it is, certainly, the most unpardonable folly." Quoted in Bridget G. MacCarthy, *Later Women Novelists, 1744-1818* (Cork: Cork University Press, 1947), p. 75.

6. Robert Bage, *Barham Downs,* quoted in J. M. S. Tompkins, *The Popular Novel in England, 1770-1800* (Lincoln: University of Nebraska Press, 1961), p. 171.

7. Robert Bage, *Hermsprong, or Man as He Is Not,* ed. Vaughan Wilkins (New York: Library Publishers, 1951), pp. 136, 233. Laura Stanley of *Mount Henneth* complains that modesty restrains women from talking or, if they can help

it, thinking, and points out that truth, as well as piety, is a valuable quality in women (p. 132). Harrison R. Steeves discusses Bage's feminism in *Before Jane Austen: The Shaping of the English Novel in the Eighteenth Century* (New York: Holt, Rinehart and Winston, 1965), pp. 274-91. Turning to other radical writers, we find in Thomas Holcroft's *Anna St. Ives* (1792) a heroine who could be considered liberated were she not, like the hero, such a slave to rational duty. Placed in a situation similar to Clarissa's, she is capable of escaping by climbing over a wall, and would have been able to survive rape unashamed even if she had not escaped. Holcroft's villain, Clifton, constantly voices male-chauvinist prejudices. Thomas Day's *The History of Sandford and Merton* (1783-89), commended by Wollstonecraft in her *Vindication*, contains brief but enlightened comments on the education of girls (New York: Garland, 1977, II, 226-29; III, 205-8).

8. Mary Wollstonecraft, *A Vindication of the Rights of Men* (London: J. Johnson, 1790), pp. 49-51. She also trenchantly attacked Burke's theory, advanced in his *Philosophical Inquiry into . . . the Sublime and Beautiful*, that women should cultivate littleness and weakness in order to be lovable (pp. 105-8).

9. Wollstonecraft had had her fill of feminine sensibility in the many novels she reviewed for the *Analytical Review* in the late 1780s. Consistently she condemned authors who praised weakness under the name of delicacy, idealized extravagant emotionality in women, and encouraged them to expect ecstasy instead of rational domestic happiness. Cf. her almost savage imagining of a dead young mother whose corpse reveals that she was weakly delicate, in "Extract of The Cave of Fancy, A Tale," in *Posthumous Works of the Author of a Vindication of the Rights of Woman* (Clifton, Eng.: Augustus M. Kelley, 1972), IV, 122-25.

10. Mary Wollstonecraft, *A Vindication of the Rights of Woman*, ed. Carol H. Poston (New York: W. W. Norton, 1975), p. 26 (cited hereafter as *Vindication*).

11. *Ibid.*, pp. 19, 34, 95.

12. *Ibid.*, pp. 3, 143, 145.

13. *Ibid.*, pp. 117, 187. Wollstonecraft quotes Jonathan Swift's "Furniture of a Woman's Mind," line 1, and John Milton's *Paradise Lost*, IV, 636-38.

14. Mary Hays, *An Appeal to the Men of Great Britain in Behalf of Women* (New York: Garland, 1974), p. 250.

15. Wollstonecraft, *Vindication*, pp. 145, 147-49.

16. Hays's *Female Biography,* the work that kept her name known through the nineteenth century, constantly emphasizes not only the achievements of its subjects, but the particular difficulties they had to contend with as women. Hays also notes that several women, such as Lady Elizabeth Hastings, preferred to remain single so as to remain mistresses of their actions and incomes.

17. Mary Hays, *Letters and Essays* (New York: Garland, 1974), pp. 34-41, 80-82.

18. Hays, *Appeal,* pp. 51-52, 72, 76-77, 122-23.

19. *Ibid.,* pp. 116-18, 141, 288-89.

20. *Ibid.,* pp. 160, 275-76.

21. *Ibid.,* pp. 194-99. In *Thoughts on the Education of Daughters,* Wollstonecraft described the humiliations of working as a companion, a teacher, and a governess—the only positions open to a lady (New York: Garland, 1974, pp. 69-73).

22. Priscilla Wakefield, *Reflections on the Present Condition of the Female Sex; with Suggestions for Its Improvement* (New York: Garland, 1974), pp. 1-2, 4-5, 39-40, 46.

23. *Ibid.,* pp. 66-68, 71-73.

24. Mary Ann Radcliffe, *The Female Advocate* (New York: Garland, 1974), pp. 397-99, 434, 446. In connection with the unfair treatment of prostitutes, she points out that no one would present a petition to Parliament from "a body of miserable women, be they really virtuous or not," but "were a body of men artificers (be their conduct or morals as they may) to offer a representation of grievances, doubtless their case would be heard, and considered" (p. 433).

25. Wollstonecraft, *Vindication,* pp. 30, 32, 50-51.

26. She wrote to Imlay of "the ineffable delight, the exquisite pleasure, which arises from a unison of affection and desire, when the whole soul and senses are abandoned to a lively imagination, that renders every emotion delicate and rapturous." Though she resisted marriage, she rejoiced in conjugal affection and prided herself on "a heart feelingly alive to all the affections of my nature" (*Posthumous Works,* II, 128, 188-89). Cf. William Godwin, *Memoirs of the Author of a Vindication of the Rights of Woman* (New York: Garland, 1974), pp. 111-12, and Ralph M. Wardle, *Mary Wollstonecraft: A Critical Biography* (Lawrence: University of Kansas Press, 1951), pp. 69-78. Wollstonecraft's first novel, *Mary: A Fiction* (1788) is a conventional novel of sensibility, though it makes the same moderate feminist claims as other novels of its type: e.g., that insipid passivity should not be the feminine ideal.

27. Mary Wollstonecraft, *Maria; or, The Wrongs of Woman*

(New York: W. W. Norton, 1975), pp. 149-50.

28. *Ibid.,* pp. 8, 102, 105.

29. *Ibid.,* p. 101. Cf. Charlotte Smith, *The Young Philosopher* (London: T. Cadell, 1798), II, 14-15.

30. Wollstonecraft, *Maria,* pp. 7, 104; *Vindication,* p. 110.

31. Hays's correspondence with John Eccles, written when she was about twenty, shows them both glorying in their unusually sensitive feelings and treating the real and imaginary difficulties in their courtship as tragedies. See *The Love-Letters of Mary Hays,* ed. A. F. Wedd (London: Methuen, 1925).

32. Mary Hays, *Memoirs of Emma Courtney* (New York: Hugh M. Griffith, 1802), I, 4 (Preface).

33. *Ibid.,* II, 15, 38. Finally she demonstrates why he should marry her: surely he knows no other woman so deserving; he cannot fail to love her when they are so perfectly matched; he could not be so unworthy as to avoid her because she is poor or to cling to any low sensual attachment. She concludes by virtuously assuring him that his cruelty will not drive her to suicide (II, 42-49).

34. Mary Hays, *The Victim of Prejudice* (London: J. Johnson, 1799), I, 8. Only in the last part of the book, after Mary, the heroine, has been raped by the baronet and refuses to accept support from him (in a crude imitation of *Clarissa*), is there convincing social criticism, as Mary finds it impossible to support herself in any respectable occupation because her reputation has been ruined.

35. Eliza Fenwick, *Secresy; or, The Ruin on the Rock* (New York: Garland, 1974), II, 39.

36. *Ibid.,* III, 273. Sibella's suitor points out the usefulness of traditional feminine moral training to self-seeking men: "if the dear creature is but any thing like what her uncle intended to make her . . . I shall be the least noosed of any married man in England. She will want no more than a cage . . . and one smile a month from her sovereign Lord and master" (II, 84).

37. Mary Ann Hanway, *Ellinor, or The World as It Is* (New York: Garland, 1974), III, 241. Hanway lightly qualifies Lady John's feminism by calling it a hobbyhorse (II, 303), but what sticks with the reader is her eloquent case for feminism. Hanway echoes the usual radical protest against repressing one's own feelings in deference to conventional opinion (II, 105-6) and the usual female resentment of the insults and exploitations suffered by ladies' companions (I, 95-96, 133-34). Ellinor herself is a typical heroine of the period, beautiful and accomplished, fortified with every vir-

tue, and credited with intellect (not demonstrated). Her only slight deviation from the type is that she actually is illegitimate, rather than merely suspected of being so.

38. Elizabeth Inchbald, *Nature and Art* (New York: Cassell, n.d.), pp. 149, 161.

39. Elizabeth Inchbald, *A Simple Story*, ed. J. M. S. Tompkins (London: Oxford University Press, 1967), pp. 72, 148.

40. *Ibid.*, pp. 33-34.

41. Moreover, in the second part of this novel, Inchbald practically denied the unconventional value of Miss Milner by replacing her with her daughter, a model of passive feminine virtue. Inchbald's many plays show a pleasant liberalism, but no evidence of feminism except for the lenient presentation of a fallen and a forward woman in *Lovers' Vows* (1798), adapted from the German of August von Kotzebue. Her editorial remarks in *The British Theatre* (1808) on plays dealing with unhappy marriages are severe on adultery by wives, however ill-treated: she condemns George Farquhar's Mrs. Sullen (*The Beaux' Stratagem*) and John Vanbrugh's Lady Brute (*The Provok'd Wife*), and commends the antifeminist morality of Colley Cibber's *Careless Husband*.

42. Charlotte Smith, *The Banished Man* (London: T. Cadell and W. Davies, 1794), II, 217.

43. Charlotte Smith, *Desmond* (London: G. G. J. and J. Robinson, 1792), I, iii-v; II, 62 ff.; III, 71-72, 271.

44. Lady Adelina in *Emmeline*; Wollstonecraft's review appeared in the *Analytical Review* of July, 1788. Cf. Smith's sympathetically presented Mrs. Vyvian in *Montalbert*, who conceived the heroine before marrying, and the hero's mother in *Ethelinde*, who lived as mistress to a lord whose wife was an idiot; Ethelinde herself has a prolonged friendship with a married man, who is in love with her. Smith admired Wollstonecraft and in *The Young Philosopher* praised *Maria; or, The Wrongs of Woman*. Wollstonecraft also reproached Inchbald for weakening the moral lesson of *A Simple Story* by making Miss Milner too amiable. Her whole review—in *Analytical Review*, X (May-August, 1791), 101-2—is curiously imperceptive.

45. Smith, *Banished Man*, I, vi-vii; II, 224-28.

46. Charlotte Smith, *Marchmont* (London: Sampson Low, 1796), I, 177-79. She made the same claim, equally unjustified, for her Ethelinde and Medora of *The Young Philosopher*.

47. Hays, *Emma Courtney*, II, 46-47.

~~~ [7] ~~~

CONSOLIDATION
AND MODERATE PROGRESS:
How Women Saw Themselves at the End
of the Eighteenth Century

It is true that the most widely respected women of later eighteenth-century England pointedly dissociated themselves from the radicals. Hannah More proudly declared that, though "much pestered to read the *Rights of Woman*," she was "invincibly resolved not to do it. . . . I am sure I have as much liberty as I can make use of, now I am an old maid; and when I was a young one, I had, I dare say, more than was good for me. . . . To be unstable and capricious . . . is but too characteristic of our sex; and there is, perhaps, no animal so much indebted to subordination for its good behaviour as woman."[1] More's disdain was intensified by outrage at Wollstonecraft's sexual freedom and her radicalism, for More was a friend and admirer of Burke, whom Wollstonecraft had attacked.

Nevertheless, More's own outstanding success as a writer and an organizer of Sunday schools must have demonstrated to everyone that women could lead virtuous independent lives and could equal men in efficiency. Moreover, despite her disclaimers, her personal competence and self-esteem produced moderate feminism in her *Strictures on the Modern System of Female Education* (1799). Though she was writing in conscious reaction to Wollstonecraft, she was equally critical of the superficial education that prepared women more to be harem slaves than to be rational wives and mothers, equally insistent that woman's mission on earth is not to please men. Her ideal wife is not radically different from Wollstonecraft's: a man of sense wants to marry "not merely a creature who can paint, and play, and dress, and dance," but "a being who can comfort and counsel him; one who can reason and reflect, and feel, and judge, and discourse, and discriminate; one who can assist him in his affairs, lighten his cares, soothe his sorrows, strengthen his principles, and educate his children." More sounds much like Wollstonecraft when she condemns "baby balls," for which little girls "Instead of bounding with the unrestrained freedom of little wood-nymphs over hill and dale, their cheeks flushed with health and their hearts overflowing with happiness . . . are shut up . . . demurely practising the *pas grave*, and transacting the serious business of acquiring a new step for the evening, with more cost of time and pains than it would have taken them to acquire twenty new ideas."[2]

More said that ladies should be educated to be good daughters, wives, mothers, and mistresses of families; but her insistence on genuine, solid development of the mind clearly went beyond the aim of mere utility to men. Far from being trained to parrot facts and quotations, a girl must read books that "exercise the reasoning faculties, teach the mind to get acquainted with its own nature, and to stir up its own powers," such as Locke's *Essay Concerning Human Understanding*. Such "tough reading" will correct "that spirit of trifling which she naturally contracts from the frivolous turn of female conversation, and the petty nature of female employments." A girl should study history "not merely to store her memory with facts and anecdotes . . . but . . . also to trace effects to their causes, to examine the secret springs of action, and to observe the operation of the passions." Like Wollstonecraft, More deplored the lack of order and precision in women's mental training, which she believed made it difficult for them to reason systematically.[3]

Occasionally, More's speculations on education led her into feminism, despite her vigorous iteration of conventional principles. Thus, a long discussion of the supposedly natural distinctions between the sexes ultimately leads to a radical questioning: "till women shall be more reasonably educated, and till the native growth of their mind shall cease to be stinted and cramped, we have no juster ground for pronouncing that their understanding has already reached its highest attainable perfection, than the Chinese would have for affirming that their women have attained the greatest possible perfection in walking." She went on to commend the "many women nobly rising from under all the pressure of a disadvantageous education and a defective system of society" to exhibit "the most unambiguous marks of a vigorous understanding, a correct judgment."[4]

She condemned as decidedly as Hays or Wollstonecraft men's habit of patronizing women: when Pope compliments women with being "Fine by defect, and delicately weak," is he not holding out "a standard of feebleness... to which vanity will gladly resort, and to which softness and indolence can easily act up, or rather *act down?*" She deplores the tendency of "many men, even of distinguished sense and learning... to consider the society of ladies, rather as a scene in which to rest their understandings, than to exercise them." This encourages ladies "to talk below their natural and acquired powers of mind; considering it as a tacit and welcome flattery to the understanding of men, to renounce the exercise of their own." If men would only keep "up conversation to its proper standard," they "would not only call into exercise the powers of mind which women actually possess; but would even awaken energies which they do not know they possess." Though she does not go so far as to condemn the custom of ladies' withdrawing after dinner, she does deplore men's constant tendency "to postpone every thing like instructive discourse till the ladies are withdrawn." Even when "Strong truths... happen to be addressed" to women, they "are either diluted with flattery, or kept back in part, or softened to their taste." If women ask for information, "they are put off with a compliment, instead of a reason," being "considered as beings who are not expected to see and judge of things as they really exist."[5]

However More objects to women's disputing or showing off their wit, she still wishes to see their conversation "rescued from vapid common places." She would have women live and converse "up to their understandings" and urges them to aspire;

for, even if they do not attain all they wish, yet they will gain something. "The mind, by always applying itself to objects below its level, contracts . . . itself to the size, and lowers itself to the level, of the object . . . while the mind which is active expands and raises itself, grows larger by exercise, abler by diffusion, and richer by communication."[6]

An intelligent husband is, in fact, obligated to improve a "helpless, fretful, and dawdling" wife. He should strive to form her mind and strengthen her character instead of slothfully accepting her as she is. Of course vanity may help out his good-natured indulgence, as "he feels a self-complacency in his patient condescension to her weakness, which tacitly flatters his own strength." He tells himself that women "are all pretty much alike, and that, as a man of sense, he must content himself with what he takes to be the common lot. Whereas, in truth, by his misplaced indulgence, he has rather *made* his lot than *drawn* it."[7] Maria Edgeworth and Jane Austen were to make the same point in fiction. Edgeworth's Vivian (1812) humors or avoids his boring, conventional wife instead of working to broaden her mind, and thereby throws away his opportunity to save his marriage and himself.[8] Mr. Bennet in *Pride and Prejudice* (1813) comes close to ruining his whole family because he sneers at his wife and younger daughters instead of trying to improve them.

Like all eighteenth-century advocates of learning for women, More argued that it improved the character, which cannot be formed just by closing out temptations: "we shall never obtain a fair garden merely by rooting up weeds—we must also plant flowers."[9] Learning does not cause women to neglect their families: "for one literary slattern who now manifests her indifference to her husband by the neglect of her person, there are scores of elegant spendthrifts who ruin theirs by excess of decoration." More exposes, as waspishly as Astell, women who take pleasure in ridiculing intellectually superior members of their sex, "while they exclaim with much affected humility, and much real envy, that 'they are thankful *they* are not geniuses.' Now, though one is glad to hear gratitude expressed on any occasion, yet the want of sense is really no such great mercy to be thankful for." "Vanity," she adds, "is not the monopoly of talents," any more than "humility is the exclusive privilege of dulness."[10]

More was the least feminist of the Bluestockings—partly because of her middle-class social origin and her fervent narrow piety—but in many ways she was typical of their limits as well as their contributions to the improved status of women. They would all have agreed with her dictum that "in this land of civil and religious liberty, where there is as little despotism exercised over the minds as over the persons of women, they have every liberty of choice, and every opportunity of improvement; and how greatly does this increase their obligation to be exemplary in their general conduct."[11] All rejected "Mrs. Wollstonecraft's wild theory concerning the 'Rights of Women,'" all paid scrupulous attention to the moral tendency of their writings (Elizabeth Carter said "she never wrote a line without considering ... whether it could ... by any construction ... be made to have a bad tendency"),[12] and all led lives of irreproachable propriety. Elizabeth Montagu was punctiliously dutiful to her estimable husband, and Elizabeth Carter scrupulously consulted her father on all important questions of propriety (although this deference did not significantly restrain her, for he always left the final decision to her).

In general, the Bluestockings were so fortunately circumstanced that they could live much as they liked. All were financially comfortable. More and Carter remained single, and Montagu married a rich, scholarly man nearly thirty years her senior, who made few demands and was glad to supply money for her lavish entertaining and literary patronage. Even so, she would not consider remarriage after his death; for, "with all due respect to the superior sex, I do not see how they can be necessary to a woman unless she were to defend her lands and tenements by sword or gun," she wrote to Carter. She confided that she was not like a mutual friend whom she ironically described as "the perfection of the female character," one who "could not stir till she received the word of command" and, just like Milton's Eve before the Fall, "would have preferred her husband's discourse to the angel's." Montagu herself and Carter, on the contrary, "should have entered into some metaphysical disquisitions with the angel, we are not so perfectly the rib of man as woman ought to be."[13]

It was this unabashed intellectuality that distinguished the Bluestockings from their predecessors and constituted their contribution to the progress of women. While Lady Mary Wortley Montagu had warned her granddaughter to conceal her learning lest she antagonize the he- and she-fools, the scholar Carter assured Catherine Talbot that there was no "deference due either to the ignorance of trifling heads, or the perverseness of worthless hearts, which will always find something or other to exercise their folly or ill nature about." She has "borne with great tranquillity the scandal of absurdities I never committed, and of nonsense that I never wrote."[14]

Hester Mulso Chapone, in her rather conservative *Letters on the Improvement of the Mind* (1773), argued against the traditional view that "a very young woman can hardly be too silent and reserved in company." Actually, a young girl who speaks "without conceit or affectation" is always "more pleasing than those, who sit like statues." Not only should she "appear to be interested in what is said," but, if she understands the subject well enough, she should "ask now and then a pertinent question" or contribute her own observations.[15] Chapone discerned "some strong sense" in Wollstonecraft's *Vindication*, "amidst many absurdities, improprieties, and odious indelicacies." (Wollstonecraft considered her *Letters* modest and inoffensive, though uninspired.)[16]

The Bluestockings took pride in their published works and rejoiced when other women cast credit on their sex by writing, so long as it was moral. Montagu made a point of reading a laborious tome by a local learned woman because she had "always a love to see Phoebus in petticoats." Talbot wrote that Carter's translation of Epictetus would "do honour to Epictetus, yourself, your country, and womankind"; and Chapone playfully but significantly suggested that the translation would provoke an act of Parliament to banish Carter "this realm, as an invader of the privileges and honours of the lords of the creation, and an occasion of stumbling to women, in the article of acknowledging their superiority."[17]

The voluminous correspondences among these women friends show that they took their reading as seriously as a modern scholar would. Every once in a while it led them to feminist insights, such as Montagu's sympathy for Medea as a learned lady before her time or Talbot's indignation that Thucydides did not mention a single Grecian woman throughout his history, but only quoted Pericles' dictum that women should "keep themselves in quiet, and make themselves as little talked of as possible."[18]

Naturally, these intellectual women resented being looked down upon by men. Carter complained of one who "so far condescended to my capacity, as to talk nothing but nonsense" and indignantly described a party at which, "As if the two sexes had been in a state of war, the gentlemen ranged themselves on one side of the room, where they talked their own talk, and left us poor ladies to twirl our shuttles, and amuse each other, by conversing as we could. By what little I could overhear, our opposites were discoursing on the old English poets, and this subject did not seem so much beyond a female capacity, but that we might have been indulged with a share of it."[19]

The great achievement of the Bluestockings was to establish a mode of social life in which such treatment was not the norm. The Bluestocking parties brought men out of their taverns and coffeehouses, not for cards or flirtation, but for intelligent conversation, and thereby established that women were capable of conversation that men of wit and learning could enjoy. As hostesses, Montagu and Vesey were of course filling women's traditional role; but they transformed it into an intellectually satisfying one. If they had radically questioned women's position in society or had flouted conventional morality, they could not have exerted the influence they did on eminent men.

Besides abstaining from protests against the status quo, the Bluestockings tacitly sacrificed emotional to intellectual emancipation. Having achieved self-respect and independence through suppressing their sexuality (Mrs. Montagu remarked to Miss Carter, "You and I . . . have never been in love"[20]), they prized emotional control as an essential virtue. As they saw it, women could be strong and rational, and therefore equal to men, only through rising above their sexual nature. This was why they turned so savagely on Hester Thrale, one of their number, when she fell helplessly in love with Gabriel Piozzi. Her marriage to this man, who could bring her no social or economic advantages, proved her to be under control of her emotions; and a middle-aged intellectual who behaved in this way was jeopardizing the intellectual respect the Bluestockings had striven so hard to attain. Montagu became almost hysterical over the marriage, which "has taken such horrible possession of my mind I cannot advert to any other subject." It would be easier to bear her friend's death than her falling into "an object of contempt and scorn," she wrote. "I respected Mrs. Thrale, and was proud of the honour she did to the human and female character in fulfilling all the domestick duties and cultivating her mind with whatever might adorn it. I would give much to make everyone think of her as mad . . . if she is not considered in that light she must throw a disgrace upon her sex."[21]

It is obvious that a value system in which women demonstrated their reason by suppressing their passions was very convenient to a patriarchal society. Reason as well as modesty is supposed to dictate to Burney's Camilla that it is not appropriate for a woman to choose her husband; rather, she "should retire to be chosen." Good sense will tell her "that where allowed only a negative choice, it is your own best interest to combat against a positive wish."[22] Edgeworth's Leonora (1805) demonstrates her rational morality by maintaining flawless sweetness and self-control while her beloved husband intrigues with her friend under her roof. Olivia, the false friend, incongruously combines Wollstonecraftian rhetoric with the very faults the feminists traced to the subjection of women: frivolity, dependence on male admiration, and pride in her inability to think precisely or control her emotions.[23] The Bluestockings were all too eager to demonstrate that developing woman's intellect would not jeopardize the status quo. Internalizing male standards, they turned restrictions on women into a source of pride.

Thrale recognized this ambiguity under stress of her passion for Piozzi: "I married the first Time to please my Mother. I must marry the second Time to please my Daughter. I have always sacrificed my own Choice to that of others ... but why? Oh because I am a Woman of superior Understanding, & must not for the World degrade my self from my Situation in Life." But then she looked at the other side: "if I *have* superior Understanding, let me at least make use of it for once; & rise to the Rank of a human Being conscious of its own power to discern Good from Ill—the person who has uniformly acted by the Will of others, has hardly that Dignity to boast."[24]

The Bluestockings' apparent restrictiveness must not, however, be seen as entirely antifeminist. Surely there is something positive in their insistence that women are to be regarded as intellectual beings, as capable as men of strength and self-discipline, and that they owe it to themselves to be virtuous and reasonable. A woman may indeed elope because she has "ceased to respect herself."[25] An Edgeworth or Austen heroine is more free as well as more dignified than an Emma Courtney "enslaved by passion." Many sentimentalists had supported a damaging double standard, which accorded women unlimited indulgence while assuming them to be weak and dependent. By exalting feeling over realism and good sense, they confirmed the stereotype that women are emotional creatures, unable to judge what is important or to face facts. By presenting love as the dominant force in human life, they overemphasized a woman's sexual role and made her helplessly dependent on man. In reaction, women novelists tended to disparage romantic passion in favor of sensitive consideration and rational esteem. Hanway's Ellinor at first rejects the estimable Mr. Howard because she does not feel "that electric fluid that shakes reason on her throne," but in the end she prefers him to the fascinating young lord she has been in love with.[26]

Moreover, the conservatives saw that the radicals' glorification of emotional freedom could imperil women as well as liberate them. For it could lead to relaxation of the moral principles necessary to protect women in a society that deprived them of power. The hero of Mary Robinson's *Walsingham* (1797) tramples upon the rights of several women as he follows his well-intentioned but undisciplined heart. After seducing a worthy young woman by mistake, he refuses to marry her because he loves her as a brother but not as a husband.[27]

Anna Laetitia Aikin Barbauld trenchantly exposed the exploitative attitudes lurking beneath sentimentalism in many novels. In her fifty-volume edition of *The British Novelists; With an Essay; and Prefaces Biographical and Critical* (1810), she deplored the novel's tendency to center on love. She saw as clearly as any modern feminist the patronage and disparagement underlying Fielding's sentimental idealization of women. "Fielding uniformly keeps down the characters of his women, as much as Richardson elevates his. A yielding easiness of disposition is what he seems to lay the greatest stress upon." After pointing out that the Booths' distresses, in *Amelia*, "arise from the vicious indulgencies of the husband, combined with unfortunate circumstances," she remarked: "Amelia is such a wife as most men of that stamp would deem the model of female perfection." She dryly commented that Sophia had not much opportunity for forming that reverence for masculine opinions for which Allworthy commends her, and noted that Fielding "constantly united" learning in women "with something disagreeable." In fact, Mrs. Bennet, a character who had let herself be seduced and becomes a domineering wife, seems to have been introduced into *Amelia* "purely to show the author's dislike to learned women."[28]

Barbauld greatly admired Wollstonecraft's writings, though she was "too correct in [her] conduct to visit her."[29] More conservative women also showed a remarkable sympathy for a person whose life was even more shockingly unconventional than her theories on marriage and feminine behavior. (Wollstonecraft had lived unmarried with Gilbert Imlay and had a child with him; when he left her, she had attempted suicide. Far from being chastened by that experience, she married Godwin belatedly and reluctantly, only to save their coming child from illegitimacy.) Wollstonecraft was vilified by conservative men— Horace Walpole called her a hyena in petticoats, and the Reverend Richard Polwhele said her death in childbed was richly deserved.[30] But women recognized Wollstonecraft's essential purity and uprightness, even when they believed her theories to be dangerous and wrong. This is evident from the sympathetic criticism of her ideas in women's novels, which introduce radical feminist characters who are usually misguided but always virtuous.

It is to be expected that Amelia Opie, a friend of the Godwins, would present the heroine of *Adeline Mowbray*, who was loosely modeled on Mary Wollstonecraft Godwin, as an admirable as well as lovable character. Adeline is destroyed through her own error—her defiance of society and traditional wisdom in refusing to legalize her union with Glenmurray—and ultimately admits she was wrong. But Opie insists on Adeline's pure intentions and constantly shows her goodness, both in the form of general benevolence and of punctilious fulfillment of her duties to her family. So much more does Opie criticize the simpleminded morality of expediency that condemns Adeline than she does the ill-judged idealism that causes her to oppose the law, that one could almost read the book as an indictment of the importance society attaches to marital law.

Even Elizabeth Hamilton's *Memoirs of Modern Philosophers* (1800), a reasoned conservative satire on radicalism which pillories Godwin and Holcroft, treats an idealistic feminist with respect. Her Julia Delmond, who is deluded by their grandiose "philosophical" ideal of general utility, is completely virtuous in intention. Sincerely aspiring to free herself from prejudice and narrow morality, she runs away from her parents because she believes (like Wollstonecraft) that independence is "essential to virtue"; she elopes with a lover because she wants to rise above the "sexual character" that makes chastity all-important in women.[31] Her tragic error results not from vice or weakness, but from her idealistic desire to rise to a higher ideal than domestic duty.

Julia's downfall is attributed to inadequate education resulting from having as a mother an insipidly correct woman who lacked intelligence to teach her the rational religion that would have safeguarded her from the philosophers. In a comic parallel to Julia's case, Bridgetina Botherim's well-intentioned but foolish mother is unable to restrain her daughter's extravagancies.[32]

Bridgetina, who demands that the hero marry her because she needs him to develop her social utility, is a devastating caricature of Mary Hays. But she is neither a genuine feminist nor a demonstration that women cannot be intellectuals. She merely uses feminist theory to advance her own ends; and her conceit, self-indulgence, and foolish ideas are not connected with her sex. She is a ludicrous person rather than a pretentious female.

Burney's *The Wanderer* offers the most striking example of feminism in a highly conservative author. Elinor Joddrel, an enthusiastic advocate of French Revolutionary principles and the equality of women, is a caricature of the candor and independence that Wollstonecraft preached; but she was not meant to be a figure of fun (though, unfortunately, she often is, especially when she pursues the hero in the manner of Emma Courtney pursuing Augustus). Rather, she is supposed to exemplify the tragic misuse of high gifts. She is clearly a superior woman, since most of those around her are petty and mindlessly conventional; and judicious characters constantly assert her nobility of soul. Occasionally, Elinor says something that Burney would probably endorse, as when she protests the imprisonment of women by public opinion: "to escape mockery, we must all be guided one by another; all do, and all say, the very same thing. Yet why? Are we alike in our thoughts?"[33] Burney's journals, which contain several similar protests, reveal that she at least was capable of thinking as an individual.

However Burney disapproved of most of Elinor's opinions, she placed her in a social setting that could not fail to give them an awkward credibility. Burney shows us the inadequacy of ladies' education, the inaccessibility of gainful employment, the predatory attitude of some men and the willful blindness of all to woman's real situation. Society disarmed women of the means to look after themselves, justifying this mutilation by the myth that they could always depend on men. The plot of *The Wanderer* shows—regardless of its factitious happy ending—that women could not rely on men for protection. We are left with the conclusion that their only real security can come from developing the assertiveness and disregard for inhibiting propriety which Elinor advocates. As Wollstonecraft declared that women should not depend on men, Burney implied that they could not.

Maria Edgeworth also created (and gently corrected) an attractive radical feminist in Angelina of *Moral Tales for Young People* (1801).[34] Educated by a radical father but conservative herself, Edgeworth well illustrates the progress women had made by the end of the eighteenth century. By learning from and then working with her father, Richard Edgeworth, she acquired a thorough understanding of education, which she used in bringing up her numerous brothers and sisters and expounded in *Practical Education* (1798), an enlightened book bearing her name and her father's, but written mostly by her.[35] Richard Edgeworth actively encouraged her to enlarge her views and to "read the papers constantly—to keep up the knowledge of all the *real* interests of the world and to exercise the judgment daily upon the great subjects on which the minds of the first people in the country are exercised."[36] Consequently, her novels capably present a wider world than that of traditional ladies' fiction. Yet, though she publicly demonstrated woman's intellectual capability and defended it in her educational works, she accepted the established social order and maintained a rigorous position on sexual morality. One of her characters is supposed to be justified in saying that "no man of sense would venture to marry the daughter of a divorcée."[37] She shared the conservatives' distrust of theory, making one of her spokesmen say, "I am more intent upon [women's] happiness than ambitious to enter into a metaphysical discussion of their rights."[38]

The first section of Maria Edgeworth's first signed work, *Letters for Literary Ladies* (1795), refutes the usual arguments against educating girls: that women are intrinsically inferior and those few who have any mental distinction are unhealthy, that failure to imbue girls with salutary prejudices renders their chastity vulnerable, that public appearance in print would jeopardize their weak fortitude and delicate reputations, and that no one would marry a literary lady because men prefer in women "a certain degree of weakness, both of mind and body."

An enlightened father, based on Richard Edgeworth, rejoins that educated women are less tenacious of their will than ignorant ones, since "People, who have reasons for their preferences and aversions, are never so zealous in the support of their own tastes, as those who have no arguments either to convince themselves or others that they are in the right." It is repressive upbringing that causes women to identify pleasure "with the mere exercise of free-will"; by never tyrannizing his daughter, he hopes to "prevent her acquiring any unconquerable prejudice in favour of her own wishes, or any unreasonable desire to influence the wishes of others." Rational conviction of the utility of preserving chastity and managing their families conscientiously is a more secure foundation than mere automatic habit. Finally, intelligent men want a wife "who can sympathize in all their thoughts and feelings; who can converse with them as equals, live with them as friends; who can assist them in the important and delightful duty of educating their children; who can make their family their most agreeable society"—and this cannot be achieved without an education sufficiently solid to "give her the habit of industry and attention, the love of knowledge and the power of reasoning."[39]

The next section of Edgeworth's book, "Letters of Julia and Caroline," was "intended to expose the absurd notion, that the sole object of a woman's life is to please, and to point out the ruinous consequences of despising reason, and indulging a morbid sensibility."[40] It narrates the disastrous career of Julia, a young woman who rejects rational analysis and confuses benevolent impulses with virtue: "I profess only to *feel*." "What has woman to do with philosophy?" she asks; "a woman's part in life is to please," which she can do better without "grave sense, and solid merit." Since our *"amiable defects* win more than our noblest virtues," let us "content ourselves to gain in love what we lose in esteem."[41] Caroline's sensible arguments have no effect on Julia, who marries the wrong man, elopes with a lover, and dies of remorse.

Practical Education shows even more clearly the Edgeworths' single standard for excellence in men and women, as they simply assume that teaching methods and aims are the same for a child of either sex. Curiosity and activity are always to be encouraged; every child is to understand how a steam engine works and "to examine carefully before he admits any thing to be a fact, or any assertion to be true." Maria specifically notes that "The masculine pronoun *he*, has been used [throughout our discussion] for grammatical convenience, not at all because we agree with the prejudiced, and uncourteous grammarian, who asserts 'that the masculine is the more worthy gender.' "[42]

She explicitly denies that superficial or imprecise knowledge is becoming to women. A girl with a smattering of every subject is "in danger of becoming ridiculous, and insupportably tiresome to men of sense and science. But let a woman know any one thing completely, and she will have sufficient understanding to learn more, and to apply what she has been taught so as to interest men of generosity and genius in her favor."[43] Edgeworth's expectation that men would be happy to instruct women shows the progress both sexes had made.

Solid intellectual training will make women useful wives and entertaining companions to men, but will also give them independent worth. On the other hand, the traditional training in accomplishments can aim only at pleasing men and therefore reveals "a degrading anxiety to attract worthless admiration." This in turn encourages "every young man, who has any pretensions to birth, fortune, or fashion" to "consider himself as the arbiter of their fate, and the despotic judge of their merit." Cultivation and enlargement of women's understandings will do more for them than "all that modern gallantry or ancient chivalry could devise in favour of the sex."[44]

On the other hand, since Maria Edgeworth does not question that a woman's primary function is to be a chaste and dutiful wife, she argues that girls must be trained to be more cautious than boys, since "They cannot rectify the material mistakes in their conduct" and are more constrained to adapt themselves to things as they are. Similarly, command of temper is more important in girls than in boys, because their amiability and influence, and therefore their happiness, depend upon gentleness and good humor. Still, she gives this compliance a self-respecting turn; for she does not mean "that women should yield their better judgment to their fathers or husbands; but, without using any of that debasing cunning which Rousseau recommends, they may support the cause of reason with all the graces of female gentleness."[45] She wishes to educate women so that they may be happy within the constraints that society will impose upon them. She does not consider the possibility that these constraints might be removed.

The same conservatism governed the presentation of women in her novels, stiffened by the conventional restrictions on the eighteenth-century heroine. Edgeworth did not modify the heroine, even though (like several predecessors) she recognized her dullness, even to admitting "the cold tameness of that stock or stone" her own Belinda (1801).[46] Her heroines remain rational, self-controlled, strong, and uninteresting, as they admirably fulfill a lady's traditional role. Belinda is distinguished by invariably right conduct and a creative tact that always tells her how to reconcile people—admirable qualities, indeed, but not what can hold our interest in her as a breathing, thinking person. Madame de Fleury (1812) is resolute enough to deal with a broken arm until the doctor comes and capable enough to organize an excellent school for poor children, but would never meddle with politics, "in which no amiable or sensible woman would wish to interfere."[47] Caroline Percy of Patronage (1814) shows her superior intellect by valuing everything correctly, for example by distinguishing between the attentiveness of courtship and that of simple courtesy and esteem.

Still, these characters are noticeably rational. Caroline declares that she would rather convince her father than persuade him.[48] All Edgeworth's heroines are happily free of weak sensibility. The character in Belinda who faints with emotion when she meets her long-lost father, as Burney's Evelina did, is not the heroine but the conspicuously simpleminded Virginia, and her reaction is shown to be faintly ridiculous.[49]

Like her predecessors, Edgeworth satirizes those who encourage weakness as a becoming womanly attribute. A nearly successful suitor of Belinda's, Vincent, is punished for his conceited patronage of women, his preference for passive Creoles over useful English ladies, and his thought "that if Belinda had more faults she would be more amiable."[50] The scheming mother of Manoeuvring (1809) is rightly foiled when she tries to alienate her son from one young woman by leading her into rational argument and to ingratiate another with him by urging her to simper "that she thought a woman who really loved *any body* was always of that person's opinion."[51] Unthinking virtue is made to appear stupid and repulsive in Lady Glistonbury of *Vivian*, who, classing any attempt to educate women with the radical philosophy she abhors, has brought up her daughter Lady Sarah "in all the ignorance and all the rigidity of the most obsolete of the old school ... with virtue, stiff, dogmatical, and repulsive; with religion, gloomy and puritanical; with manners, cold and automatic."[52] Lady Glistonbury's propriety has made a stick of her older daughter and a rebel of her younger, and has hopelessly antagonized her husband.

The novels of Jane Austen obviously benefited from the feminine awareness developed by earlier women writers. Like them, she focused on an intelligent young woman, through whose eyes she presented women, men, and the world. She took pleasure in deflating masculine complacency, as when she commented on Henry Tilney's pleasure in Catherine's unformed taste: "though, to the larger and more trifling part of the [male] sex, imbecility in females is a great enhancement of their personal charms, there is a portion of them too reasonable and too well informed themselves, to desire anything more in a woman than ignorance."[53] Austen wickedly exposed the enforced triviality of ladies' social lives by describing in detail the pointless visits in which the intelligent Dashwood ladies (of *Sense and Sensibility*, 1811) must take part. She recognized the mortifying dependency of woman's position, remarking in one story that Emma Watson's conceited sister-in-law "could not but feel how much better it was to be the daughter of a gentleman of property in Croydon, than the niece of an old woman who threw herself away on an Irish captain."[54]

The opening of *Mansfield Park* (1814) makes the same point, as it defines three sisters in terms of the men they have married—even more tellingly, in terms of the men's incomes. Austen presented the familiar theme of women's economic plight with brilliant ruthless realism, as she demonstrated that women were practically forced to marry and yet were hobbled in their opportunities to get a husband. Though she pilloried the mercenary, mechanistic view voiced by Mrs. Bennet (*Pride and Prejudice*, 1813), who assumes that marriage (to anyone) is the primary aim of a woman's existence, she recognized that not everyone was in a position to be fastidious. Elizabeth Watson has "not much" inclination for matrimony, "but my father cannot provide for us, and it is very bad to grow old and be poor and laughed at." Her younger and more fortunate sister Emma is shocked at the idea of pursuing "a man merely for the sake of situation"; but Elizabeth answers: "I should not like marrying a disagreeable man any more than yourself,—but I do not think there *are* very many disagreeable men;—I think I could like any good humoured man with a comfortable income."[55]

Women had to marry because they were not only disabled from supporting themselves but often deprived of their fair share of inherited wealth. The entail in *Pride and Prejudice*, which takes their rightful inheritance from Elizabeth and her sisters to bestow it on Mr. Collins, neatly symbolizes the inequity of a system that deprived of money those very people who could not be expected to make it for themselves. In *Sense and Sensibility* the property that should rightly go to Mrs. Dashwood and her daughters is irresponsibly willed to a male child who does not need it, and his father salves his conscience with the thought that women do not need money as men do. Somehow they are to support themselves by properly managing their income, but, as Emma Watson tells a complacent lord who urges her to buy a horse, "Female economy will do a great deal ... but it cannot turn a small income into a large one."[56]

Yet, despite her awareness of women's disadvantages and women's intelligence, Austen rejected systematic feminism. Although we see the unfairness of the entail on the Bennet estate, Elizabeth accepts it; it is her foolish mother who keeps protesting against it and the stupid autocrat Lady Catherine who voices disapproval of "entailing estates from the female line." The only Austen character to stand up for women is the obtuse and aggressive Mrs. Elton in *Emma* (1816).[57] Her intelligent women never discuss ethics or politics, and she makes no distinction between genuine learning and fashionable accomplishments. Mary, the most intellectual of the Bennet sisters, has studied only to compensate for her plainness, while Elizabeth, the most intelligent of the five, eagerly disclaims a serious interest in books. Though Austen recognized that ladies may be subject to boredom, she evidently expected them to spend their days in "work" (that is, useless sewing) and courtesy calls. Realizing the bleak situation of a Charlotte Lucas, forced to accept Mr. Collins as her "pleasantest preservative from want,"[58] she did not suggest any better solution.

Austen's ideal marriages are those in which husband and wife gracefully fill their traditional roles. All her heroines but Anne Elliot marry men who are decidedly their superiors in age, experience, and wisdom, who will obviously guide them after marriage. Even independent Elizabeth Bennet acknowledges that the sense of humor she will bring Darcy is less valuable than the judgment he will bring her, and her father tells her she "could be neither happy nor respectable, unless you truly esteemed your husband," by which he means "unless you looked up to him as a superior."[59] Of course Austen did not believe, any more than other intelligent conservative women of her time, that wives should be passive or blindly worshipful. A woman should be able to exert an improving influence on her husband. As a more intelligent Mrs. Bennet could have developed her husband's responsibility to his family, "a woman of real understanding" might have made something more than an easygoing sportsman of Charles Musgrove; she "might have given more consequence to his character, and more usefulness, rationality, and elegance to his habits and pursuits."[60]

Austen's insistence that her heroines learn self-discipline, humility, duty to others, and sober acceptance of reality[61] is not antifeminist, though it is opposed to the radicals' claims for freedom, self-fulfillment, and enlarged aspirations for women. For it was not based on a double standard, but on her rational estimate of the self-control necessary to all people living in society; it is clearly applied to men as well as women. With the usual feminine stress on the small virtues that are more important in daily living than heroic ones, Austen insisted on consideration and adaptability in both sexes. She condemned arrogant disregard of other people's feelings whether it appeared in Marianne Dashwood or Fitzwilliam Darcy. As masculine virtue should include self-control, feminine virtue should include rationality: Mary Musgrove's ceaseless selfish complaints proceed from her incapacity to view a situation objectively; and Lydia Bennet's elopement, from her empty-headed superficiality. Increased knowledge has the natural effect of making Kitty Bennet "less irritable," as well as "less ignorant, and less insipid."[62]

Although Austen's view of the position of women was less advanced than those of many predecessors, her superior artistry made her fiction more convincing, in terms of asserting female worth as well as of presenting life. Her insights are incorporated into the total structure of her novels, and her plots are realistic rather than tritely romantic. This effect is overt in *Northanger Abbey*, where Catherine Morland's melodramatic illusions about General Tilney, derived from her gothic reading, reflect the reality of his arbitrary power in her patriarchal society.[63]

More important, Austen transformed the insipidly perfect heroine of the earlier women novelists into a real woman who could function as a convincing model and spokesperson for her sex. While quite as virtuous as their predecessors, her heroines all have enough imperfections to make them lifelike and interesting. Elizabeth Bennet, like Burney's Evelina, makes embarrassing errors of judgment and suffers from vulgar relatives. But Elizabeth's liabilities are part of her: she misjudges because she is too proud of her discernment; and she has grown up in the Bennet family. Evelina, on the other hand, errs solely through inexperience with the situations into which she is forced, and she is practically dissociated from her vulgar grandmother and cousins, since she has just met them. Unlike most of her predecessors, Austen endowed her heroines with unconventional assertiveness and spirit, rather than isolating these qualities in disapproved characters such as Burney's Mrs. Arlbery (though she followed the old pattern with Fanny Price and Mary Crawford).

All Austen's heroines—even self-effacing Fanny Price—are assertive and passionate enough to recognize their love for men who are not yet official suitors. Catherine is unabashedly interested in Tilney from the first time they meet; he becomes serious about her only in response to her obvious partiality. Austen points out that Catherine would have been blamed for indelicacy by many moralists, who pronounced "that no young lady can be justified in falling in love before the gentleman's love is declared."[64] Even so sensible an authority as Edgeworth could present as ideal the incredibly unfeeling passivity of Caroline, heroine of *Patronage,* who responds to her sister's suggestion that a certain man loves her: "I cannot forget that the delicacy, honour, pride, prudence of our sex, forbid a woman to think of any man, as a lover, till he gives her reason to believe that he feels love for her." For a woman's love "should *not unsought be won*"; in other words, she must not love spontaneously, but only in response to a man. Thus, in the name of delicacy and proper pride, women were to be denied even the freedom to wish in the most important decision of their lives. Caroline goes on to reveal that her principle rests on a belief in woman's weakness: she fears that, if she allows herself to love a man who does not love her, she will sink into "an object of pity and contempt, the victim, the slave of an unhappy passion."[65]

How different is Elizabeth Bennet, who actively forms opinions and retains her independence of male approval, although she needs a good marriage as much as any other young lady of small income. She laughs at Darcy's original slight to her attractiveness and does not grasp at him even when he has cleared his character; acknowledging his general superiority and grateful for his continued attention, she still pauses to consider whether she would be happy with him. After she knows she loves him, but fears he may abandon her because Lydia has disgraced the family, she does not droop but thinks: "If he is satisfied with only regretting me, when he might have obtained my affections and hand, I shall soon cease to regret him at all."[66] Contrast this sturdy confidence with Caroline's assumption that a woman once in love is not capable of controlling her feelings.

Even Austen's later heroines who lack Elizabeth's wit and spirit express woman's point of view more effectively than the heroines of earlier female novelists, simply because they are more solidly imagined. Anne Elliot of *Persuasion* is a model of feminine propriety, always doing what she ought and never making claims on anyone. She has accepted her adopted mother's prudential advice against marrying the man she loves and does not resent it even though she now faces a single life of dreary dependency. But Anne is by no means a cypher. Although she keeps her opinions to herself, she is quite capable of forming them. She has become mentally independent of her adopted mother, even though that is the only older person she can look up to. She would like to respect her father and sisters, but recognizes that she has no relatives "which a man of sense could value." She is quietly disgusted when they toady to aristocratic connections, for she has the sense to see that good company consists of "clever, well-informed people, who have a great deal of conversation."[67]

By focusing on Anne's consciousness, Austen forces us to feel her as a person rather than a convenience. However gracefully Anne may resign herself, we are made aware that she does not enjoy being never considered and always made use of, and that no one should be taken for granted in this way, not even a dependent single woman. We learn that one of the burdens of a single woman's life is its uselessness: made to feel useless at home, Anne is happy to go to a married sister who needs her; and once there, she greatly prefers making herself genuinely useful by nursing a sick child to merely listening to her sister's chronic complaints. Without directly protesting society's attitude toward women like Anne, Austen shows its unfairness, simply by making the reader thoroughly aware of her mind and feelings.

The articulate women discussed in this chapter, personally fortunate and identified with the upper classes, felt that they had gained a great deal—and they had, in terms of the share they could expect in men's intellectual life and the respect they could claim from men as husbands or friends. Recognizing that their position rested on men's good will—and not envisioning any possibility of changing this situation—they feared to jeopardize their improved position and that of their sex. Moreover, as conservatives, they distrusted theory: as they saw it, the radicals were imperiling the real progress and security women enjoyed by their demands for abstract rights of no practical consequence. The conservatives failed to see that oppression of woman could not be eliminated without recognition of her equality and her rights.

It is obvious that these women were far from feminists in the modern image. Some of them explicitly defended the patriarchal status quo, allowing feminist protests to slip out only in unguarded moments. None of them competed professionally with men, for even those who did not confine themselves to intellectual entertaining and dilettante writing stayed within the pale of acceptable feminine pursuits: writing of novels or educational works for Austen, Edgeworth, and Hamilton; philanthropy and writing of conventional moral treatises for More. They gained intellectual freedom by sacrificing their emotional lives, whether they remained single or made a loveless marriage as Montagu did. All were careful to avoid radical opinions— none questioned that women belonged in private life, that they should not concern themselves with politics, that there could be no excuse for a lapse from chastity. But the respectability thus insured by limited claims may have been more useful to the cause of women than more liberated views, especially after the conservative reaction of the later 1790s had discredited all radicalism. People like Montagu and More, Edgeworth and Austen, had to be respected both as virtuous ladies and as strong, rational human beings.

NOTES

1. Letter to Horace Walpole, quoted in Eleanor Flexner, *Mary Wollstonecraft* (Baltimore: Penguin Books, 1973), pp. 164-65.
2. Hannah More, *Strictures on the Modern System of Female Education* (New York: Garland, 1974), I, 86-87, 98.
3. *Ibid.*, I, 98, 161, 164, 166-67, 175-76, 198-99; II, 63. Cf. Mary Wollstonecraft, *A Vindication of the Rights of Woman*, ed. Carol Poston (New York: W. W. Norton, 1975), p. 22.
4. More, *Strictures*, II, 28-29.
5. *Ibid.*, II, 42-43, 45-46, 129.
6. *Ibid.*, II, 47, 52-53.
7. *Ibid.*, II, 127-28. Cf. Elizabeth Montagu: "Sure the men are very imprudent to endeavour to make fools of those to

whom they so much trust their honour and happiness and fortune, but it is in the nature of mankind to hazard their peace to secure power, and they know fools make the best slaves," in *Elizabeth Montagu, the Queen of the Blue-Stockings: Her Correspondence from 1720 to 1761*, ed. Emily Climenson (New York: Dutton, 1906), I, 155.

8. Maria Edgeworth, *Vivian*, in *Tales and Novels* (New York: AMS Press, 1967), V, 406. The whole novel shows Vivian repeatedly destroying himself by throwing away the support he could have had from women of stronger principles than his own.

9. Hannah More, *Essays*, in *The Complete Works* (New York: Harper, 1835), II, 339.

10. More, *Strictures*, II, 70-72, 150-51. Cf. Wollstonecraft, *Vindication*, pp. 169-70. Of course More's work also includes much restrictive antifeminism, resulting in part from her excessive and simplistic religiosity. When she exhorts ladies to exert their proper influence in society, all she means is that they should support the status quo and discountenance adultery. (A virtuous woman should pity a remorseful adulteress, but see to it that she remains remorseful by preventing her reentry into society.) Propriety "is the first, the second, the third requisite to a woman," without which no qualities are amiable (*Strictures*, I, 6). More greatly admired Milton's characterization of Eve, which Wollstonecraft had found so demeaning, and dismissed the rights of woman as an even more absurd concept than the rights of man (I, 7; II, 135). She constantly insisted that woman has a character distinct from man's and a divinely limited role to fulfill (II, 20-22). It should be noted, however, that radical writers such as Mary Hays also devoted more attention to moral than intellectual education. See, e.g., Hays's summary of what education should produce in women, in *An Appeal to the Men of Great Britain in Behalf of Women* (New York: Garland, 1974), p. 252.

11. More, *Essays, Works*, II, 339.

12. *Memoirs of the Life of Mrs. Elizabeth Carter, with . . . Poems . . . [and] Essays*, ed. Montagu Pennington (London: F. C. and J. Rivington, 1808), I, 236, 447-48.

13. *Mrs. Montagu, "Queen of the Blues": Her Letters and Friendships from 1762 to 1800*, ed. Reginald Blunt (Boston: Houghton Mifflin, 1923), II, 119-20. Although Montagu's marriage was generally happy, her husband did occasionally exert an arbitrary authority which she resented, though she complained only privately to her sister: "Do you not ad-

mire these lovers of liberty! What do the generality of men mean by a love of liberty but the liberty to be saucy to their superiors, and arrogant to their inferiors, to resist the power of others over them, and to exert their power over others. I am not sure that Cato did not kick his wife" (*ibid.*, I, 264-66).

14. *A Series of Letters Between Mrs. Elizabeth Carter and Miss Catherine Talbot ... 1741 to 1770*, ed. Montagu Pennington (London: F. C. and J. Rivington, 1819), I, 157. Cf. More, *Essays, Works*, II, 343-44.

15. Hester Mulso Chapone, *The Works* (Boston: Wells and Wait, 1809), III, 131. Chapone's view of the scope and purpose of women's learning was unusually wide: "Whatever tends to embellish your fancy, to enlighten your understanding, and furnish you with ideas to reflect upon when alone, or to converse upon in company, is certainly well worth your acquisition" (III, 139).

16. Chapone, *Works*, II, 162; Wollstonecraft, *Vindication*, p. 105.

17. *Elizabeth Montagu*, ed. Climenson, I, 172-73; *Memoirs ... of Mrs. Carter*, I, 187; Chapone, *Works*, I, 83. Carter was delighted to discover that a highly acclaimed volume of plays was by a woman, Joanna Baillie (*Memoirs ... of Mrs. Carter*, I, 443); and Montagu proudly tells how she and Carter amazed the librarian at a Jesuits' college by asking "for Greek manuscripts for the amusement of Mrs. Carter" (*Mrs. Montagu*, ed. Blunt, I, 48).

18. *Mrs. Montagu*, ed. Blunt, II, 68; *Letters between Carter and Talbot*, I, 71. The reference to Pericles is found in Thucydides, *The History of the Peloponnesian War*, trans. Rex Warner (Harmondsworth: Penguin Books, 1954), p. 122.

19. *Letters between ... Carter and ... Talbot*, I, 101; *Letters of Mrs. Elizabeth Carter, to Mrs. Montagu*, ed. Montagu Pennington (London: F. C. and J. Rivington, 1817), III, 68. The Burneys, conventional as they were, expressed their resentment of male patronizing: see, e.g., *The Early Diary of Frances Burney: 1768-1778*, ed. Annie Raine Ellis (London: George Bell, 1907), I, 227, 301.

20. *Mrs. Montagu*, ed. Blunt, I, 2.

21. *Ibid.*, II, 274-75. Chapone agreed that "it has given great occasion to the Enemy to blaspheme and to triumph over the Bas Bleu Ladies"; see James L. Clifford, *Hester Lynch Piozzi (Mrs. Thrale)* (Oxford: Clarendon, 1952), pp. 230-31. The same drama was replayed, with a little less horror and indignation, when Burney married for love ten years later.

22. Frances Burney d'Arblay, *Camilla, or A Picture of Youth*, ed. Edward and Lillian Bloom (London: Oxford University Press, 1972), pp. 358-59.

23. Edgeworth, *Leonora*, in *Tales and Novels*, VIII, 243, 294, 320.

24. *Thraliana: The Diary of Mrs. Hester Lynch Thrale (Later Mrs. Piozzi) 1776-1809*, ed. Katharine C. Balderston (Oxford: Clarendon, 1951), pp. 544-45. When still married to Henry Thrale, she had remarked complacently, "tho *I* never was troubled with the Tender passion . . . there *is* such a Thing as violent Love I suppose . . . tho I should fancy not once for 5000, or even 500,000 Times it is imagined by People who wish for the praise of Sensibility" (*ibid.*, p. 110).

25. Elizabeth Hamilton, *The Cottagers of Glenburnie* (New York: Garland, 1974), p. 310.

26. Mary Ann Hanway, *Ellinor, or The World as It Is* (New York: Garland, 1974), III, 11-12. Cf. Jane Austen, *Pride and Prejudice* (New York: New American Library, 1961), p. 233. Even sentimental Mary Hays had pointed out that overemphasis on love can be an oppressive force on women, since they are brought up to believe it is more important than anything else (*Appeal*, pp. 133-35).

27. *Walsingham* does show some evidence of the radicals' feminist concerns, as it attacks society's persecution of unchaste women and indicts fashionable education for girls. Presumably, the worthless Bristol school attended by Isabella is modeled on the esteemed establishment of the More sisters, which Robinson attended: Isabella "had read authors, whose works she did not comprehend; prattled a foreign jargon, without knowing the meaning of the words she uttered; finished needle-work which in half a century would only adorn the lumber-room . . . and learnt, by ear, a few old lessons on the harpsichord, so little graced by science and so methodically dull, that they would scarcely have served as an opiate to a country 'squire, after the voluntary toil of a fox chase. For this lingering death of every mental blossom, Isabella's conscientious governess had received a considerable annual sum"; see Mary Robinson, *Walsingham* (New York: Garland, 1974), I, 230-31.

28. Anna Laetitia Barbauld, ed., *The British Novelists; with An Essay; and Prefaces Biographical and Critical* (London: F. C. and J. Rivington, 1810), I, 52 ff.; XVIII, xxv, xxviii, xxx. Cf. Elizabeth Inchbald's acid commentary on Edward Moore's *The Gamester*, a more egregious example of sentimental exploitation of women, in her *British Theatre; or, A Collection of Plays . . . with Biographical and Critical Remarks*.

For other women's negative reactions to Amelia, see Patricia M. Spacks, *Imagining a Self: Autobiography and Novel in Eighteenth Century England* (Cambridge: Harvard University Press, 1976), p. 280. I have followed Hannah More in classifying Barbauld with the Bluestockings ("Sensibility"), though Richard Polwhele execrated her among the radicals in his *The Unsex'd Females*. While she did sympathize with the French Revolution in its initial stages, she was suspicious of radical theorizing and opposed rights for women. See Barbauld's poem on the subject, in her *Works*, ed. Lucy Aikin (London: Longman, 1825), I, 185-87. The relative positions of these women are indicated by a letter Barbauld wrote to Maria Edgeworth, advising against a ladies' periodical: "Mrs. Hannah More would not write along with you or me, and we should probably hesitate at joining Miss Hays, or if she were living Mrs. Godwin." See Betsy Rodgers, *Georgian Chronicle: Mrs. Barbauld and Her Family* (London: Methuen, 1958), p. 133.

29. Quoted in Rodgers, *Georgian Chronicle*, p. 189. The poet Anna Seward, no radical, called the *Vindication* a "wonderful book. . . . Though the ideas of absolute equality in the sexes are carried too far," for they contradict St. Paul; yet "It applies the spear of Ithuriel" to the systems of "the sophist Rousseau, or the plausible Gregory." Quoted in Ralph M. Wardle, *Mary Wollstonecraft* (Lawrence: University of Kansas Press, 1951), pp. 158-59.

30. *Letters of Horace Walpole*, ed. Mrs. Paget Toynbee (Oxford, 1905), XV, 337-38; Richard Polwhele, *The Unsex'd Females* (New York: Garland, 1974), pp. 29-30.

31. Elizabeth Hamilton, *Memoirs of Modern Philosophers* (New York: Garland, 1974), III, 310-11.

32. Hamilton comments: ". . . surely the man does great injustice to his children, who gives them a mother so weak, or so ignorant, as to render her despicable in their eyes; not that to a well-regulated mind the weakness of a parent will ever be made the obstacle [sic] of contempt; but how should the children of a fool come by the information necessary to point out the line of duty?" (*Memoirs*, III, 52-53). Hamilton praised the *Vindication*, though she believed Wollstonecraft's zeal carried her into "expressions which have raised a prejudice against the whole. To superficial readers it appears to be her intention to unsex women entirely" (I, 196).

33. Frances Burney d'Arblay, *The Wanderer; or, Female Difficulties* (London: Longman, Hurst, 1814), III, 37. Elinor is

commended by both the hero (e.g., I, 376-77) and the heroine (e.g., V, 209).

34. Angelina has resolved "to *act* and *think* upon every occasion for myself; though I am well aware that they who start out of the common track ... are exposed to the ridicule and persecution of illiberal minds." She flies to join a female soul mate who extols "shackle-scorning Reason" and exclaims, "Oppressed, degraded, enslaved—must our unfortunate sex for ever submit to sacrifice their rights, their pleasures, their *will* at the altar of public opinion"; see Maria Edgeworth, *Moral Tales for Young People* (New York: Garland, 1974), II, 155. Though Angelina is comically disillusioned, she is presented as mentally and morally superior; only empty-headed ladies of fashion laugh at her.

35. Maria Edgeworth and Richard Lovell Edgeworth, *Practical Education* (New York: Garland, 1974).

36. Maria Edgeworth, letter of 1819, quoted by Marilyn Butler, *Maria Edgeworth: A Literary Biography* (Oxford: Clarendon, 1972), p. 303.

37. Maria Edgeworth, *Patronage*, in *Tales and Novels*, VII, 53. Similarly, the right-minded hero of *The Absentee* (1812) will not propose to Grace Nugent, although he loves her, until he is assured that her mother was indeed married to her father. Almost all the women novelists went to great lengths to make their heroines legitimate, however mysterious the circumstances of their birth. This attitude reflects actuality, for Lord Mulgrave said in the House of Lords in 1800 that "bastardy if of little comparative consequence to the male children," but of great consequence to females because it impairs their chances in marriage. See Lawrence Stone, *The Family, Sex and Marriage In England 1500-1800* (New York: Harper & Row, 1977), p. 534.

38. Maria Edgeworth, *Letters for Literary Ladies* (New York: Garland, 1974), pp. 45-46.

39. *Ibid.*, pp. 34, 54-55, 62, 72-74.

40. Anonymous reviewer in the *Analytical Review*, XXIII (May, 1796), 527.

41. "Letters of Julia and Caroline," *Letters for Literary Ladies*, pp. 3, 8, 9.

42. Edgeworth and Edgeworth, *Practical Education*, pp. 552, 676. All quoted passages are Maria's.

43. *Ibid.*, p. 515.

44. *Ibid.*, pp. 534, 549-50.

45. *Ibid.*, pp. 167, 699.

46. Quoted in Bridget G. MacCarthy, *The Female Pen* (Cork:

Cork University Press, 1947), II, 226. She contrasted her own heroines unfavorably with Inchbald's tragically imperfect Miss Milner: "I was not either in Belinda or Leonora sufficiently aware that the *goodness* of a heroine interests only in proportion to the perils and trials to which it is exposed"; quoted by Anna Letitia Le Breton, *Memoir of Mrs. Barbauld* (London: George Bell, 1874), p. 137.

47. Maria Edgeworth, *Madame de Fleury*, in *Tales and Novels*, VI, 292. Edgeworth evidently changed her opinion in the late 1820s and 1830s, when she started writing letters on specifically political or economic themes. And a lady in *Helen* (1834) tells the heroine: "the position of women in society, is somewhat different from what it was a hundred years ago, or . . . sixty, or . . . thirty years since. Women are now so highly cultivated, and political subjects are at present of so much importance . . . to all human creatures who live together in society, you can hardly expect . . . that you, as a rational being, can go through the world . . . without forming any opinion on points of public importance. You cannot satisfy yourself with the common namby-pamby little missy phrase, 'ladies have nothing to do with politics'" (quoted in Butler, *Maria Edgeworth*, p. 451).

48. Edgeworth, *Tales and Novels*, VII, 160-61. Cf. More's reproof to young ladies who prefer pretty rhetoric to reason (*Strictures*, II, 61-62).

49. *Ibid.*, III, 400.

50. *Ibid.*, III, 414.

51. Edgeworth, *Tales of Fashionable Life*, in *Tales and Novels*, V, 68.

52. *Ibid.*, V, 333.

53. Jane Austen, *Northanger Abbey*, in *Complete Novels* (New York: Random House, n.d.), p. 1124.

54. Jane Austen, "The Watsons," in *Lady Susan, The Watsons, Sanditon*, ed. Margaret Drabble (Harmondsworth: Penguin Books, 1974), p. 139.

55. *Ibid.*, pp. 109-10.

56. *Ibid.*, p. 136.

57. Nina Auerbach, *Communities of Women: An Idea in Fiction* (Cambridge: Harvard University Press, 1978), p. 51; Jane Austen, *Emma* (New York: Bantam Books, 1958), p. 217.

58. Austen, *Pride and Prejudice*, p. 107.

59. *Ibid.*, pp. 316-17.

60. Jane Austen, *Persuasion* (New York: W. W. Norton, 1958), p. 43. While Austen sympathizes with Mr. Bennet, she

shows that he is responsible for the irritations he suffers from having married a fool. She criticizes Captains Benwick and Wentworth in *Persuasion* for proposing to mediocre Louisa Musgrove when they had known intellectually superior women.

61. Developed in Marilyn Butler, *Jane Austen and the War of Ideas* (Oxford: Clarendon, 1975).

62. Austen, *Pride and Prejudice*, p. 324.

63. Sandra M. Gilbert and Susan Gubar, *The Madwoman in the Attic: The Woman Writer and the Nineteenth-Century Literary Imagination* (New Haven: Yale University Press, 1979), pp. 135-36.

64. Austen, *Northanger Abbey*, in *Complete Novels*, p. 1073. She is paraphrasing Richardson's dictum in *The Rambler*, No. 97.

65. Edgeworth, *Patronage*, in *Tales and Novels*, VII, 214-16.

66. Austen, *Pride and Prejudice*, pp. 222, 303. Far from being educated to suit whatever man might come along to propose for her, as Camilla's wise father assumed was necessary (Burney, *Camilla*, pp. 357-58), an Austen heroine develops herself and accepts the man if he suits her: most obvious in the case of Elizabeth Bennet, this is also implied in those of Elinor Dashwood, Emma Woodhouse, Anne Elliot, and even Fanny Price. Cf. Lloyd W. Brown, "Jane Austen and the Feminist Tradition," *Nineteenth Century Fiction*, 28 (1973), 338.

67. Austen, *Persuasion*, pp. 150, 251. Austen's only approaches to feminist social criticism are her defense of women's novels in *Northanger Abbey* (pp. 1077-78, 1085) and Anne Elliot's argument that women are more constant than men (*Persuasion*, pp. 232-35). What is most remarkable there is that Anne rejects the sentimental explanation that women have finer natures in favor of the realistic one that their feelings prey upon them because they must do without the distractions available to men. On this point, Austen agreed with Wollstonecraft (*Vindication*, p. 31) and disagreed with Hays (*The Love-Letters of Mary Hays*, ed. A. F. Wedd [London: Methuen, 1925], p. 29).

༚ᢏᡂᢌ CONCLUSION ᢏᢀᢌ

By the later eighteenth century, there were many articulate women in England who felt free to publish their views. Though deprived of formal education, they acquired impressive knowledge through tutoring, conversation, and independent reading. In certain distinguished circles, they were accepted as intellectuals in conversation, though not outside the private social sphere. Every one of these women was a feminist to the extent of challenging the inherited assumptions of her patriarchal society—whether, like Wollstonecraft, she publicly attacked the double sexual standard or, like Burney, she ridiculed in her diary men's patronizing chivalry toward "fair females."[1] The very fact that they had mental training, encouragement to think for themselves, and sufficient confidence to express their thoughts caused women to question conventional views of their nature and role.

Obviously, none of these women—including the radicals—was a feminist in the contemporary image. Social conditions and assumptions were too different from those of today. Of these, the most pervasively inhibiting was the exaggerated emphasis on chastity in women. Even Wollstonecraft's Maria is not justified in leaving her husband until he actually tries to sell her to another man, not justified in considering adultery until he actually imprisons her in a madhouse. Moreover, even such moderate sexual liberalism was not useful to the feminist cause, be-

cause it disproportionately shocked women who might otherwise have listened sympathetically.

Going back to the earliest moral codes, this insistence on
female chastity was enforced by religion, ethics, custom, and
economics in a society that still depended upon inheritance
through the male line. Thus even so humane and reasonable a
man as Samuel Johnson could argue that an adulterous wife
should be outlawed from society because she might endanger
legitimate inheritance. Making a woman's entire moral status
and fate depend upon her observance of a single law severely
restricted her possibilities for self-determination. A momentary
yielding to passion or pressure, or even violation against her
will, could blast a woman's character, force her into an odious
marriage, or deprive her of the opportunity for a satisfying
one.

Thus women were pressured into timid caution as the only
way to avoid a fatal misstep. No error a man could commit was
so irrevocable: he could pay his creditors after a bankruptcy or
wipe out cowardice with a heroic act, but nothing could remove a stain from a woman's chastity. Richardson's Clarissa
shows how little intelligence and integrity could avail against a
pressure that caused her loss of virginity to so debase her in
society's eyes and her own that her life became unbearable.
That unchastity was considered merely venial in men reinforced a moral double standard that made it harder to argue for
any form of equality between the sexes.

Chastity was so vital that its appearance had to be as
scrupulously preserved as its reality. The resulting concern for
reputation further inhibited women by making them dependent
upon the opinions of others, however narrow these might be.
Experience had to be avoided if it might in someone's eyes
jeopardize chastity; any enterprise or profession was condemned
if it could plausibly be called immodest. A comic exchange in
Elizabeth Hamilton's *Memoirs of Modern Philosophers*, a conservative but not benighted book, illustrates the significance of
the dread of losing reputation. When Bridgetina, the ludicrous
radical, exclaims, "What so much as the dread of censure has
cramped the energy of the female mind," a sensible young man

replies: "I never knew anyone that began in despising the censures of the world, that did not conclude in deserving them."[2] With the penalties for losing reputation so severe, most women chose to preserve it by restricting themselves.

Mary Wortley Montagu came to recognize and resent the effects of men's overemphasis on women's chastity, as she protested against "that tyrannical Sex, who with absurd cruelty first put the invaluable deposite of their precious honor in our hands, and then oblige us to prove a negative for the preservation of it." Therefore, "I hate Mankind with all the fury of an old maid (indeed most women of my age do), and have no real esteem but for those heroines who give them as good as they bring."[3] Because men regarded unchastity in their women as a reflection upon their own honor, they felt entitled to restrict their wives and daughters. And making the major law for women a negative one created inner inhibitions by causing women to think about avoiding blame rather than achieving excellence: not doing wrong became the standard, rather than doing right or cultivating positive virtues. Frances Reynolds, Sir Joshua's sister, an intellectual as well as a professional portrait painter, wrote in her "Essay on Taste": "Perhaps the most perfect feminine mind habitually aims at nothing higher than exemption from blame."[4]

This negative ideal was reinforced by the ambiguity built into the word *modesty*, which expanded from a means to safeguard chastity to become an ideal in itself. For, besides having a sexual meaning, modesty implies self-effacement, at least in women. David Hume, discussing ancient Greek society, assumed a natural connection between imposing "the strictest laws of modesty and decency" on women and excluding them from social and political life.[5] Steele defined modesty in women as "a certain agreeable fear" in all they enter upon, while "in men, it is composed of a right judgment of what is proper to attempt." Only in man is it a weakness "if it suppresses his virtue and hides it from the world."[6] Wollstonecraft made a clear distinction between modesty as chastity and modesty as self-effacement,[7] but most women were intimidated by the possibility that any attempt at self-fulfillment or public recognition could be suspected of the immodesty that savored of unchastity. Any assertiveness in women, including that necessary for achievement and independence, might be associated with unchastity, the one vice that was universally condemned out of hand.

Knowledge itself was suspect in women, perhaps because of the association of intellectual with sexual knowledge which goes back to the Biblical doctrine of the Fall. Pointing out that among the ancient Greeks only courtesans were educated, Hannah More darkly implied a causal connection and went on to warn "the Christian female, whatever her talents," to "renounce the desire of any celebrity when attached to impurity of character."[8] Even the relatively liberal Richard Edgeworth made the same association when he cautioned Anna Barbauld: "As your sex becomes more civilized every day, it is necessary that they should become more circumspect in conversation and in all the paraphernalia of modesty. A married lady in France is allowed one lover, she is pardon'd for two."[9] The example of French women, who were more free than English to display their talents, to engage in political or religious controversy, and to have extramarital affairs, suggested to many English observers that all three activities were equally dangerous. What most eighteenth-century writers vaguely feared was stated explicitly in France, by Donatien-Alphonse-François, the Marquis de Sade. In de Sade's *Philosophy in the Bedroom* (1795), Eugénie de Mistival simultaneously learns the falsity of conventional morality and the joys of unrestrained sexual activity.

Even those who did not distrust knowledge *per se* were apt to suspect a connection of sensibility and imagination with sexual passion. All, of course, spring from the unconscious mind, which cannot be controlled by propriety and good sense. Accordingly, women felt that imagination and emotional warmth, two potential liberating forces, should be repressed like guilty passion. In *Memoirs of Modern Philosophers*, the heroine's wise aunt warns her against imagination, lest it delude her reason to make her yield to passions she could otherwise easily resist.[10] When Burney's Evelina is warned not to let her imagination run away with her, the warning is provoked not by any evidence of imagination, but by her sexual attraction to a man who does not seem about to propose marriage. In the same way, Camilla's uncontrollable imagination must be a euphemism for the warm feelings which might lead her into sexual impropriety.[11]

The association of imaginative freedom with sexual indulgence made it harder for women writers to free themselves from the bad reputation of the early female professionals—so much so that even the witty intellectual Elizabeth Montagu wrote that "the generality of women who have excelled in wit have failed in chastity; perhaps it inspires too much confidence in the possessor, and raises an inclination in the men towards them without inspiring an esteem so that they are more attacked and less guarded than other women."[12] No wonder, then, that women felt guilty about expressing themselves and went out of their way to assure the world of their personal modesty and the unexceptionable propriety of their works. It is only to be expected that a shy woman like Burney would be genuinely distressed to be recognized as the author of *Evelina* and that all women would impose rigorous morality on their heroines (and thus offer restrictive role models to their readers). Although some women struggled to free themselves, they still had to contend with an ideology that censored every independent thought, every imaginative flight, every spontaneous feeling, that declared a woman was safe only when acting, thinking, and feeling in rigid observance of convention.

It is not surprising, then, that both fact and fiction show women to be more inhibited than men, and that it was men more than women who helped women toward freedom and self-development. Hester Thrale's mother exhorted her to respond to her husband's neglect by sinking herself in her children; it took Johnson to tell her that she could not hope to hold her husband's interest unless she developed her mind.[13] Few women who achieved had strong, beloved mothers. For, generally speaking, such mothers would restrict their daughters by imposing a conventional ego ideal upon them. It was usually fathers who developed their daughters' minds, either through active teaching or indulgence. This is probably why the radical Hays draws a surprisingly glowing picture of the relationship between father and daughter.[14] The writer who had the most liberating influence on women was Samuel Richardson, who not only set the example for a novel that would express women's insights and values, but in *Clarissa* at least presented more feminist views than any female follower was prepared to advance. (*Sir Charles Grandison*, written under female influence, centers on a dominant male and is much less feminist.) Female authority figures in women's fiction are generally negative, revealing the authors' observation that women used power to inhibit women or their self-destructive belief that women's power had better be inhibited lest it be abused. Sheridan's Mrs. Bidulph destroys her daughter's chance for happiness and fulfillment by imposing narrow conventional morality upon her. Jane Austen's mothers and mother-surrogates are at best misguided, like Lady Russell in *Persuasion*; at worst, foolish and tyrannical, like Mrs. Bennet and Lady Catherine de Bourgh.[15] Burney has only praise for the conventionally virtuous mother of her Camilla, but the picture she draws of her influence is bone-chilling, as Camilla reflects that her mother's unfailing kindness to her from childhood on "seemed to say, Camilla, be blameless—or you break your Mother's heart!"[16]

Several other traditional assumptions, almost as deep-rooted as the insistence on female chastity, were necessarily opposed to the idea of sexual equality. Without being explicitly antifeminist, many people assumed that a system of subordination was essential to produce peace and order, and therefore happiness, in any social group, from the nation to the family. This system included men along with women—tenants, employees, sons, as well as wives and daughters. The son of poor parents was as restricted as a woman, though in different ways; and both were expected to be satisfied with their lot. Richardson's paragon Sir Charles Grandison is as submissive to his unworthy father as Clarissa is to hers—although of course he is not required to make anything like the same sacrifices. Still fixed in a clearly defined class structure, the eighteenth century saw in graceful submission in certain relationships a fitness and beauty not visible to us today. Women were particularly drawn to this view because, being placed in subordinate positions, they needed, as J. M. S.

Tompkins has written, "to idealize submission to preserve their self-respect.... The submission is generous... not the collapse of the weak... but the abnegation of the strong.... Such submission was not a degradation, but a spiritual grace."[17] Of course the rationalization that made their oppression easier to bear simultaneously made it harder to reject.

Thus Hannah More was expressing conservatism more than antifeminism when she wrote: "The more a woman's understanding is improved, the more obviously she will discern that there can be no happiness in any society where there is a perpetual struggle for power."[18] Sharing the same assumption, Elizabeth Carter argued that a family has greater potentiality for harmony than a purely voluntary society since, "In family connections... all goes quietly on, from that subordination by which most points are regulated and determined."[19] If it is once granted that either husband or wife must rule the family, the grounds of argument shift from female equality to female dominance. This was harder to justify and, indeed, could be reasonably contested on the grounds that women's relative lack of education and experience made them less qualified to rule than men.

The same conservatism led people to doubt that the social order could be changed. Therefore, it was surely more kind, as well as more realistic, to prepare women for the position they were destined to occupy. Again, the motive was not antifeminist, though the effect might seem so. When More argues that girls should not be accustomed to being the center of attention and should learn "to expect and to endure opposition," it is not to disparage and humiliate them, but to prepare them for "a lesson with which the world will not fail to furnish them." For most women it must have been the sober truth that happiness depended on acquiring "a submissive temper and a forbearing spirit."[20] The more liberal Maria Edgeworth, who agreed that girls needed to learn more control of temper than boys, made a similar point when she argued that women's happiness, meaning their contented adjustment to their inevitable place in society, was more important than their abstract rights.

Here the conservatives differed from radical writers, who believed that social institutions could and should be reformed:

subordination by birth was not necessary for social harmony; inheritance of property need not be safeguarded, because it was unjust in the first place; and marriage could be questioned because it was neither sacred as a religious ordinance nor essential to preserve decency in sexual relationships. Rejecting conservative assumptions about woman's role in society, they were more free to reject the inhibiting "sexual character" that prescribed to women a self-effacing modesty, meek passivity, and anxious concern for others' opinions which would all effectively prevent their achievement outside the home, or self-assertion within it.

Even the radicals, however, remained too bound by social assumptions to envision a convincing liberated female character. The only social change they developed in detail was reform of education for girls—and here many conservatives agreed with them. The radicals more explicitly traced the weaknesses of contemporary women to poor education and disparaging social attitudes, but this awareness was increasing among all people who thought about women. Like their contemporaries, the radicals assumed that woman's primary role is in the family, and they saw paid employment mainly as the means to avoid degrading dependence on men. Wollstonecraft based her arguments in the *Vindication* on fitting women to be good mothers. It is significant, however, that she emphasized motherhood over wifehood, reflecting the increasing concern for children characteristic of the later eighteenth century. For she used this concern to emphasize women's contribution to society as opposed to their ministrations to one of its members. She redefined woman's domestic role to make her a useful member of society rather than a dependent on a man who keeps her as an ornament, a housekeeper, or a comfort to himself. As a citizen, woman is equivalent to man; as a wife, she is an adjunct to him.

This redefinition is only one example of the ways in which eighteenth-century women, feminists declared or undeclared, anticipated the concerns of contemporary feminism. Like women today, they objected to being treated as sexual objects or servants and insisted that they had the same mental qualities, aspirations, and needs that men do. They protested against being trivialized—whether this meant patronage by men or pressure to waste their lives in pointless needlework or empty formal visits. They questioned men's unfavorable assumptions about women's capacity to reason or endure, seeing that these might be based on nothing more than a need to rationalize their subjection. (Mary Wortley Montagu whimsically claimed that, in "a Common-wealth of rational Horses . . . it would be an establish'd maxim . . . that a mare could not be taught to pace.") They recognized the humiliations of dependency, though most accepted it in a loving marriage. Then as now, some feminists asserted the importance of traditionally feminine values, such as personal emotion, sensibility, and spontaneity, while others preferred to emphasize woman's equal claims to qualities shared with men. Both views opened vistas, neither insured enlightened feminism—but alike they challenged a patriarchal order in which woman's passivity and subjection is justified by man's law.

NOTES

1. Frances Burney d'Arblay, *Diary and Letters of Madame d'Arblay*, ed. Charlotte Barrett (London: Swan Sonnenschein, 1893), I, 202-4.
2. Elizabeth Hamilton, *Memoirs of Modern Philosophers* (New York: Garland, 1974), II, 218-19.
3. Quoted in Patricia M. Spacks, *The Female Imagination* (New York: Knopf, 1975), pp. 295-96.
4. Quoted in *Bluestocking Letters*, ed. R. Brimley Johnson (London: John Lane, 1926), p. 8.
5. David Hume, "A Dialogue," in *The Philosophical Works*, ed. Thomas Hill Green and Thomas Hodge Grose (Darmstadt: Scientia Verlag Aalen, 1964), IV, 301.
6. Richard Steele, *The Tatler*, No. 52.
7. Mary Wollstonecraft, *A Vindication of the Rights of Woman*, ed. Carol Poston (New York: W. W. Norton, 1975), pp. 121-25.
8. Hannah More, *Strictures on the Modern System of Female Education* (New York: Garland, 1974), I, 74-75.
9. Anna Letitia Le Breton, *Memoir of Mrs. Barbauld* (London: George Bell, 1874), p. 94.
10. Hamilton, *Modern Philosophers*, II, 125-26.
11. Frances Burney, *Evelina: or The History of a Young Lady's Entrance into the World* (New York: W. W. Norton, 1965),

p. 290; *Camilla, or A Picture of Youth,* ed. Edward and Lillian Bloom (London: Oxford University Press, 1972), p. 84. Patricia Spacks points out that Burney connects "sexual passion, the unconscious mind, the imagination" by calling Cecilia's heart the seat of her imagination; see "Ev'ry Woman is at Heart a Rake," *Eighteenth-Century Studies,* VIII (Fall, 1974), pp. 41-42. Cf. Charlotte Smith's more favorable association of romantic imagination with generous imprudence and warm feelings in *The Young Philosopher:* "if affection for merit, if admiration of talents, if the attachments of friendship are romantic; if it be romantic to dare to have an opinion of one's own, and not to follow one formal tract, whether wrong or right, pleasant or irksome, because our grandmothers and aunts have followed it before; if not to be romantic one must go through the world with prudery, carefully settling our blinkers at every step ...if a woman, because she is a woman, must resign all pretensions to being a *reasoning* being... oh! may my Medora still be the child of nature and simplicity, still venture to express all she feels, even at the risk of being called a strange romantic girl"; *Young Philosopher* (London: T. Cadell, 1798), II, 14-15.

12. Quoted in Laetitia Pilkington, *Memoirs,* ed. Iris Barry (New York: Dodd, Mead, 1928), p. 472.

13. *Thraliana: The Diary of Mrs. Hester Lynch Thrale (Later Mrs. Piozzi) 1776-1809,* ed. Katharine C. Balderston (Oxford: Clarendon, 1951), p. 309.

14. Mary Hays, *An Appeal to the Men of Great Britain in Behalf of Women* (New York: Garland, 1974), p. 260. In *Philosophy in the Bedroom,* de Sade shows Eugénie's hatred (justified, in his view) for her conventionally virtuous mother.

15. Nina Auerbach, *Communities of Women: An Idea in Fiction* (Cambridge: Harvard University Press, 1978), pp. 50-51. Auerbach further points out that Lady Catherine bases her claim to social distinction on the female line; Elizabeth, on the male.

16. Frances Burney d'Arblay, *Camilla,* p. 866.

17. J. M. S. Tompkins, *The Popular Novel in England 1770-1800* (Lincoln: University of Nebraska Press, 1961), pp. 86-88.

18. More, *Strictures,* II, 14.

19. *Letters of Mrs. Elizabeth Carter to Mrs. Montagu,* ed. Montagu Pennington (London: F. C. and J. Rivington, 1817), II, 16.

20. More, *Strictures,* I, 142-43.

❧❧ APPENDIX ❧❧

Women Writers in Britain, 1660–1800

This appendix is designed to indicate the scope of women's achievement as writers from 1660 to 1800 and the factors that may have encouraged or inhibited their achievement: socio-economic background (as indicated by father's occupation), relationship with parents, education, political and religious beliefs, means of support, literary friendships, and family circumstances. Many sketches are necessarily incomplete, since only partial information is available. All of these women produced at least one significant work after 1660 and before 1800. I have included all authors mentioned in the text, as well as other significant ones, omitting those of whom nothing is known but a name and a list of works, on the grounds that such listings add nothing to our understanding of the situation of the woman writer. I have aimed at wide representation rather than completeness, but I have tried to include all the women whose lives or works remain of particular interest today.

AIKIN, ANNA LAETITIA. *See* Barbauld, Anna Laetitia Aikin

ANSPACH, ELIZABETH BERKLEY CRAVEN, MARGRAVINE OF
   Elizabeth Berkley (1750-1828), daughter of the Earl of Berkley and a mother who (she said) disliked her, married William Craven (1767), who became the Earl of Craven. They had six children. Her comedy *The Miniature Picture* was produced at Drury Lane (1780), but lasted only a few days. At this time the Cravens were still affectionate, but, after affairs on both sides, they separated (1783). She traveled through Europe and became the mistress of the Margrave of Anspach, whom she married on Craven's death (1791). At his Court, and after the two moved to England, she wrote and performed in many plays, which were

privately produced and not printed. She published a travel book, *A Journey Through the Crimea to Constantinople* (1789), and her *Memoirs* (1826).

D'ARBLAY, FRANCES BURNEY

Frances Burney (1752-1840), daughter of a fashionable musician and member of Johnson's circle, had practically no systematic education. But she was part of a close group of sisters and brothers (her mother had died young), and the most eminent Londoners of the day regularly visited her home. She developed her talent by writing voluminous and delightful journal-letters to her intimates, a practice she continued all her life. *Evelina* (1778), published with elaborate secrecy, quickly made her a celebrity in the society of Johnson and the Bluestockings. Her next work, the comedy "The Witlings," she suppressed as imprudent. Though her second novel, *Cecilia* (1782), was successful, it did not provide financial security, so at her father's urging she became Second Keeper of the Robes to Queen Charlotte, a post she resigned after five miserable years. In 1793 she married a French émigré, Alexandre d'Arblay; they were very happy together and had one son. *Camilla* (1796), published by subscription, earned her £2000. Her last novel, *The Wanderer* (1814), was published after the family had spent many years in France.

ASTELL, MARY

Mary Astell (1666-1731), from a middle-class provincial family, was probably educated by a clergyman uncle. Moving to London at the age of twenty, she became a good friend of aristocrats such as Lady Mary Wortley Montagu and Lady Elizabeth Hastings, who contributed to her support; for she did not write for money. Astell had a distinguished career in controversial writing, ranging from scholarly works such as *Letters Concerning the Love of God* (1695) to polemical ones such as *A Fair Way with the Dissenters* (1704), but always defending the established order in Church and State. Many clergymen respected her intellect and valued her contributions in support of the Church of England. Her two feminist treatises, *A Serious Proposal to the Ladies* (1694; Part II, 1697) and *Some Reflections upon Marriage Occasioned by the Duke and Duchess of Mazarine's Case* (1700), were popular enough to go through several editions.

AUBIN, PENELOPE

Penelope Aubin, a married woman, began writing seriously about 1720, though not, she claimed, "for bread." A Roman Catholic, she made a point of sympathetically presenting Catholic clergy and religious experience. She wrote romantic novellas, such as *The Life of Madame de Beaumont* (1721), *The Strange Adventures of the Count de Vinevil* (1721), and *The Life and Adventures of the Lady Lucy* (1726). She also gave public speeches, which people paid to hear.

AUSTEN, JANE
Jane Austen (1775-1817), daughter of a prosperous country clergyman, was part of a large, close-knit, clever family. She lived among them all her life, generally in villages, country towns, and the city of Bath. She attended boarding school for a year or two, voraciously read popular fiction, and wrote brilliant burlesques of it in her teens to amuse her family, who remained an appreciative audience for all her works in progress. Her father recognized her gifts, encouraged her to write, and made the initial overtures to publishers. She began to write seriously in the 1790s, but because of her own diffidence and rewriting, as well as publishers' delays, her novels were published much later: *Sense and Sensibility* (1811), *Pride and Prejudice* (1813), *Mansfield Park* (1814), *Emma* (1816), *Northanger Abbey* and *Persuasion* (1818). She published all her books anonymously and did not wish to be recognized as an author outside her own family.

BAILLIE, JOANNA
Joanna Baillie (1762-1851), daughter of a distinguished Scottish clergyman, lived with her family all her life. She was educated at school, where she showed aptitude for acting and improvisation of dialogue. Her *Fugitive Verses* (1790) were well received, as were her anonymously published *Plays on the Passions* (First Series, 1798), which included *De Monfort*, a tragedy on hatred. John Kemble produced this at Drury Lane, with, however, only moderate success (1800). Baillie went on to publish more *Plays on the Passions*, as well as other plays—a total of twenty-six, of which only five were produced. She was a good friend of Barbauld and Scott.

BAILLIE, LADY GRIZEL (OR GRISELL) HUME
Grizel Hume (1665-1746), daughter of an aristocratic family of Scottish Covenanters, adventurously shielded her relatives from government persecution in her youth. She married George Baillie (1692), had three children, and spent the next forty years running a large estate. She wrote much prose and verse, but her only surviving song is "Werena my heart licht I wad die" (published in Allan Ramsay's *Tea Table Miscellany*, 1724).

BARBAULD, ANNA LAETITIA AIKIN
Anna Laetitia Aikin (1743-1825) managed to persuade her

father, a clergyman and schoolmaster, to teach her Latin and a little Greek. Though her conventional mother discouraged her, she absorbed an education from her father's colleagues at the excellent Dissenting academy at Warrington. Her brother John, three years younger, recognized her ability and encouraged her to publish her poems (1773), which were very successful; then he got her to collaborate with him on *Miscellaneous Pieces, in Prose* (1773). The next year she married Rochemont Barbauld, a Dissenting clergyman. They had no children, although they adopted her nephew. She significantly helped her husband run a boarding school for boys, but she declined an opportunity to found a school for young ladies. Rochemont Barbauld gradually became insane, and she was finally forced to separate from him. She published very popular books for children, works of religious and political controversy (on the liberal side), and editions of several eighteenth-century authors with critical prefaces, of which the most interesting is her *British Novelists* (1810). She knew Johnson and the Bluestockings, Priestley, Edgeworth, Joanna Baillie, Scott, and Wordsworth.

BARBER, MARY

Mary —— *(1690?-1757)* married Barber, a wool clothier, and helped him significantly in his business in Dublin. They had several children, including two sons who attained success in art and medicine. She began writing poetry to enliven her children's lessons. A poem she wrote to help a poor widow (c. 1724) brought her to the attention of Swift, who became her good friend. He invited her to the Deanery, where she acquired the name "Sapphira" and her poems were read and corrected; he introduced her to his friends in England and Ireland and helped her get subscriptions for her *Poems*; when she fell into poverty, he gave her the manuscript of his *Polite Conversation* to sell for her own benefit. She, in turn, conveyed some of his dangerous writings to English publishers, for which she was on one occasion imprisoned. Her *Poems on Several Occasions* was published in 1734, with new editions in 1735 and 1736; and a selection was included in *Poems by Eminent Ladies* (1755).

BARKER, JANE

Jane Barker (1660-?), born into a Roman Catholic Royalist family, was educated by a clergyman. She wrote for a rural literary circle modeled on that of Katherine Philips, adopted the pen name "Galesia," corresponded in poetry with several gentlemen, and published the results as *Poetical Recreations* (1688). She had a small inherited income, probably enjoyed the patronage of a neighboring noblewoman, and presumably earned something from her short novels: *Love Intrigues; or, The History of the Amours of Bosvil and Galesia* (1713), *Exilius* (1715), *A Patch-Work Screen for the Ladies* (1723), and *The Lining for the Patch-Work Screen* (1726).

BARNARD, LADY ANNE LINDSAY

Anne Lindsay (1750-1825), a Scottish earl's daughter, knew the leading intellectuals of Edinburgh in her youth and Burke, Sheridan, and the Prince of Wales in later life. She married Andrew Barnard (1793) and, when he was appointed colonial secretary, moved with him to the Cape of Good Hope, where she wrote "Journals and Notes," illustrated with sketches. They had no children. She composed a sentimental ballad "Auld Robin Gray" (1772), which was immensely popular; but she revealed her authorship only shortly before her death.

BEHN, APHRA JOHNSON (?)

Aphra Johnson (?) (1640-89), possibly an illegitimate child of the noble Willoughby family, lived in Surinam for a few years in her youth and on her return married a merchant named Behn (1664?), who died in 1665(?). She went to Antwerp as a spy during the Dutch War (1666), and on returning to London became a professional writer. She wrote eighteen plays, chiefly comedies, which were successful and often expressed her Tory sympathies. After the success of *The Rover* (1677), she published its second part with her name. Other noteworthy plays were *The Dutch Lover* (1677, produced 1673), with a vigorous feminist preface, and *Sir Patient Fancy* (1678). She also wrote romantic novellas, of which the best is *Oroonoko* (1688), one of the first treatments of black slavery in English. She was a friend of Dryden, Otway, Southerne, and Ravenscroft, and had a long unhappy affair with the cold bisexual John Hoyle. Despite her success as a playwright, she died poor.

BENNETT, AGNES MARIA

Agnes Maria Bennett (died 1808) was a married woman with many children. Her novels, most of which were extremely popular, include *Anna, or The Memoirs of a Welch Heiress* (1785; dedicated with permission to the Princess Royal, it sold out on the day of publication and was twice translated into French), *Juvenile Indiscretions* (1788), *Agnes de Courci* (1789), *Ellen, Countess of Castle Howel* (1794), *The Beggar Girl and Her Benefactors* (1797), *De Valcourt* (1800), *Vicissitudes Abroad, or The Ghost of my Father* (1806, all 2000 copies sold on publication day). Nevertheless, in the Apology to *Ellen*, the first novel published with her name, she complained of "the greatest Distress, both of Mind and Circumstances."

BONHOTE, ELIZABETH

Elizabeth —— *(1744-1818)* married Daniel Bonhote, a solicitor, and had several children. She published *The Parental Monitor* (moral essays, 1788), a poem (1810), and five novels, which were moderately well received: *Rambles of Mr. Frankley, by His Sister* (1773), *Olivia, or The Deserted Bride* (1787), *Darnley Vale, or Emelia Fitzroy* (1789), *Ellen Woodley* (1790), and *Bungay Castle* (1797).

BROOKE, CHARLOTTE

Charlotte Brooke (died 1793), daughter of the author Henry Brooke in his old age, was well educated by him in literature, art, and music; she also studied the Irish language. She devoted herself to her father until his death in 1783. Losing her money when her cousin failed in business, she turned to writing to support herself. She published by profitable subscription *Reliques of Irish Poetry; consisting of heroic poems, odes, elegies and songs, translated into English verse, with notes explanatory and historical, and the originals in the Irish character* (1789), which include an original "Irish Tale" and "Thoughts on Irish Song." She also published the *School for Christians* (1791), dialogues for the use of children, and a successful subscription edition of some of her father's works (1792).

BROOKE, FRANCES MOORE

Frances Moore (1724-89), a clergyman's daughter, married a prosperous clergyman, John Brooke (c. 1756), whom she accompanied to Quebec when he was appointed chaplain to the garrison. They had one son. She published a periodical, *The Old Maid*, which ran for thirty-seven weeks in 1755-56; translations of French sentimental fiction; three novels, *Lady Julia Mandeville* (1763, published anonymously and very successful), *The History of Emily Montague* (1769, published with her name), and *The Excursion* (1777); two undistinguished but extremely successful musical comedies, *Rosina* (1783) and *Marian* (1788); and a moderately successful tragedy, *The Siege of Sinope* (1781). She knew Johnson, Boswell, More, and Burney.

BURNEY, FRANCES. *See* d'Arblay, Frances Burney

CARTER, ELIZABETH

Elizabeth Carter (1717-1806) was the daughter of a learned clergyman who educated all his children; her mother died when she was ten. Elizabeth learned Latin, Greek, Hebrew, and French from her father and taught herself Italian, Spanish, German, and a little Portuguese and Arabic. She habitually read and wrote from eight to twelve hours a day. Edward Cave, a friend of her father, published a small collection of her poems (1738). Through him she met Johnson, who became a lifelong friend. After publishing translations from French and Italian, she translated Epictetus, at the urging of her friends and with the constant encouragement of Bishop Secker; this translation is still standard. Published by subscription (1758), it brought her almost £1000. She also published her poems (1762), which went through four editions, and contributed two essays to *The Rambler* (1750, 1751). She lived with her father in Deal, but spent much time in London, where she was a prominent member of the Bluestocking coterie and a close friend of Elizabeth Montagu. She was supported comfortably first by her father and then by the proceeds of her own writings, supplemented by annuities from wealthy friends.

CELLIER, ELIZABETH DORMER

Elizabeth Dormer married Peter Cellier, a Frenchman, and became a noted midwife in London. She converted to Roman Catholicism and helped imprisoned victims of the alleged Popish Plot, as a result of which she herself was accused of complicity in a treasonable plot. She was tried, but was acquitted when she convinced the court that her accuser was too infamous for his testimony to be accepted. However, passages in her vindication of herself, *Malice Defeated; or A Brief Relation, of the Accusation and Deliverance of Elizabeth Cellier*, describing the treatment of prisoners in Newgate, exposed her to a trial for libel (1680); this time she was condemned to pay a fine of £1000 and stand three times in the pillory. Considering the problem of establishing professional standards for midwives, she addressed to King James II *A Scheme for the Foundation of a Royal Hospital, and Raising a Revenue of 5,000£ or 6,000£ a Year by and for the Maintenance of a Corporation of Skilful Midwives, and Such Foundlings or Exposed Children as Shall Be Admitted Therein* (1687), in which she argued that midwives were capable of organizing and licensing themselves without male supervision. She defended her views in *To Dr. —— An Answer to his Queries Concerning the Colledg of Midwives* (1688).

CENTLIVRE, SUSANNAH FREEMAN (?)

Susannah Freeman (?) (1669-1723) was orphaned at twelve

and fled to London. After an affair followed by two marriages that soon ended in widowhood, she became an indifferent actress and a very successful author. However, her most successful play, *The Busy Body* (1709), almost failed on the first night because many people stayed away on hearing it was a woman's work. Accordingly, she published many of her works anonymously. Of her nineteen plays, the comedies *The Busy Body*, *The Wonder* (1714), and *A Bold Stroke for a Wife* (1718) are the best. She married Joseph Centlivre (1707), principal cook to Anne and George I, who had fallen in love with her after seeing her act at Windsor. She propagandized for the Whigs and the House of Hanover, and was a friend of Farquhar, Rowe, and Steele.

CHALLINOR, HANNAH WOOLLEY

Hannah ——— *(born c. 1623),* whose parents died when she was young, worked as a schoolmistress and governess, and became adept in needlework, medicine, cooking, and household management. At the age of twenty-four she married Woolley, a schoolmaster. After his death she married Francis Challinor (1666). She wrote five successful books on housewifery, primarily cooking. In the last, *The Gentlewoman's Companion* (1673), she advocated intellectual development for women.

CHANDLER, MARY

Mary Chandler (1687-1745), daughter of a dissenting minister, suffered from a crooked spine. She set up a millinery shop in Bath c. 1705 and spent her leisure time reading poetry and writing rhyming riddles and poems to her friends. She was a friend of Mary Barber and Elizabeth Rowe and enjoyed the patronage of the neighboring gentry. After her volume of poems, *A Description of Bath* (c. 1733; other poems were added in later editions) went into its sixth edition (1744), she retired from business. Her poems went into an eighth edition in 1767.

CHAPONE, HESTER MULSO

Hester Mulso (1727-1801), a precocious child, was discouraged by her mother, who, however, died young, and left Hester to take over the management of her father's household and to educate herself. She was a good friend of Richardson, with whom she argued in letters over the limits of filial and marital obedience, and she also knew Carter and Johnson. She made minor contributions to Johnson's periodicals. Her happy marriage to the lawyer Chapone (1760), who died ten months later, left her with a modest but sufficient income, though no children. Her

Letters on the Improvement of the Mind (1774), written for her niece and published anonymously, were extremely successful.

CHARKE, CHARLOTTE CIBBER

Charlotte Cibber (?-1760), daughter of the actor, author, and Drury Lane manager Colley Cibber, spent two years at boarding school. She showed troublesome eccentricity from youth, particularly in masquerading as a man. She married Charke, a violinist at Drury Lane (probably 1729) and had one daughter; but the marriage soon failed. Deserted by her husband and eventually cast off by her father, she struggled to survive as an actress; she had a few successes, notably as Macheath, but then sank to the lowest level of strolling player. Her farce *The Art of Management; or, Tragedy Expell'd* was produced with some success and printed (1735). *A Narrative of the Life of Mrs. Charlotte Charke* (1755) and *The History of Henry Dumont, Esq.; and Miss Charlotte Evelyn . . . with Some Critical Remarks on Comic Actors* (1756), written in a desperate effort to make money, had some success as scandal, but yielded little profit to their author.

CHUDLEIGH, LADY MARY LEE

Mary Lee (1656-1710) acquired some education, but lamented its limitations. She married Sir George Chudleigh (c. 1685) and had three children. Unhappy in her marriage, she found consolation in study and lived a life of retirement. In two feminist pamphlets, *The Female Preacher* (1699?) and *The Ladies' Defence* (1701), she refuted a misogynistic marriage sermon. Her *Poems on Several Occasions* (1703) and *Essays upon Several Subjects in Prose and Verse* (1710) were published with her name. She was strongly religious and royalist.

CLIVE, CATHERINE RAFTOR

Catherine Raftor (1711-85), daughter of an Irish lawyer of good family, had little education. She went on the stage at seventeen and soon became an outstanding comic actress. She married George Clive, a barrister, but they soon separated by mutual consent, though her character remained unblemished. She wrote a pamphlet, *The Case of Mrs. Clive, Submitted to the Public* (1744), and four dramatic sketches: *The Rehearsal, or Bayes in Petticoats* (1753), *Every Woman in Her Humour* (1760), *Sketch of a Fine Lady's Return from a Rout* (1763), and *The Faithful Irish Woman* (1765).

COCKBURN, ALICIA (OR ALISON) RUTHERFORD

Alicia Rutherford (1712?-94) wrote poems all her life, but only a few were published, of which the best known was "I've see the smiling of Fortune beguiling" (1765). She married Patrick Cockburn, an advocate (1731), and had one son. Her salon in Edinburgh was frequented by Hume and other celebrities, and she was a friend of Scott.

COCKBURN, CATHERINE TROTTER

Catherine Trotter (1679-1749), daughter of a naval captain, wrote five plays before she was twenty-seven, including Agnes de Castro (1695), The Fatal Friendship (1698), and Revolutions of Sweden (1706). All were produced and published. She supported Manley's play The Royal Mischief (1696) with verses lauding her as the champion of their sex. When Locke's theories were called materialistic, she published a defense (1702) that he warmly acknowledged; she also published an explanation of her reasons for converting to Roman Catholicism and back to the Church of England (1707). After her marriage in 1708 to a clergyman, Patrick Cockburn, she gave up writing and even had to ration her reading. (They had many children and a small income.) After eighteen years of silence she published another defense of Locke (1726), an essay on moral obligation (1737, published 1743), and a defense of Clarke (1747), as well as a poem to Queen Caroline asking her to help their sex (1732).

COLLIER, JANE

Jane Collier (1710?-1754 or '55) was the daughter of Arthur Collier, a clergyman and writer on philosophy, who tutored her, her sister Margaret, Sarah Fielding, and Hester Salusbury (Thrale). She and Margaret were friends both of the Fieldings and of Richardson. She published An Essay on the Art of Ingeniously Tormenting (1753) and, in collaboration with Sarah Fielding, The Cry: A New Dramatic Fable (1754).

COLLYER, MARY MITCHELL

Mary Mitchell (died 1763) married Joseph Collyer, a compiler and translator, and had at least one son. She translated several works, most notably Solomon Gessner's Death of Abel (1761). Her anonymously published novel Felicia to Charlotte: Being Letters from a Young Lady in the Country to Her Friend in Town (or Letters from Felicia to Charlotte, Vol. I, 1744; Vol. II, 1749) recommended her to the Bluestockings. According to Carter, she wrote to support her family.

CONWAY, ANNE FINCH, VISCOUNTESS

Anne Finch (died 1679), daughter of the Speaker of the House of Commons, was taught the learned tongues and early formed a taste for mystical philosophy. In 1651 she married Edward Conway (created Earl of Conway, 1679). Despite constant suffering from headaches, she assiduously studied metaphysics. She regularly corresponded with Henry More on theology. Ultimately she converted to Quakerism. She wrote numerous works, only one of which was published, a collection of philosophical treatises in Latin by an English countess "learned beyond her sex," printed in Amsterdam (1690).

COOPER, ELIZABETH

Elizabeth Cooper, the widow of an auctioneer, wrote *The Rival Widows, or the Fair Libertine. A Comedy*, which ran for nine nights; she took the lead on her benefit nights. More significant, she edited *The Muses Library; or A Series of English Poetry, from the Saxons, to the Reign of King Charles II* (Vol. I, 1737; no later volumes issued), an anthology of poetry with biographical-critical prefaces. William Oldys assisted her in this project.

COWLEY, HANNAH PARKHOUSE

Hannah Parkhouse (1743-1809), a bookseller's daughter, married Cowley, a captain in the service of the East India Company, when she was about twenty-five. They had two children. Her first play, *The Runaway*, was a great success at Drury Lane (1776). Of her twelve other plays, the best are *The Belle's Stratagem* (produced 1780, printed 1782), which remained a stock piece for a century, and *A Bold Stroke for a Husband* (1783). She published book-length poetic narratives and, writing under the name Anna Matilda, exchanged sentimental poetical epistles with Robert Merry, "Della Crusca." Her plays were printed with her name.

COWPER, MARY CLAVERING, COUNTESS

Mary Clavering (1685-1724) married William, Earl of Cowper (1706), who became Lord Chancellor (1707). On the accession of George I, she was appointed Lady of the Bedchamber to the Princess of Wales and began a diary recounting the intrigues at Court (printed in 1864).

DAVYS, MARY

Mary ——— (born 1674) married Peter Davys, a clergyman friend of Swift and headmaster of the school attached to St. Patrick's Cathedral. Widowed early, she moved to Cambridge, England, and ran a coffeehouse, whose young patrons subscribed to her works. Her comedy *The Humours of York* was produced in 1716, but most of her work was short fiction, notably *The*

Reform'd Coquet (1724) and *The Accomplish'd Rake, or The Modern Fine Gentleman* (1727).

DELANY, MARY GRANVILLE PENDARVES

Mary Granville (1700-88), born into a distinguished aristocratic family, was forced into a political marriage at the age of seventeen. After many years of widowhood, she married the clergyman Patrick Delany for love when she was forty-three. She had no children by either marriage. After Patrick Delany's death, she lived with the Duchess of Portland, and finally was pensioned by George III. Though she never published, she wrote numerous letters and an autobiography, and was universally admired for her wit and intelligence. In youth, she was a friend of Swift; in old age, of the Bluestockings, Burney, and the royal family.

EDGEWORTH, MARIA

Maria Edgeworth (1767-1849) was the oldest child in a family of Anglo-Irish gentry; her mother died when she was five, and her father was a distinguished liberal author and educator, Richard Lovell Edgeworth. She attended several schools, but it was her father who educated her—remarkably well—both by direct lessons and by enlisting her collaboration in teaching her numerous younger siblings and in writing *Practical Education* (1798). He also got her to help manage the family estate and urged her to take an interest in politics. He encouraged her writing and closely supervised most of her novels. From 1800, when she published her first novel, *Castle Rackrent*, to 1814, when Scott's *Waverley* appeared, she was "easily the most celebrated and successful of practising English novelists" (Marilyn Butler). Courted by the best society on her visits to London, she knew most of the leading intellectuals. Among her many works are *Letters for Literary Ladies* (1795), *Moral Tales for Young People* (1801), *Belinda* (1801), *Tales of Fashionable Life* (First Series: *Manoevring*, etc., 1809; Second Series: *The Absentee*, etc., 1812), *Patronage* (1814), and *Helen* (1834, her last novel).

ELLIOT, JEAN (OR JANE)

Jean Elliot (1727-1805), daughter of a Scottish judge, lived with her family all her life. She apparently wrote just one famous poem, the earlier set of words to "The Flowers of the Forest" ("I've heard the lilting at our yowe-milking," 1756), which was published anonymously with great secrecy.

ELSTOB, ELIZABETH

Elizabeth Elstob (1683-1756) was first inspired to study by her mother, who died when she was eight. She later went to live with her brother William, a clergyman at Oxford, who encouraged her to learn eight languages and to become a scholar of Old English. She published *An English-Saxon Homily on the Birth-Day of St. Gregory,* with an English translation and preface (1709), and *Rudiments of Grammar for the English-Saxon-Tongue, First Given in English; With an Apology for the Study of Northern Antiquities* (1715). In the preface to the *Homily,* issued with her name, she vigorously defended women's right to learning. After her brother's death (1715), she supported herself by setting up a cheap elementary school, and in 1738, through Mary Delany, was appointed governess to the children of the Duchess of Portland, a position she held till her death. Although various friends helped Elstob financially, she never had sufficient money to publish her edition of the homilies of Aelfric or, after her brother's death, to free herself from teaching small children in order to pursue her scholarship.

FALCONBRIDGE, ANNA MARIA

Anna Maria —— married Alexander Falconbridge in 1790. She accompanied him when he was sent to organize a commercial colony in Sierra Leone (1791). He was displaced from authority, took to drink, and died in 1792; she stayed in the colony and promptly remarried. Then she returned to England and, obtaining no recompense for her husband's services, published a *Narrative of Two Voyages to the River Sierra Leone, during the Years 1791, 1792, and 1793 . . . in a Series of Letters* (1794).

FANSHAWE, LADY ANNE HARRISON

Anne Harrison (1625-80), born to an aristocratic Royalist family, which was to be ruined in the Civil War, was well trained in the fashionable accomplishments. She married Richard Fanshawe in 1644 and bore fourteen children, of whom nine died young; the Fanshawes were poor and constantly moved around in the service of Prince Charles. Nevertheless, their marriage was idyllically happy. She wrote a *Memoir* of her husband to preserve his memory for their son (written 1676, published 1829).

FELL, MARGARET. *See* Fox, Margaret Askew Fell

FENWICK, ELIZA

Eliza —— *(died 1840)* married John Fenwick, an editor and translator, in the late 1780s. They were friends of Godwin, Wollstonecraft, and Hays; Eliza nursed Wollstonecraft on her deathbed. Eliza's novel, *Secresy; or The Ruin on the Rock* (1795) was praised by two reviewers. In 1800 she separated from her alcoholic husband and, to support herself and their two children, wrote seven books for children, most of them educational. She launched her daughter as an actress and herself worked as a governess. When her daughter's marriage broke up, Eliza followed her to America, where they struggled unsuccessfully to support themselves and the daughter's four children by running schools.

FIELDING, SARAH

Sarah Fielding (1710-68), three years younger than her brother Henry, grew up with him in the country. Their mother died when Sarah was eight. She attended boarding school and learned Latin from Dr. Arthur Collier, a friend of the family, who was greatly impressed by her ability. She lived with Henry off and on, and they made minor contributions to each other's works; she was also a good friend of Richardson and defended Clarissa in her anonymously published Remarks on Clarissa (1749). She published several novels, of which the most important is David Simple (1744; sequel and additions, 1747, 1752). Her book for children, The Governess (1749), was reprinted well into the nineteenth century, and she also published a successful translation of Xenophon (1762). She was supported by the modest proceeds of her writings, contributions from her brothers, and annuities from friends.

FIENNES, CELIA

Celia Fiennes (1662-1741), daughter of a distinguished Puritan family, traveled all over England and into Scotland and Wales, usually on horseback and accompanied only by servants. She kept extensive travel journals (probably written 1685-1703), showing particular interest in the local industries; she left these in publishable form at her death.

FINCH, ANNE KINGSMILL. See Winchilsea, Anne Kingsmill Finch, Countess of

FOSTER, ANNE EMELINDA MASTERMAN SKINN

Anne Emelinda Masterman (1747-89) was disinherited by her grandfather for a false step committed before she was sixteen. On the death of her first husband, Skinn, an attorney, she married Nicholas Foster, a well-born officer, who abandoned her. She struggled to support herself by writing, needlework, and keeping a day school, but died in great distress. She published a novel, The Old Maid; or, History of Miss Ravensworth (1771).

FOX, MARGARET ASKEW FELL

Margaret Askew (1614-1702), daughter of a prosperous country gentleman, married Judge Thomas Fell before she was eighteen, and had nine children. Deeply religious, she inquired for "the right way" for twenty years and encouraged preachers to come to her house. George Fox came in 1652 and converted her and most of the family. Judge Fell gave the Quakers the use of his house for their meetings. Margaret exerted herself for the relief and release of imprisoned Friends, including Fox himself (1660). She had several interviews with King Charles II, on one occasion successfully petitioning him for the release of four thousand imprisoned Friends. She herself was imprisoned for allowing illegal religious meetings in her home. Judge Fell died in 1658, and in 1669 she married Fox. She wrote many religious tracts, including *False Prophets, Antichrists, Deceivers Which Are in the World* (1655) and *Women's Speaking Justified, Proved and Allowed of by the Scriptures* (1666), and left an autobiography (published in 1710).

GODWIN, MARY WOLLSTONECRAFT

Mary Wollstonecraft (1759-97), daughter of a brutal, improvident tradesman and a weak mother, knew the oppression of women at first hand. After working as a companion, a schoolmistress, and a governess, she became a professional writer. She wrote extensively for *The Analytical Review*, and at the home of its publisher, Joseph Johnson, met radical thinkers such as Paine and Godwin. From her *Vindication of the Rights of Men* (1790), the first answer to Burke's *Reflections on the Revolution in France*, she logically progressed to *A Vindication of the Rights of Woman* (1792). She went to Paris to observe the French Revolution and gather material for a history to justify it. There she fell in love with Gilbert Imlay, with whom she bore a daughter. A business trip she took for Imlay produced *Letters Written during a Short Residence in Sweden, Norway, and Denmark* (1796). Imlay deserted her, and she fell in love with Godwin. For seven months they lived happily as lovers, though keeping separate households, until they married to legitimize their coming child. She died eleven days after giving birth to a daughter, Mary, who was to become an author and the wife of Shelley. Wollstonecraft left an unfinished novel, *Maria; or, The Wrongs of Woman*, published in 1798.

GRAHAM, CATHARINE SAWBRIDGE MACAULAY

Catharine Sawbridge (1731-91), whose mother died young, educated herself in the library of her father, a wealthy squire.

She developed a passion for history and the republican form of government, and started a liberally oriented *History of England* (Vol. I, 1763). She married George Macaulay, a medical doctor fifteen years older than she, who was sympathetic to her intellectual activities; they had one child. After Macaulay died, she published seven more volumes of the *History* (1766-83), and wrote pamphlets denouncing monarchy (1769) and defending the French Revolution (1791), and a conventional work on education for girls (*Letters on Education*, 1790). She was a celebrity in her day, conducting a salon in which (unlike those of the Bluestockings) political discussion was encouraged. Her *History* was enthusiastically received, partly because its political teaching provided welcome support to the Whigs. Her personal and professional prestige declined when she married William Graham, a young and undistinguished man; but she was well received by Washington and others when she and Graham made a tour to America.

GRIERSON, CONSTANTIA PHILLIPPS (?)
Constantia Phillipps(?) (1706?-33) was the daughter of poor parents, but her father encouraged her love of learning. After studying obstetrics in her teens, she married George Grierson, an eminent Dublin printer. She knew Hebrew, Greek, Latin, French, and mathematics; and she wrote verse and prose. She edited Latin classics published by her husband, notably Terence (1727) and Tacitus (1730). She was a friend of Swift, Thomas Sheridan, and Patrick Delany. Her son was also a scholar.

GRIFFITH, ELIZABETH GRIFFITH
Elizabeth Griffith (1720?-93) was encouraged by her father and educated largely by her fiancé, Richard Griffith. Their correspondence during their long engagement and after their marriage (1751) was published in six volumes of *Genuine Letters between Henry and Frances* (1757-70), widely admired because they sustained sentimental romance over many years. The Griffiths supported themselves and their two children by writing. Her most significant works were successful comedies, such as *The Double Mistake* (1766), and the novels *The History of Lady Barton* (1771) and *The Story of Lady Juliana Harley* (1776).

GUNNING, SUSANNAH MINIFIE
Susannah Minifie (1740?-1800) wrote *The Histories of Lady Frances S—— and Lady Caroline S——* (1763) and three other novels in collaboration with her sister Margaret. She married John Gunning, an army officer of distinguished family, in 1768 and had one daughter. When the daughter, Elizabeth (1769-

1823), caused a scandal involving an abortive courtship, her father threw her out of the house, and her mother went with her. Susannah continued to write novels during her marriage and after the separation; the best is *Memoirs of Mary* (1793), inspired by the family scandal. Elizabeth also wrote novels and translations from the French; she married a Major Plunkett.

HALKETT, LADY ANNE MURRAY

Anne Murray (1622-99), whose parents were tutors to the children of James I, was given a careful fashionable education by her mother. She studied medicine to help the poor and ultimately was consulted by people from all over Britain. During the Civil War, she helped the Duke of York escape from England, and she nursed wounded soldiers. She married Sir James Halkett (1656) and had several children. After his death, she supplemented her income by educating upper-class children in her home. She published a volume of religious meditations (1701) and left twenty more volumes in manuscript at her death, as well as her autobiography (written c. 1678).

HAMILTON, ELIZABETH

Elizabeth Hamilton (1758-1816), orphaned at nine, was raised by her aunt and her uncle, prosperous farmers. She attended boarding school and then educated herself. She corresponded voluminously with her brother Charles, an official in India, and published some prose and poetry in the *Lounger* (1785). Her *Letters of a Hindoo Rajah* (1796), strongly influenced by her brother's opinions and experiences, was well reviewed; and *Memoirs of Modern Philosophers* (1800), a satire on Godwin's radical circle, was a best-seller. Her best known work was *The Cottagers of Glenburnie* (1808). Besides these didactic novels, she wrote several books on education. She lived with her uncle in Scotland until his death, then in London with her brother and sister, and finally settled in Edinburgh with her sister; the Scottish government gave her a pension.

HANWAY, MARY ANN

Of *Mary Ann Hanway* nothing is known except that she wrote several novels, of which *Ellinor, or The World as It Is* (1798) drew the most critical notice. She also published *Andrew Stuart, or the Northern Wanderer* (1800) and *Falconbridge Abbey; A Devonshire Story* (1808). *Christabelle, the Maid of Rouen* (1815) and *A Journey to the Highlands of Scotland, with Occasional Remarks on Dr. Johnson's Tour, by a Lady* (1796?) have been attributed to her.

HAYS, MARY

Mary Hays (1760-1843) was born into a family of London Dissenters, who encouraged her intellectual development. An intense sentimental romance ended when her fiancé died. She read widely under the guidance of a radical Baptist preacher and pseudonymously published a defense of the Unitarians (1791), which was enthusiastically received. This introduced her to the circle of the radical publisher Joseph Johnson, where she met Paine, Holcroft, Godwin, and Wollstonecraft. After falling in love with a man who did not reciprocate, she put her passion into *Memoirs of Emma Courtney* (1796). All her life she campaigned for women's rights, in *Emma Courtney* and her other novel, *The Victim of Prejudice* (1799), in *Letters and Essays, Moral and Miscellaneous* (1793), in *An Appeal to the Men of Great Britain in Behalf of Women* (1798, published anonymously), in *Female Biography* (1803, a reference work that kept her name alive through the nineteenth century), and in *Memoirs of Queens* (1821). She lived on her earnings as a writer of books and contributor to periodicals, perhaps supplemented by an allowance from her family. Though her sexual principles shocked the conservatives, her practice was invariably correct.

HAYWOOD, ELIZA FOWLER

Eliza Fowler (1693?-1756?), daughter of a small shopkeeper, married Valentine Haywood before she was twenty. She eloped from him in 1721 and then had to support herself and their two children. (There is no evidence, apart from enemies' charges, that they were illegitimate.) She tried acting and playwriting, but soon turned to salacious romances—of which the most popular was *Love in Excess* (1719)—and scandal chronicles, such as *Memoirs of a Certain Island Adjacent to the Kingdom of Utopia* (1725-26). These sold well but paid badly; she had to churn out an average of one novella per month during the years 1724 to 1726 and published a total of at least seventy books. She generally published her early works with her name, but after Pope pilloried her in the *Dunciad* (1728), she disappeared from the literary scene. When she began to publish again, it was often anonymously, though her later works were not scandalous. They included a periodical, *The Female Spectator* (twenty-four monthly parts, 1744-46), several domestic handbooks, and, most notably, two novels, *The History of Miss Betsy Thoughtless* (1751) and *The History of Jemmy and Jenny Jessamy* (1753).

HERSCHEL, CAROLINE LUCRETIA

Caroline Lucretia Herschel (1750-1848), daughter of a German music teacher, had little education because her mother was determined to restrict her to household drudgery. She joyfully accepted her brother William's invitation to live with him in Bath (1772). He taught her singing, English, and arithmetic, and from 1773 enlisted her help in his study of astronomy. Meanwhile, she sang successfully in oratorios that William conducted. She worked constantly with him on astronomy, writing down his observations and doing extensive calculations afterward. Becoming interested in the subject on her own, she discovered three nebulae in 1783 and eight comets between 1786 and 1797. In 1787 the King settled £50 a year on her as her brother's assistant—her first money of her own. After William's marriage (1788) she moved into lodgings, but continued to work with him as before. Her *Index to Flamsteed's Observations of the Fixed Stars*, with her corrections, was presented to the Royal Society (1798) and published at their expense. Her most valuable contribution, though never published, was "Reduction and Arrangement in the Form of a Catalogue in Zones of all the Star Clusters and Nebulae observed by Sir William Herschel" (1828). She was made an honorary member of the Royal Astronomical Society in 1835.

HUTCHINSON, LUCY APSLEY

Lucy Apsley (c. 1620-1675?), daughter of the Lieutenant of the Tower of London, was carefully educated, both in fashionable accomplishments and languages. Her father's chaplain taught her Latin, and she was also versed in Greek and Hebrew, as well as classics and theology. She married Colonel John Hutchinson (1638), who fought on the Puritan side in the Civil War. He tolerated her literary ambitions, and they were very happy together. She translated Lucretius, wrote on moral and religious subjects, and honored her husband with a volume of *Memoirs* (1664-71). She left all her writings in manuscript.

INCHBALD, ELIZABETH SIMPSON

Elizabeth Simpson (1753-1821), from a family of Catholic farmers, was self-educated. Determined to see the world, she ran away from home and became an actress, despite the handicap of a speech impediment. She married Joseph Inchbald, but had no children. They joined a provincial touring company, where she played leading roles. In addition to a rigorous repertory schedule, she kept up a systematic reading program and taught herself French. After Joseph's death (1779), she resisted several offers of marriage and numerous attempts at seduction; though she enjoyed flirtation, she remained strictly virtuous, and managed to retain as friends the men she rejected as lovers. Meanwhile she tried to establish herself as a playwright, since she was never really successful as an actress. Her first play accepted, the farce *The Mogul Tale* (1784), brought her 100 guineas. She continued to write successful plays (nineteen produced), of which the best are the comedies *Such Things Are* (1787; she made £900 on it) and *Every One Has His Fault* (1793, £700). She wrote a novel, *A Simple Story* (1791), and a philosophical tale, *Nature and Art* (1796); and she edited the twenty-five-volume *British Theatre* (1806-9). She worked hard, with consistent success, and lived frugally, leaving £6000 at her death. At the same time, she maintained an active social life, both in aristocratic society and in the radical circle of Godwin, though her disapproval of Mary Wollstonecraft's common-law marriages caused a break in their friendship. She was friendly with Sarah Siddons and romantically involved with John Philip Kemble, who was the model for the hero of *A Simple Story*.

JEMMAT, CATHERINE YEO

Catherine Yeo, whose mother died young, was the daughter of an admiral. After several abortive romances, she married Jemmat, a mercer, mainly to escape from her tyrannical father. The marriage proved unhappy, because of Jemmat's jealousy and drunkenness; and when he went bankrupt three years later, she apparently left him. When her family refused to help her, she published by subscription *The Memoirs of Mrs. Catherine Jemmat* (1765), a defense of her conduct. Both these and her *Miscellanies, in Prose and Verse* (1766) were dedicated to members of the royal family and included many aristocrats among their subscribers.

KILLIGREW, ANNE

Anne Killigrew (1660-85), the daughter of Dr. Henry Killigrew, a prominent clergyman, became maid of honor to Mary of Modena, wife of the future James II. She wrote poems and painted portraits, of the King and Queen among others. A small volume of her poems, published posthumously (1686), was prefixed by an engraving of her self-portrait and a eulogistic ode by Dryden.

KNIGHT, ELLIS CORNELIA

Ellis Cornelia Knight (1757-1837) was educated at a school kept by a clergyman and became a good Latin scholar. Her father was a rear admiral and her mother, an accomplished woman, was a friend of Reynolds's sister, through whom the family met Johnson. An only child, Knight lived with her mother in Italy, then was appointed companion to Queen Charlotte (1805), transferred to the household of Princess Charlotte, and eventually moved back to the continent. She published *Dinarbas* (1790, a sequel to *Rasselas*), *Marcus Flaminius; or A View of the Military, Political and Social Life of the Romans, in a Series of Letters from a Young Patrician to His Friend* (1792, a didactic romance), a *Description of Latium* (1805, a travel book valuable in its own day), and *Sir Guy de Lusignan* (1833, a romance). She left an autobiography in manuscript.

LEAD (OR LEADE), JANE WARD

Jane Ward (1624-1704), the conventionally educated daughter of a good family, heard a miraculous voice when she was fifteen and devoted herself (despite family protests) to a religious life. She married William Lead (c. 1643) and had four daughters. On his death (1670), she dedicated herself to spiritual meditation; she regularly had visions, which she recorded and interpreted in her journal, *A Fountain of Gardens* (published 1697-1701). She formed a theosophical congregation with a dissident clergyman, Dr. John Pordage, and other followers of the mystical teachings of Jacob Boehme. She published *The Heavenly Cloud Now Breaking* (1681) and *The Revelation of Revelations* (1683), both in poetic prose with poems. The congregation dwindled after Pordage's death, and in 1692 Lead was living alone in a charitable institution, though she continued to publish her works. These aroused interest on the continent, where they were discovered by an English scholar, Dr. Francis Lee, who sought her out. When she became blind, he acted as her secretary; together they reorganized her congregation as the Philadelphian Society.

LEAPOR, MARY

Mary Leapor (1722-46), a gardener's daughter, had little education but did have a passion for reading. At an early age, she composed verses in the manner of Pope; these came to the attention of upper-class people who resolved to publish them by subscription. Leapor died before her *Poems on Several Occasions* appeared (1748, 1751).

LEE, HARRIET

Harriet Lee (1757-1851), daughter of a mother who died young and John Lee, an actor and theatrical manager, helped her older sister, Sophia (q.v.), run a successful school in Bath. Her first novel, *The Errors of Innocence* (1786), attacks injustice to women. She published another novel, a comedy, and a melodrama; but her best work is in the short fiction of *Canterbury Tales* (not related to Chaucer's), written in collaboration with Sophia and published with their names. Harriet wrote most of

Volumes I (1797) and III (1799) and all of Volumes IV (1801) and V (1805); the best tales are hers (most notably "The German's Tale: Kruitzner"). William Godwin proposed to her, but she rejected him for his vanity and for his unorthodoxy in religion.

LEE, SOPHIA

Sophia Lee (1750-1824) was educated by her father, the actor and manager John Lee, and early took over as mother to her four younger sisters. With the sizable profits of a comedy, The Chapter of Accidents (1780), she established in Bath a girls' school that she and Harriet Lee (q.v.) ran successfully from 1781 to 1803, when the two sisters retired with a comfortable income. Her historical romance The Recess (1783-85) was well received, and she wrote a few other novels and plays, all published with her name. She collaborated with Harriet on Canterbury Tales, writing parts of Volumes I (1797) and III (1799) and all of Volume II (1798).

LENNOX, CHARLOTTE RAMSAY

Charlotte Ramsay (1729?-1804), daughter of an army officer stationed in America, came to England in her teens, wrote poetry and was helped by two noblewomen, worked unsuccessfully as an actress, and became a professional writer. She married Alexander Lennox (c. 1748), probably an employee of the printer William Strahan. She met Johnson, who proved to be a good friend: he arranged a celebration in honor of her first novel (Harriot Stuart, 1750), wrote seven prefaces and dedications for her, and helped her with translations and scholarly work; he quoted her in his Dictionary and seems to have used her Shakespeare Illustrated (1753-54) in his own edition of Shakespeare. Both Johnson and Richardson helped her with her best novel, The Female Quixote (1752); she published this anonymously, but was generally known as the author. Among her other works are The Lady's Museum (a periodical which ran for eleven monthly numbers, 1760-61), the novel Euphemia (1790), and several plays. Her marriage was unhappy, and in 1792 she seems to have separated permanently from her husband. She had a son and a daughter. Despite constant and generally successful writing, Lennox was usually hard up; she died penniless.

MACAULAY, CATHARINE. See Graham, Catharine Sawbridge Macaulay

MAKIN, BATHSUA PELL

Bathsua Pell Makin, the daughter of a clergyman and sister of an eminent mathematician, was appointed tutor to the daughters of Charles I; she taught classical and modern languages and mathematics to the Princess Elizabeth. She corresponded with the famous Dutch scholar Anna Maria von Schur-man. She ran several girls' schools and in 1673 issued a prospec-tus for one which would offer a truly solid curriculum. She in-cluded with this *An Essay to Revive the Antient Education of Gentlewomen.*

MANLEY, MARY DE LA RIVIÈRE

Mary de la Rivière Manley (1663-1724), daughter of a dis-tinguished knight, was orphaned at fourteen and at fifteen was deceived into a bigamous marriage by her cousin, John Manley. He then deserted her and their child. Although she became the mistress of several men, she lived only with men she loved, and she supported herself by writing. She wrote plays and epistolary fiction in the 1690s, but made her name with scandalous ro-mances attacking the Whigs, of which the most famous was *Secret Memoirs and Manners of Several Persons of Quality, of Both Sexes; From the New Atalantis* (1709; continuations, 1710, 1711). In 1711 Swift chose her to succeed him as editor of the Tory paper, *The Examiner.* She was lampooned anonymously, along with her fellow playwrights Catherine Trotter (Cockburn) and Mary Pix, in *The Female Wits* (1696). She argued for wom-en's rights in the prologue to *The Lost Lover* (1696), *The New Atalantis,* and *Memoirs of Europe* (1710-11). Her *Adventures of Rivella* (1714) is a glamorized autobiography.

MASHAM, LADY DAMARIS CUDWORTH

Damaris Cudworth (1658-1708), daughter of the Cambridge scholar Ralph Cudworth, was educated by him and Locke. She married Sir Francis Masham (1685) and had one son, whom she educated. Locke, who lived with them from 1691 until his death in 1704, greatly admired her intellect. She published, anony-mously, *A Discourse Concerning the Love of God* (1696), which carried on the debate between Astell and Norris, and *Occasional Thoughts in Reference to a Virtuous Christian Life* (1700), which included an argument for educating women.

MEADES, ANNA

Anna Meades, a young woman in her twenties who was just publishing a romance (*The History of Cleanthes*), wrote to Richardson in 1757, asking him to correct and publish her Rich-ardsonian novel *Sir William Harrington.* He suggested detailed revisions, some of which were incorporated in the final version (1771, published anonymously).

MEEKE, MARY

Mary Meeke (died 1816?) was probably the wife of the Reverend Francis Meeke. She published translations and many shoddy but popular novels, of which the best known is *Count St. Blanchard* (1795). Twenty-four of her books were published under her own name and four under the pseudonym Gabrielli.

MILLER, LADY ANNA RIGGS

Anna Riggs (1741-81), daughter of a wealthy family, brought a fortune to John Miller, a retired army officer (later created a baronet), whom she married in 1765; they had two children. Her letters describing their tour of Italy (1770-71) were published anonymously (1776). On their return from Italy, she established a literary salon at their villa at Batheaston, near Bath. She invited everyone of wit and fashion in Bath, asking each to bring a poem and place it in an antique urn. Then the poems were read aloud and discussed, and the authors of those judged best were awarded myrtle wreaths. She published annual volumes of selections from these competitions under the title *Poetical Amusements at a Villa near Bath* (1775, 1776, 1777, 1781). Lady Miller's poetical competitions were ridiculed but were also fashionable.

MINIFIE, SUSANNAH. *See* Gunning, Susannah Minifie

MONTAGU, ELIZABETH ROBINSON

Elizabeth Robinson (1720-1800), of a distinguished family, grew up in an intellectual household where daughters were encouraged to think and compete with their brothers; she was educated by her father and her stepgrandfather, the scholar Conyers Middleton. She married Edward Montagu, a wealthy scholar twenty-nine years her senior (1742); they had lasting affection and esteem for each other, but there was no mention of romantic love. They had one child, who died young. A brilliant conversationalist, Montagu became the leading Bluestocking hostess from 1750; the foremost intellectuals of her day, including Johnson, Burke, Garrick, and Reynolds, were regular guests. Elizabeth Carter was a close friend. Montagu published only an *Essay on the Writings and Genius of Shakespeare* (1769) and three dialogues in the *Dialogues of the Dead* of her friend Lord Lyttelton (1760), all anonymously. She capably managed her husband's farms and collieries and organized munificent charities, of which the most appealing was an annual dinner for the boy chimney sweepers of London.

MONTAGU, LADY MARY PIERREPONT WORTLEY

Lady Mary Pierrepont (1689-1762), a beautiful and precocious child whose mother died when she was four, was early introduced to society by her father, the Earl of Kingston. She educated herself by reading voluminously in his library, and even taught herself Latin. In 1712 she eloped with Edward Wortley Montagu, a rising Whig politician; they had two children. She accompanied him on his embassy to Constantinople (1716), whence she sent back brilliant travel letters; she brought back to England the Turkish method of inoculation for smallpox. Acquainted with all the London wits, she was a particular friend of Pope; later they quarreled, and he lampooned her as "Sappho." She wrote essays and poems, including five satirical "town eclogues" and a periodical supporting Walpole's ministry, *The Nonsense of Common Sense* (1737-38). In 1739 she separated from her husband and went to live in Italy. Her best work is her letters, especially the ones from Turkey and those written to her daughter during her exile on the continent. Her works were published anonymously or circulated in manuscript, but she intended the Turkish Letters to be published after her death.

MORE, HANNAH

Hannah More (1745-1833), daughter of the master of a charity school, was the fourth of five sisters and from childhood was regarded as the genius of the family. Her father taught her Latin, but stopped her mathematics lessons when she showed "unfeminine" aptitude. The older sisters established a very successful school in Bristol (c. 1757), where the younger ones joined them; in 1790 they were all able to retire comfortably. Hannah had entrée to the best London society through her Bristol connections and soon established herself by her knowledge, wit, charm, and deference. She was a friend of Johnson, Garrick, Horace Walpole, and the Bluestockings. Garrick shepherded her tragedy, *Percy*, to triumphant success (1777); it gained her £750. Always pious, she became increasingly interested in evangelical religion. In 1789 she started establishing Sunday schools for the poor, bringing civilization into utterly barbarous areas. She also proselytized among her fashionable friends for the abolition of the slave trade. After publishing *Village Politics, by "Will Chip"* (1792), she organized the writing, editing, distribution, and financing of the *Cheap Repository Tracts* (1795-98), designed to counteract the influence of radical propaganda on the lower classes. These proved to be as successful as their sensational or Jacobinical rivals. More wrote many volumes of didactic works, including *Thoughts on the Importance of the Manners of the Great to General Society* (1788), *Strictures on the Modern System of Female Education* (1799), and the moral novel *Coelebs in Search of a Wife* (1809). All were phenomenally successful; her writing earned her more than £30,000.

MULSO, HESTER. *See* Chapone, Hester Mulso

NEWCASTLE, MARGARET LUCAS CAVENDISH, DUCHESS OF
   Margaret Lucas (1624?-74), one of eight children in an aristocratic family, was raised by her capable mother in loving freedom. She insisted on becoming a Maid of Honor to Queen Henrietta Maria, whom she accompanied in exile to Paris. At Court
she met William Cavendish, Marquis (later Duke) of Newcastle;
they married for love (1645), though he was thirty years older,
and were blissfully happy together. They had no children. She
began to write, and between 1653 and 1668 published twelve
large volumes of poems, plays, essays, and philosophical voyages,
filled with philosophical and scientific speculations and characteristically centering on a wise, learned, beautiful, and universally admired lady. The most readable is a *Life* of her husband
(1667). She argued for the improvement of women's education
and lamented the deficiencies of her own. William consistently
encouraged his wife to write and publish, and her brother, a
member of the Royal Society, helped her with scientific reading.
On their return to England at the Restoration, she became a celebrity, treated with respect because of her rank but privately
ridiculed as eccentric because of her peculiar dress, manners, and
intellectual aspirations.

OPIE, AMELIA ALDERSON
   Amelia Alderson (1769-1853) was the devoted daughter of a
medical doctor, who was radical in politics and Unitarian in religion. Her mother died when she was fifteen. She had little serious education. She entered radical circles in London, meeting
Barbauld, Inchbald, Wollstonecraft (whom she greatly admired),
Godwin, and Holcroft. The latter two are said to have proposed
to her, but she rejected them for the painter John Opie, whom
she married in 1798. They were very happy, and he encouraged
her to continue her writing. Her novel *Father and Daughter*
(1801) was warmly received, as were her equally sentimental
poems (1802) and her best novel, *Adeline Mowbray* (1804, inspired by the character and ideas of Wollstonecraft). Her works
were published with her name. She continued to publish fiction
until she converted to Quakerism (1825), after which she devoted herself mainly to philanthropic work, such as visiting pris-
ons and hospitals; in 1840 she was the Norwich delegate to the
antislavery convention in London.

PARSONS, ELIZA PHELP
   Eliza Phelp (died 1811), whose father was a wine merchant,
married Parsons, a turpentine merchant, at an early age. After

his death, she supported herself and their eight children by writing about sixty volumes of mediocre novels, of which the best known are *The Castle of Wolfenbach* (1793) and *The Mysterious Warning* (1796).

PEACOCK, LUCY

Lucy Peacock kept a bookshop in Oxford Street and wrote tales for children, such as *The Adventures of the Six Princesses of Babylon in Their Travels to the Temple of Virtue* (1785; third edition, 1790), *The Knight of the Rose* (1793; second edition, 1807), and *Emily, or The Test of Sincerity* (1816). Most were published anonymously. She edited *The Juvenile Magazine* for the year 1788.

PHILIPS, KATHERINE FOWLER

Katherine Fowler (1631-64), daughter of a merchant, was educated at a fashionable boarding school. She married a landed gentleman, James Philips (1647), and had two children. She gathered about her a "society of friendship," whose members she endowed with fanciful names. Hers was Orinda, and she became known as "the matchless Orinda." She wrote verses from an early age and circulated them among her friends, but claimed that their publication in 1664 was against her will. She was encouraged by friends to complete her translation of Corneille's *Pompée*, which was produced successfully in Dublin (1663).

PHILLIPS, CATHERINE PAYTON

Catherine Payton (1727-94), the daughter of devout Quakers, entered the ministry in 1748. She went on annual preaching tours to all parts of Britain, Carolina and New England, and Holland. She married William Phillips, who was in the copper-mining business (1772). She published tracts on the *Causes of the High Price of Grain* (1792), on missionary efforts in Africa (1792), and on other subjects.

PILKINGTON, LAETITIA VAN LEWEN

Laetitia Van Lewen (1712-50), daughter of a successful Dublin obstetrician, was encouraged to learn by her father, but harshly disciplined by her mother, who would not let her read lest she spoil her eyes. She married a penniless clergyman, Matthew Pilkington (1729), and had several children. She and her husband were befriended by Swift, who was delighted by her intelligence. Her husband divorced her for adultery (1738), on what she claimed were trumped up charges. Dropped by all her respectable friends, she fled to London, where she supported herself and her children by any means she could. She wrote everything, from amusing letters to long solemn poems to tracts abusing her husband; and she got money from men by flirtation, cajolery, and threats of exposing them in print. Her best work is *Memoirs of Mrs. Laetitia Pilkington, Wife to the Reverend Matthew Pilkington, Written by Herself* (1748). Though Cibber and Richardson helped her, she was always on the edge of poverty and died destitute.

PIOZZI, HESTER LYNCH SALUSBURY THRALE

Hester Lynch Salusbury (1741-1821), the daughter of upper-class but impoverished parents, was a bright, petted child, educated largely by her mother. She adored her mother, a model of conventional virtue, and always consciously accepted her self-sacrificing precepts. Dr. Arthur Collier, a family friend, taught her Latin. She married Henry Thrale, a rich brewer (1763), mainly to please her mother, and had twelve children. Samuel Johnson practically lived in the Thrale home from 1766, and through him she came to know the leading intellectuals of the day. She knew the Bluestockings, but was not included in their inner circle. After Thrale's death, she married Gabriel Piozzi, an Italian Catholic music teacher (1784), for which she was ostracized by her friends, including Johnson, and her own daughters. Though she kept an extensive diary (*Thraliana*), she did not publish anything until *Anecdotes of the Late Samuel Johnson* (1786). This was followed by a travel book, *Observations and Reflections Made in the Course of a Journey through France, Italy, and Germany* (1789), and several other works of nonfiction.

PIX, MARY GRIFFITH

Mary Griffith (1666-1720?), a vicar's daughter, married George Pix, a merchant tailor (1684) and had one child, who died young. She wrote twelve plays that were produced and printed, generally with her name. The best are the comedies *The Spanish Wives* (1696) and *The Innocent Mistress* (1697). She supported one of Mary Manley's plays with verses praising her as the "Pride of our Sex" (1696), and her tragedy *Queen Catherine* (1698) had an epilogue by Catherine Trotter (Cockburn). The three women were lampooned in the anonymous *The Female Wits* (1696).

PLUNKETT, ELIZABETH GUNNING. *See under* Gunning, Susannah Minifie

POLWHELE, ELIZABETH

Elizabeth Polwhele wrote a high-flown melodrama, *The*

Faithful Virgins (probably 1670), which was almost certainly produced, and a comedy of intrigue, *The Frolicks, or The Lawyer Cheated* (1671), which may have been. She wrote because "haunted with poetic devils." Neither play was printed. This author may be the Elizabeth Polwhele (died 1691), daughter of a prominent nonconformist clergyman, who married the Reverend Stephen Lobb before 1678 and had five children.

RADCLIFFE, ANN WARD

Ann Ward (1764-1823), daughter of a genteel tradesman, probably attended the Lee sisters' school in Bath. At twenty-three she married William Radcliffe, a journalist who became editor of the *English Chronicle;* their marriage, though childless, was happy. She began writing Gothic novels while her husband was away on business, and they proved enormously popular and profitable. Her first success was *The Romance of the Forest* (1791), followed by *The Mysteries of Udolpho* (1794, for which she got £500) and *The Italian* (1797, £600). She also published a travel book, *A Journey Made in the Summer of 1794 through Holland and the Western Frontier of Germany* (1795). She was universally praised, but never entered literary society. She did, however, put her name on the title page of all her books from the second edition of *The Romance of the Forest.* Though conservative in religion and politics, she expressed indignation at the slave trade and other examples of injustice toward people without power.

RADCLIFFE, MARY ANN

Mary Ann Radcliffe, a gentlewoman with a kindly but incompetent husband and many children, had to find some way to support the family; the only obvious one, she discovered, was prostitution. This moved her to write *The Female Advocate; or, An Attempt to Recover the Rights of Women from Male Usurpation* (1799), which she later incorporated into her *Memoirs* (1810). She may be the Mary Anne Radcliffe who published *Manfroné; or, The One-Handed Monk* (1809), as well as two other gothic novels in 1790.

REEVE, CLARA

Clara Reeve (1729-1807), the daughter of a clergyman, was well educated by her father. Her novel *The Champion of Virtue, a Gothic Story* (1777, later titled *The Old English Baron*) was very popular. Her many other works include *The Progress of Romance* (1785, literary criticism), *The School for Widows, a Novel* (1791), and its continuation, *Plans of Education* (1792). She did not publish with her full signature until her sixtieth year.

ROBINSON, MARY DARBY

Mary Darby (1758-1800), the daughter of a whaling captain, attended several schools, including that kept by the More sisters. She married Thomas Robinson (1774), an articled clerk, and had one daughter. When he was arrested for debt, she wrote poems that won the patronage of the Duchess of Devonshire. Then she made a successful acting debut as Juliet at Drury Lane (1776), and played leading roles there until 1780. George, Prince of Wales, fell in love with her in the role of Perdita and persuaded her to become his mistress. But he soon grew tired of her and left her, without money and too compromised to return to the stage. She became a professional author, producing more poems and novels such as *Vancenza* (1792) and *Walsingham, or The Pupil of Nature* (1797), as well as two feminist pieces: *Thoughts on the Condition of Women* (n.d.) and a *Letter to the Women of England on the Injustice of Mental Subordination, with Anecdotes by Anne Frances Randall* (1799). She joined the radical circle of Godwin and the Fenwicks. She died crippled and impoverished. Her daughter, Mary (or Maria) Elizabeth Robinson (died 1818), published *The Shrine of Bertha* (1794), a novel, and *The Wild Wreath* (1805), a poetical miscellany.

ROBINSON, MARY ELIZABETH. *See under* Robinson, Mary Darby

ROCHE, REGINA MARIA DALTON

Regina Maria Dalton (1764?-1845) published two novels before she married Roche, but it was *The Children of the Abbey* (1796) that made her famous. She turned out similar novels for the rest of her life—a total of sixteen, generally published with her name.

ROWE, ELIZABETH SINGER

Elizabeth Singer (1674-1737), the daughter of an upper-class nonconformist minister, had little education. Her *Poems on Several Occasions by Philomela* (1696) attracted the attention and patronage of a neighboring noble family. She was a friend of Isaac Watts and admired by Matthew Prior. She was happily married to a young scholar, Thomas Rowe (1710); but he died after five years, and she retired to her small estate in the country, where she devoted herself to writing pious works and keeping up extensive friendships by correspondence. She deliberately abstained from trying to make money by writing, but her meditations, prayers, and pious romances were all best sellers. Her most lastingly popular works were edifying fiction, *Friendship in Death: In Twenty Letters from the Dead to the Living* (1728) and *Letters Moral and Entertaining* (1729, 1731, 1733).

ROWSON, SUSANNA HASWELL

Susanna Haswell (1762-1824) was the daughter of a naval lieutenant; her mother died at her birth, and her father soon remarried. She was born at Portsmouth, but grew up in Massachusetts, where the statesman James Otis called her his little scholar. The family returned to England during the Revolutionary War. She worked as a governess until she married William Rowson, a hardware merchant (1786). Her first novel, *Victoria*, published by subscription in 1786, was followed by schoolbooks, farces, and other novels, of which the best is *Charlotte Temple, or A Tale of Truth* (1790); this was very successful in England and the United States. William Rowson went bankrupt, and Susanna became an actress. After touring the United States from 1793 to 1797, she opened a successful girls' school in Boston, which closed only when she retired in 1822. She also edited the Boston *Weekly Magazine* (1802-5) and contributed to other periodicals.

SCOTT, SARAH ROBINSON

Sarah Robinson (1723-95), younger sister of Elizabeth Montagu (q.v.), married George Lewis Scott, a tutor to the royal princes (c. 1751). They parted after a year, evidently for incompatibility, and she went to live with a woman friend on their pooled income. They established a school for twenty-four poor children. Scott published nine novels and histories, all anonymously, of which the best known is the novel *Millenium Hall* (1762).

SEWARD, ANNA

Anna Seward (1747-1809), the daughter of a prominent clergyman in Lichfield, was educated by him and lived with him most of her life. She had a long, presumably platonic, romance with a married clergyman attached to the cathedral. Known as "the Swan of Lichfield," she was the most praised woman poet of her day. Her *Monody on the Unfortunate Major André* (1781) was particularly admired; George Washington cared enough about an attack in this poem that he sent an officer to her to clear himself of the charge. Liberal in politics, she knew Helen Maria Williams and Richard Lovell Edgeworth, as well as Johnson and Boswell. She was an early admirer of Scott.

SHERIDAN, FRANCES CHAMBERLAINE

Frances Chamberlaine (1724-66), whose mother died soon after her birth and whose father disapproved of educating women, was taught writing, Latin, and botany by her brothers. After she published a poem and a pamphlet supporting Thomas

Sheridan, manager of the Dublin theater, in a theatrical quarrel (1746), he met, courted, and married her (1747). They were very happy and had three children, including Richard Brinsley Sheridan. She gave up writing when she married, but was glad to return when the family needed money. Encouraged by Richardson, she published, anonymously, the successful novel *Memoirs of Miss Sidney Bidulph* (1761; second part, 1767). Her other works include an Oriental tale, *The History of Nourjahad* (1767), and a successful comedy, *The Discovery* (1763).

SMITH, CHARLOTTE TURNER

Charlotte Turner (1749-1806), daughter of a landed gentleman, received a conventional fashionable education. Her mother died when she was three, and at fifteen, spurred by her father's impending remarriage, she married Benjamin Smith. The son of a wealthy merchant, he had no turn for business himself and dissipated the family fortune. Charlotte turned to writing, first a book of poems and then a series of novels. She left Smith after more than twenty miserable years and thenceforth was the major support of herself and their nine surviving children. Though she was a popular and hard-working novelist, producing an average of one four-volume novel per year from 1788 to 1798, she was chronically pressed for money; one son died because, lacking money to educate him for the Church, she had to send him into the army. William Hayley befriended her, and she also knew Cowper and Romney. She took particular pride in her poems (notably sonnets), but her major achievement was in the novel. She wrote ten novels, of which the most important are *Emmeline* (1788), *The Old Manor House* (1793), and *The Banished Man* (1794).

STARKE, MARIANA

Mariana Starke (1762?-1838), daughter of the governor of Fort St. George in Madras, wrote a comedy about India, *The Sword of Peace; or, A Voyage of Love* (acted 1788, published anonymously 1789), in the preface of which she protested against hostility to women authors. She also wrote two tragedies and several useful guide books.

TALBOT, CATHERINE

Catherine Talbot (1721-70), born of an aristocratic family, spent most of her life in the household of Thomas Secker, who became Archbishop of Canterbury. He educated her in Scripture and languages and introduced her into distinguished literary circles. She was a lifelong friend of Elizabeth Carter, and knew Richardson and other celebrities. She never published during her lifetime, apart from some slight anonymous contributions to *The Rambler* and *The Adventurer*; but after her death Carter published her *Reflections on the Seven Days of the Week* (1770), which was often reprinted.

THOMAS, ELISABETH
   Elisabeth Thomas (1677-1731), a lawyer's daughter, got the name "Corinna" from Dryden, whom she inveigled into a correspondence. She led a disreputable life and was pilloried in *The Dunciad* for selling twenty-five of Pope's letters to the publisher Curll. Her *Critical Remarks* on four popular plays appeared in 1719 and *Poems on Several Occasions, by a Lady* in 1722. Curll published her love correspondence as *Pylades and Corinna: Or, Memoirs of the Lives, Amours, and Writings of Richard Gwinnett, Esq. . . . and Mrs. Elizabeth Thomas* (1731-32).

THRALE, HESTER. *See* Piozzi, Hester Lynch Salusbury Thrale

TRIMMER, SARAH KIRBY
   Sarah Kirby (1741-1810), daughter of a painter and author, attended a provincial school. She married James Trimmer (1762) and they had twelve children. She educated their six daughters and helped to educate the sons. She published an *Easy Introduction to the Knowledge of Nature* (1782), based on these lessons, and six volumes of Bible stories for young people (1782-84). Active in the Sunday School movement, she was consulted by Queen Charlotte and published *The OEconomy of Charity* (1786), on the promotion and management of Sunday Schools. She wrote several other moral works for children and edited two periodicals: *The Family Magazine* (1788-89), to instruct and amuse cottagers and servants; and *The Guardian of Education* (1802-6), to monitor books for children.

TROTTER, CATHERINE. *See* Cockburn, Catherine Trotter

WAKEFIELD, PRISCILLA BELL
   Priscilla Bell (1751-1832), a Quaker, married the merchant Edward Wakefield in 1771, and had three children. Her many philanthropic activities included establishing savings banks and a lying-in hospital. She wrote fifteen successful children's books and *Reflections on the Present Condition of the Female Sex* (1798).

WALKER, LADY MARY HAMILTON
   Lady Mary Hamilton Walker, an earl's daughter, wrote *Letters from the Duchess of Crui and Others* (1776) "in her nursery,

surrounded by her children, for whose use only they were intended." She also published *Memoirs of the Marchioness de Louvoi* (1777) and *Munster Village* (1778), all three books anonymously.

WALLACE , LADY EGLANTINE MAXWELL

Eglantine Maxwell (d. 1803), daughter of a baronet, married Thomas Dunlop, who took the name of Wallace with the title of baronet (1770), and had two sons. She got a legal separation on grounds of cruelty (c. 1783) and subsequently traveled around the continent with the revolutionary general Charles-François Dumouriez. She defended him in *The Conduct of the King of Prussia and General Dumouriez* (1793), published with her name. She published poems, pamphlets, and plays. Her comedy *The Ton, or Follies of Fashion* (1788) was produced, but damned as dull.

WARDLAW, LADY ELIZABETH HALKET

Elizabeth Halket (1677-1727), daughter of a baronet, married Sir Henry Wardlaw (1696). Her imitation ballad *Hardyknute* (written c. 1710, published 1719) was long accepted as genuine.

WARWICK, MARY BOYLE RICH, COUNTESS OF

Mary Boyle (1625-78), daughter of the Earl of Cork, lost her mother when she was three. Before she was thirteen, her father tried unsuccessfully to force her into marriage. Instead, she married Charles Rich against the wishes of her father, who wanted a wealthier match; but he was persuaded to give her a large dowry. The marriage was happy and produced two children. Living generally in the country with her husband's family, she devoted much of her time to meditation, entertainment of ministers, and works of charity. A volume of her religious writings was published after her death (1686).

WEST, JANE

Jane—— (1758-1852), who was self-educated, married a local farmer, Thomas West, and had several children. In addition to caring for them and supervising the dairy, she wrote voluminously—poems, plays, novels, and educational tracts. All of them sold well. The best of her novels are *A Gossip's Story* (1797) and *A Tale of the Times* (1799). Her volume of *Letters to a Young Lady* (1806) was dedicated to the Queen. She was rigorously conservative on questions of politics, religion, and women's rights.

WILLIAMS, ANNA

Anna Williams (1706-83), daughter of a physician and inventor, was well educated. She looked after her father until his death and struggled to support herself by needlework and translation even when her vision was failing. After the death of Mrs. Samuel Johnson, her close friend (1752), she lived with Johnson whenever he had a house. Even when she was in separate lodgings, Johnson would drink tea with her every night. Her *Miscellanies in Prose and Verse*, to which Johnson contributed several pieces and Hester Thrale one, was advertised in 1750 and finally published by subscription in 1766. She lived on the proceeds of this, together with a benefit Garrick gave her and small annuities from friends.

WILLIAMS, HELEN MARIA

Helen Maria Williams (1762?-1827), daughter of an army officer, was educated (inadequately) by her mother. In the 1780s she established herself in London as a poet (she published several volumes by subscription, very profitably) and, with her sisters, as a literary hostess; she was a friend of liberal writers like Godwin and Smith. She went to Paris to observe the French Revolution at first hand, and was enthusiastic. In 1792 she established there a salon frequented by the Girondists, including Mme. Roland, and visiting republicans from England, such as Wollstonecraft and Fox. She was imprisoned by Robespierre in 1793. On her release she formed a liaison with a married man, John Hurford Stone, with whom she lived for the rest of his life. Her works include, besides *Julia, a Novel* (1790), a long series of *Letters* describing and justifying the French Revolution (1790-1801).

WINCHILSEA, ANNE KINGSMILL FINCH, COUNTESS OF

Anne Kingsmill (1661-1720), orphaned at three, became a maid of honor to Mary of Modena, wife of the Duke of York (later James II). At Court she met Heneage Finch, her future husband. Their marriage was childless, but blissfully happy. When James was deposed, the Finches retired to the country seat of the Earl of Winchilsea (Heneage later succeeded to the title). Anne had been writing poetry from her days at Court, though at first she kept it secret lest she be known as "a Versifying Maid of Honour." Encouraged by her husband, by the Earl, and by a group of congenial friends, she steadily wrote poetry, publishing a volume in 1713, but leaving many of her best works in manuscript. She knew Pope, Swift, Gay, and Rowe. She wrote lyrics of love and friendship, odes, fables, satires, meditative nature pieces, religious poetry, and closet dramas.

WOLLSTONECRAFT, MARY. *See* Godwin, Mary Wollstonecraft

YEARSLEY, ANN
   Ann Yearsley (1752-1806), "the Bristol milkwoman," made her living selling milk from door to door. Her brother taught her to write, and her mother, also a milkwoman, borrowed books for her. She married an honest but stupid man and bore six children in seven years. Nevertheless, she found time to write poems. The family was almost destitute when Hannah More's cook showed Yearsley's poems to her employer. More worked hard to correct the poems and obtain subscribers for an edition (1785). The volume made £600, but More infuriated Yearsley by her patronizing attitude and her refusal to give her control over the money. After this bitter rupture, Yearsley continued to publish poems, a tragedy, and a novel, *The Royal Captives* (1795), which were moderately profitable and well received.

৵৴₰ঌ INDEX ঌ৵₰ঌ

Women are referred to in the text by the name by which they are most commonly known; in the index, as in the appendix, they are listed under their latest married name.

A Note on the Author

KATHARINE MUNZER ROGERS is professor of English at Brooklyn College and the Graduate School of the City University of New York. Her particular interests are Restoration and eighteenth- and nineteenth-century literature, and women's studies. After receiving her B.A. from Barnard College, she spent a year in Cambridge, England, as a Fulbright Scholar. She received her Ph.D. from Columbia University. Her first book, *The Troublesome Helpmate: A History of Misogyny in Literature*, was published in 1966, her study of *William Wycherley* in 1972. She has published numerous articles on eighteenth- and nineteenth-century writers, and has edited five books, including the *Signet Classic Book of Eighteenth and Nineteenth Century British Drama* (1979), *Before Their Time: Six Women Writers of the Eighteenth Century* (1979), and *Selected Writings of Samuel Johnson* (1981). She provided the foreword to the 1978 edition of Ruth Kelso's *Doctrine for the Lady of the Renaissance*.